OF MATHEMATICIANS

A QUOTATION BOOK FOR PHILOMATHS

Rosemary Schmalz

MAA
SPECTRUM

The Mathematical Association of America
1529 Eighteenth Street, N.W.
Washington, D.C. 20036

LATEX macros by Michael Downes

Current Printing (last digit):
10 9 8 7 6 5 4 3 2 1

OUT OF THE MOUTHS
OF MATHEMATICIANS

A Quotation Book for Philomaths

"OUT OF THE MOUTHS

SPECTRUM SERIES

The Spectrum Series of the Mathematical Association of America was so named to reflect its purpose: to publish a broad range of books including biographies, accessible expositions of old or new mathematical ideas, reprints and revisions of excellent out-of-print books, popular works, and other monographs of high interest that will appeal to a broad range of readers, including students and teachers of mathematics, mathematical amateurs, and researchers.

Complex Numbers and Geometry, by Liang-shin Hahn
From Zero to Infinity, by Constance Reid
I Want to be a Mathematician, by Paul R. Halmos
Journey into Geometries, by Marta Sved
The Last Problem, by E. T. Bell (revised and updated by Underwood Dudley)
Lure of the Integers, by Joe Roberts
Mathematical Carnival, by Martin Gardner
Mathematical Circus, by Martin Gardner
Mathematical Cranks, by Underwood Dudley
Mathematical Magic Show, by Martin Gardner
Mathematics: Queen and Servant of Science, by E. T. Bell
Memorabilia Mathematica, by Robert Edouard Moritz
Numerical Methods that Work, by Forman Acton
Out of the Mouths of Mathematicians, by Rosemary Schmalz
Polyominoes, by George Martin
The Search for E. T. Bell, also known as John Taine, by Constance Reid
Shaping Space, edited by Marjorie Senechal and George Fleck
Student Research Projects in Calculus, by Marcus Cohen, Edward D. Gaughan, Arthur Knoebel, Douglas S. Kurtz, and David Pengelley

Mathematical Association of America
1529 Eighteenth Street, NW
Washington, DC 20036
800-331-1MAA   FAX 202-265-2384

Preface

When Robert Moritz compiled his book of quotations, *Memorabilia Mathematica,* which first appeared in 1914, he stated that his primary objective was to seek out the exact statement of and exact references for famous passages about mathematics. He searched the writings not only of mathematicians but of poets, philosophers, historians, statesmen, and scientists as well. His sources ranged from the works of Plato to the writings of Hilbert and Whitehead. His second objective was to produce a volume that would be a source for pleasure, encouragement and inspiration to mathematicians and non-mathematicians alike.

This work is a similar compilation of quotations, more limited in many ways yet expanded in others. First, I have limited my sources, with a few exceptions, to the writings of mathematicians of this century. For the most part, these are not well-known quotations; in fact, some of them are from sources published in very recent years! Thus my primary objective is more in keeping with Moritz's second objective: to compile a volume that can be used by researchers to facilitate a literature search, by writers to emphasize or substantiate a point, by teachers to encourage or amuse their students, and by all readers, and in particular young readers, to get the flavor of mathematics and to whet their appetites and make them eager to learn more about it.

A further objective emerged as I worked on the volume. I realized that through researching the quotations, I myself developed a sense of the *whole* of mathematics of the 20th century, something which in this era of knowledge explosion is almost impossible. The mathematicians of this century, their collaborations and disputes, the movement from abstractions to applications, the emergence of new areas of research, the impact of computers on mathematics, the challenges in mathematics education—all this came alive for me as I worked. I hope that the reader will have a similar experience from perusing the pages of this book.

How were quotations chosen for this text? Against what criteria was an entry judged? My main criterion for including a passage was not only the merit of its message or the fame of the writer, but also its style of expression. I chose passages that exhibited the vitality of both mathematics and mathematicians. No one is more aware than I that the work is incomplete. The task is an infinite one and I am forced to follow the advice of Paul Halmos in "How to Write Mathematics" [*L'Enseignement Mathématique* 16 (May-June 1970) 151], namely, "There is always something left undone, always either something more to say, or a better way to say something, or, at the very least, a disturbing vague sense that the perfect addition or improvement is just around the corner, and the dread that its omission would be everlasting cause for regret ... There is no solution to this problem except the obvious one; the only way to stop is to be ruthless about it."

I wish to thank my colleagues at Eastern Illinois University for their interest and encouragement, in particular James Glazebrook who gave me invaluable suggestions and Duane Broline who, in introducing me to Moritz's volume, gave me the initial idea.

Contents

Preface vii

1   Mathematics in General 1

2   The Development of Mathematics 19

3   Particular Disciplines in Mathematics 35

4   Doing Mathematics 47

5   Exhortations to Aspiring Mathematicians 77

6   The Creative Process in Mathematics 83

7   Moments of Mathematical Insight 93

8   The Love of Mathematics 101

9   Pure and Applied Mathematics 115

10   Mathematics and the Arts 131

11   Mathematics and Matters of the Spirit 145

12   Mathematics and the Computer 153

13   About Mathematicians, A–L 163

14   About Mathematicians, M–Z 191

15 Anecdotes and Miscellaneous Humor 221

16 Mathematics Education 243

Author Index 277

Topic Index 283

Mathematics in General

1   Mathematics is the instrument by which the engineer tunnels our mountains, bridges our rivers, constructs our aqueducts, erects our factories and makes them musical by the busy hum of spindles. Take away the results of the reasoning of mathematics, and there would go with it nearly all the material achievements which give convenience and glory to modern civilization.   —Edward Brooks
Mental Science and Culture, Philadelphia: Normal Publishing, 1891, p. 255.

2   Mathematics is the most abstract of all the sciences. For it makes no external observations, nor asserts anything as a real fact. When the mathematician deals with facts, they become for him mere "hypotheses"; for with their truth he refuses to concern himself. The whole science of mathematics is a science of hypotheses; so that nothing could be more completely abstracted from concrete reality.   —C. S. Pierce
"The Regenerated Logic," *The Monist* 7 (October 1896) 23.

3   Mathematics has not only commercial value, but also educational, rhetorical, and ethical value. No other science offers such a rich opportunity for original investigation and discovery. While it should be studied because of its practical worth, which can be seen about us every day, the primary object of its study should be to obtain mental power, to sharpen and strengthen the powers of thought, to give penetrating power to the mind which enables it to pierce a subject to its core and discover its elements; to develop the power to express one's thoughts in a forcible and logical manner; to develop the memory and the imagination; to cultivate a taste for neatness and a love for the good, the beautiful, and the true; and to become more like the greatest of mathematicians, the Mathematician of the Universe.

—Samuel I. Jones
Mathematical Wrinkles, Gunter, TX: Samuel I. Jones,
1912, p. 257.

4   I may perhaps describe it [my part in the progress of mathematics] as that of a long-robed priest who simply lights, in some little chapel, seven small candles. And to these seven candles I may give fanciful names, just to increase your interest in my humble task.

I may speak of the first as the *lampas utilitatis,* because we cannot convey mathematics to the great mass of people unless we first dwell upon the utility of the subject and imagine what would happen to the world if every trace of mathematics and of mathematical knowledge were blotted out tonight.

The second candle has been the *lampas decoris,* the lamp of beauty; because if we are to teach mathematics at all, real success is not possible unless we know that the subject is beautiful as well as useful. Mere utility of the moment without any feeling of beauty, becomes a hopeless bit of drudgery, a condition which leads to stagnation.

The third has been the *lampas imaginationis,* which has always seemed to me especially appropriate in referring to a medieval cathedral in which we set our lamps, and which seems equally so in respect to our chosen science; for what would mathematics have amounted to without the imagination of its devotees—its giants and their followers? There was never a discovery made without the urge of imagination—of imagination which broke the roadway through the forest in order that cold logic might follow.

The fourth candle has been the *lampas poesis,* the lamp of poetry; because if one does not feel the poetry in mathematics, one may as well cease teaching the science. What, after all, is mathematics but the poetry of the mind, and what is poetry but the mathematics of the heart?

The fifth of the candles that we all seek to light is the *lampas mysteriae.* This it is that reveals to us one of the great charms of the science—that in working in the domain of mathematics you are surrounded by clouds, and success drives back those clouds a little way, and a discovery is made; then someone makes another discovery and drives them back a little more; and at rare intervals in time a Newton comes and drives them back, what seems a long, long way—and still there is the surrounding mist of mystery . . .

The next lamp has been and is the *lampas infinitatis,* the lamp of the infinite. A writer not long ago . . . spoke of mathematics as the science which lassos the flying stars. It means much to have played even a little around the outskirts of "the science venerable," to have seen how it reveals something of our own position on the great macrocosmos, and to see what an infinitesimal thing we seem when we look at ourselves in the light that mathematics sheds upon this cosmos . . .

And the seventh of the candles that this humble priest in the little chapel of the great cathedral has essayed to light is the *"lampas religionis."* We may wonder if such a candle burns and sheds its light, but I have an idea that we all feel that, while a mathematician may not necessarily be a very religious man, on the other hand no man can appreciate religion to the full unless he has to assist him some knowledge of the great field which mathematics opens to his vision. Mathematics may not make any man more religious, but if he is religiously inclined it makes him see the grandeur of religion as nothing else can.

—D. E. Smith
"Dinner in Honor of Professor David Eugene Smith,"
Math. Teacher 19 (May 1926) 279.

5   A mathematic may be established through the free choice of a logic, and of primitive ideas and primitive propositions; if this choice is guided by wisdom, the mathematic will be capable of development and application. The application will then, sometimes directly, but more frequently through a chain of intermediate stages, have significant bearing upon the content of human experience and furnish results which may be called true. Their truth then gives, retroactively, a sound basis for belief in the validity of the conclusions of mathematics.

—Arnold Dresden
"Some Philosophical Aspects of Mathematics," *Bull.
of the Amer. Math. Soc.* 34 (July-August 1928) 452.

6   Mathematics, by exhibiting a body of truth which can live through millenniums without needed connections, and at the same time can

grow in magnitude and range and interest, has given the human spirit new ground for believing in itself and for rejoicing in its power of consistent thought.   — R. D. Carmichael
The Logic of Discovery, Chicago: Open Court, 1930, p. 263.

7   What is the inner secret of mathematical power? Briefly stated, it is that mathematics discloses the skeletal outlines of all closely articulated relational systems. For this purpose mathematics uses the language of pure logic with its score or so of symbolic words, which, in its important forms of expression, enables the mind to comprehend systems of relations otherwise completely beyond its power. These forms are creative discoveries which, once made, remain permanently at our disposal. By means of them the scientific imagination is enabled to penetrate ever more deeply into the rationale of the universe about us.
—George Birkhoff
"Mathematics: Quantity and Order," in J. G. Crowther (ed.), *Science Today,* London: Eyre & Spottiswoode, 1934, p. 297.

8   The primary service of modern mathematics is that it alone enables us to understand the vast abstract permanences which underlie the flux of things, without requiring us to regard its self-consistent abstractions as more than specific, limited instruments of thought.
—George Birkhoff
"Mathematics: Quantity and Order," in J. G. Crowther (ed.), *Science Today,* London: Eyre & Spottiswoode, 1934, p. 317.

9   The mathematician is still regarded as the hermit who knows little of the ways of life outside his cell, who spends his time compounding incredible and incomprehensible theorems in a strange, clipped, unintelligible jargon.   —Edward Kasner and James Newman
Mathematics and the Imagination, New York: Simon and Schuster, 1940, p. xiii.

IO   Mathematics thus belongs to the great family of spiritual enterprises of man. These enterprises, all the members of the great family, however diverse in form, in modes of life, in methods of toil, in their progress along the way that leads toward logical rectitude, are alike children of one great passion. In genesis, in spirit and aspiration, in motive and aim, natural science, theology, philosophy, jurisprudence,

religion and art are one with mathematics; they are all of them sprung
from the human spirit's craving for invariant reality in a world of tragic
change; they all of them aim at rescuing man from "the blind hurry of
the universe from vanity to vanity" [Bertrand Russell]: they seek cosmic
stability—a world of abiding worth, where the broken promises of hope
shall be healed and the infinite aspiration shall cease to be mocked.

—Cassius J. Keyser
The Human Worth of Rigorous Thinking, New York:
Scripta Mathematica, 1940, p. 48.

II   Mathematics as an expression of the human mind reflects the active
will, the contemplative reason, and the desire for aesthetic perfection.
Its basic elements are logic and intuition, analysis and construction,
generality and individuality.

—Richard Courant and Herbert Robbins
What is Mathematics, London: Oxford University
Press, 1941, p. xv.

12   When we learn to drive a car
we are able to "go places"
easily and pleasantly
instead of walking to them
with a great deal of effort.
And so you will see that
the more Mathematics we know
the EASIER life becomes,
for it is a TOOL with which
we can accomplish things
that we could not do at all
with our bare hands.
Thus Mathematics helps
our brains and hands and feet,
and can make
a race of supermen out of us.   —Lillian R. Lieber

The Education of T. C. Mits, New York: W. W. Norton,
1942, p. 45.

13   Consider mathematics as a discipline in itself—that is to say, as
a body of concepts and methods which constitute a way of thinking.
Surely mathematics is such a discipline. It deals almost exclusively with
premises and conclusions, and with deductive reasoning, which is one

of the more important methods of drawing conclusions from premises. Moreover, clarity and precision of definitions and assumptions, and rigor in reasoning, can be more nearly attained and more simply studied in mathematics than in the other disciplines. Is this not the real place of mathematics in a liberal education—not simply as a subject matter, or as a discipline applicable only to its own subject matter, but as a discipline which is applicable to almost every intellectual activity of man?

—E. P. Northrop
"Mathematics in a Liberal Education," *Amer. Math. Monthly* 52 (March 1945) 133.

14 Mathematics, like any other cardinal activity of the human spirit, has an individuality of its own. A student seriously bent upon discovering that individuality—upon ascertaining what mathematics essentially or distinctively is—may hopefully follow the leading of one or another of three commanding points of view. The coveted insight may be won by contemplating mathematics as a certain kind of intellectual enterprise characterized by its aim, or by contemplating it as a body of achievements or of knowledge characterized by the type of propositions constituting the body, or by contemplating it as a certain type of thought or way of thinking characterized by its procedure or method ... the three paths of inquiry thus suggested lead to one and the same goal.

—Cassius J. Keyser
Mathematics as a Cultural Clue and Other Essays, New York: Scripta Mathematica, 1947, p. 2.

15 Mathematics is a vast adventure in ideas; its history reflects some of the noblest thoughts of countless generations.   — Dirk J. Struik
A Concise History of Mathematics, Vol. 1, New York: Dover, 1948, p. xi.

16 The first acquaintance which most people have with mathematics is through arithmetic. ... Arithmetic, therefore, will be a good subject to consider in order to discover, if possible, the most obvious characteristic of the science. Now, the first noticeable fact about arithmetic is that it applies to everything, to tastes and to sounds, to apples and to angels, to the ideas of the mind and to the bones of the body.

Thus we write down as the leading characteristic of mathematics that it deals with properties and ideas which are applicable to things just because they are things, and apart from any particular feelings, or emotions, or sensations, in any way connected with them. This is what is meant by calling mathematics an abstract science.

—Alfred North Whitehead
"The Nature of Mathematics," *An Introduction to Mathematics,* London: Oxford University Press, 1948, p. 2.

17 Mathematics is an aspect of culture as well as a collection of algorithms.

—Carl Boyer
The Concepts of the Calculus, New York: Hafner, 1949, preface to second printing.

18 Mathematics is neither a description of nature nor an explanation of its operation; it is not concerned with physical motion or with the metaphysical generation of quantities. It is merely the symbolic logic of possible relations, and as such is concerned with neither approximate nor absolute truth, but only with hypothetical truth. That is, mathematics determines what conclusions will follow logically from given premises. The conjunction of mathematics and philosophy, or of mathematics and science, is frequently of great service in suggesting new problems and points of view.

Nevertheless, in the final rigorous formulation and elaboration of such concepts as have been introduced, mathematics must necessarily be unprejudiced by any irrelevant elements in the experiences from which they have arisen . . . . Thus only may be fully appreciated the twofold aspects of mathematics: as the language of a descriptive interpretation of the relationships discovered in natural phenomena, and as a syllogistic elaboration of arbitrary premises. —Carl Boyer
The Concepts of the Calculus, New York: Hafner, 1949, p. 308.

19 From the axiomatic point of view, mathematics appears thus as a storehouse of abstract forms—the mathematical structures; and it so happens—without our knowing why—that certain aspects of empirical reality fit themselves into these forms, as if through a kind of preadaptation. Of course, it can not be denied that most of these forms had originally a very definite intuitive content; but, it is exactly by deliberately throwing out this content, that it has been possible to give these forms all the power which they were capable of displaying and to prepare them for new interpretations and for the development of their full power.

It is only in this sense of the word "form" that one can call the axiomatic method a "formalism." The unity which it gives to mathematics is not the armor of formal logic, the unity of a lifeless skeleton; it is the nutritive fluid of an organism at the height of its development, the supple and fertile research instrument to which all the great mathematical thinkers since Gauss have contributed, all those who, in the words of Lejeune–Dirichlet, have always labored to "substitute ideas for calculations."   —Nicholas Bourbaki
"The Architecture of Mathematics," *Amer. Math. Monthly* 57 (April 1950) 231.

20   Kierkegaard once said religion deals with what concerns man unconditionally. In contrast (but with equal exaggeration) one may say that mathematics talks about the things which are of no concern at all to man. Mathematics has the inhuman quality of starlight, brilliant and sharp, but cold. But it seems an irony of creation that man's mind knows how to handle things the better the farther removed they are from the center of his existence. Thus we are cleverest where knowledge matters least: in mathematics, especially in number theory.   —Hermann Weyl
"A Half-century of Mathematics," *Amer. Math. Monthly* 58 (October 1951) 523.

21   Mathematics is not a popular subject, even though its importance may be generally conceded. The reason for this is to be found in the common superstition that mathematics is but a continuation, a further development, of the fine art of arithmetic, of juggling with numbers.
—David Hilbert
D. Hilbert and S. Cohn-Vossen, *Geometry and the Imagination,* New York: Chelsea Publishing Co, 1952, p. iv.

22   Rich in its past, dynamic in the present, prodigious for the future, replete with simple and yet profound ideas and methods, surely mathematics can give something to anyone's culture.   —R. E. Langer
"The Things I Should Have Done, I Did Not Do," *Amer. Math. Monthly* 59 (September 1952) 445.

23   I propose the following, if not as a definition, then at least as a partial description; *mathematics is persistent intellectual honesty.*
—Moses Richardson
"Mathematics and Intellectual Honesty," *Amer. Math. Monthly* 59 (February 1952) 73.

24 When we consider the number of fields on which mathematics impinges and the number of these over which it already gives us mastery or partial mastery, we are tempted to call it a method of approach to the universe of physical, mental, and emotional experiences. It is distillation of highest purity that exact thought has extracted from man's efforts to understand nature, to impart order to the confusion of events occurring in the physical world, to create beauty, and to satisfy the natural proclivity of the healthy brain to exercise itself.

—Morris Kline
Mathematics in Western Culture, New York: Oxford University Press, 1953, p. 471.

25 Mathematics has determined the direction and content of much philosophic thought, has destroyed and rebuilt religious doctrines, has supplied substance to economic and political theories, has fashioned major painting, musical, architectural, and literary styles, has fathered our logic, and has furnished the best answers we have to fundamental questions about the nature of man and his universe. As the embodiment and most powerful advocate of the rational spirit, mathematics has invaded domains ruled by authority, custom, and habit, and supplanted them as the arbiter of thought and action. Finally, as an incomparably fine human achievement mathematics offers satisfactions and aesthetic values at least equal to those offered by any other branch of our culture.

—Morris Kline
Mathematics in Western Culture, New York: Oxford University Press, 1953, p. ix.

26 Mathematics, springing from the soil of basic human experience with numbers and data and space and motion, builds up a far-flung architectural structure composed of theorems which reveal insights into the reasons behind appearances and of concepts which relate totally disparate concrete ideas.   —Saunders Mac Lane
"Of Course and Courses," *Amer. Math. Monthly* 61 (March 1954) 152.

27 Science is reasoning; reasoning is mathematics; and, therefore, science is mathematics.   —Marshall H. Stone
"Mathematics and the Future of Science," *Bull. of the Amer. Math. Soc.* 63 (March 1957) 61.

28   Mathematics begins in bewilderment and ends in bewilderment.
—J. L. Synge
Kandelman's Krim, London: Jonathan Cape, 1957, p. 17.

29   That a mathematical theory is a lasting object to believe in few can doubt. Mathematical language is difficult but imperishable. I do not believe that any Greek scholar of to-day can understand the idiomatic undertones of Plato's dialogues, or the jokes of Aristophanes, as thoroughly as mathematicians can understand every shade of meaning in Archimedes' works.   —M. H. A. Newman
"What is Mathematics?," *Math. Gaz.* 43 (October 1959) 167.

30   The answer to the question *Can there be a general method for solving all mathematical problems?* is no!
Perhaps, in a world of unsolved and apparently unsolvable problems, we would have thought that the desirable answer to this question from any point of view, would be yes. But from the point of view of mathematicians a yes would have been far less satisfying than a no is . . . . Not only are the problems of mathematics infinite and hence inexhaustible, but mathematics itself is inexhaustible.   —Constance Reid
Introduction to Higher Mathematics for the General Reader, New York: Thomas Y. Crowell, 1959, p. 180.

31   Somebody once said that philosophy is the misuse of a terminology which was invented just for this purpose. In the same vein, I would say that mathematics is the science of skillful operations with concepts and rules invented just for this purpose.   —Eugene Wigner
"The Unreasonable Effectiveness of Mathematics in the Natural Sciences," *Comm. on Pure and Appl. Math.* 13 (February 1960) 2.

32   Mathematical activity—like all of Gaul—may be divided into three areas: Education, Research, and Applications . . . much of the strength of the mathematical fabric comes from the interaction among these three.   —Henry O. Pollak
"The Role of Industrial Members in the Mathematical Association of America," *Amer. Math. Monthly* 68 (June-July 1961) 551.

33   The philosopher Bertrand Russell has described the abstract nature of mathematics in the epigram: "Mathematics is the subject in which we do not know what we are talking about or whether what

we say is true." . . . A modern mathematician would prefer the positive characterization of his subject as the study of general abstract systems, each one of which is an edifice built of specified abstract elements and structured by the presence of arbitrary but unambiguously specified relations among them.   —Marshall H. Stone
> "The Revolution in Mathematics," *Liberal Education* 47 (May 1961) 307.

34   With even a superficial knowledge of mathematics, it is easy to recognize certain characteristic features: its abstractness, its precision, its logical rigor, the indisputable character of its conclusions, and finally, the exceptionally broad range of its applications.

    —A. D. Aleksandrov
> A. D. Aleksandrov, A. N. Kolmogorov, M. A. Lavrent'ev (eds.), *Mathematics: Its Content, Methods, and Meaning, Vol. I,* Cambridge, MA: MIT Press, 1963, p. 1.

35   Mathematics is loved by many, disliked by a few, admired and respected by all. Because of their immense power and reliability, mathematical methods inspire confidence in persons who comprehend them and awe in those who do not.   —Hollis R. Cooley
> "Forward," in Samuel Rapport and Helen Wright (eds.), *Mathematics,* New York: New York University Press, 1963, p. ix.

36   Mathematics is a human activity almost as diverse as the human mind itself.   —Gábor Szegö
> Jozsef Kürschak, compiler, *Hungarian Problem Book I,* Washington, DC: Mathematical Association of America, 1963, p. 6.

37   It is commonplace that mathematics is an excellent school of thinking, that it conditions you to logical thinking, that after having experienced it you can somehow think more validly than otherwise. I don't know whether all these statements are true, the first one is probably least doubtful. However, I think it has a very great importance in thinking in an area which is not so precise. I feel that one of the most important contributions of mathematics to our thinking is, that it has demonstrated an enormous flexibility in the formation of concepts,

a degree of flexibility to which it is very difficult to arrive in a non-mathematical mode.   —John von Neumann
"The Role of Mathematics in the Sciences and Society," in A. H. Taub (ed.), *John von Neumann Collected Work, Vol VI,* New York: Pergamon, 1963, p. 482.

38 Like many great temples of some religions, mathematics may be viewed only from the outside by those uninitiated into its mysteries . . . understanding [its] methods is reserved for those who devote years to the study of mathematics.   —Andrew Gleason
"Evolution of an Active Mathematical Theory," *Science* 145 (31 July 1964) 457.

39 The word "mathematics" is a Greek word, and, by origin, it means "something that has been learned or understood," or perhaps "acquired knowledge," and perhaps even, somewhat against grammar, "acquirable knowledge," that is, "learnable knowledge," that is, "knowledge acquirable by learning."   —Salomon Bochner
The Role of Mathematics in the Rise of Science, Princeton: Princeton University Press, 1966, p. 24.

40 What indeed is mathematics? . . . A neat little answer . . . is preserved in the writings of a Church Father of the 3rd century A.D.; Anatolius of Alexandria, bishop of Laodicea, reports that a certain (unnamed) "jokester," using words of Homer which had been intended for something entirely different, put it thus:

Small at her birth, but rising every hour,

While scarce the skies her horrid [mighty] head can bound,

She stalks on earth and shakes the world around.

(Iliad, IV, 442-445, Pope's translation.)

For, explains Anatolius, mathematics begins with a point and a line, and forthwith it takes in heaven itself and all things within its compass. If the bishop were among us today, he might have worded the same explanation thus: For mathematics, as a means of articulation and theoretization of physics, spans the universe, all the way from the smallest elementary particle to the largest galaxy at the rim of the cosmos.
—Salomon Bochner
The Role of Mathematics in the Rise of Science, Princeton: Princeton University Press, 1966, p. 13.

41 Mathematics is abstract thought, mathematics is pure logic, mathematics is creative art. All these statements are wrong, but they are

all a little right, and they are all nearer the mark than "mathematics is number" or "mathematics is geometric shapes." For the professional pure mathematician, mathematics is the logical dovetailing of a carefully selected sparse set of assumptions with their surprising conclusions via a conceptually elegant proof. Simplicity, intricacy, and above all, logical analysis are the hallmark of mathematics.   —Paul Halmos
>   "Mathematics as a Creative Art," *Amer. Scientist* 56
>   (Winter 1968) 380.

42   At this moment there are thousands of people around the world doing pure mathematics. A few might be doing so because they foresee a possible application. A few might be philosophers taking Bertrand Russell's advice that "to create a healthy philosophy you should renounce metaphysics but be a good mathematician." There might even be a few ascetics who are doing it to sharpen their minds. But the vast majority are doing it simply because it's fun. . . .

Pure mathematics is the world's best game. It is more absorbing than chess, more of a gamble than poker, and lasts longer than Monopoly. It's free. It can be played anywhere—Archimedes did it in a bathtub. It is dramatic, challenging, endless, and full of surprises.

Pure mathematics is a pleasant way to pass the time until the end. And to me that makes it very serious, very important indeed.
>   —Richard J. Trudeau
>   *Dots and Lines,* Kent, OH: The Kent State University
>   Press, 1976, p. 9.

43   Mathematics abounds in bright ideas. No matter how long and hard one pursues her, mathematics never seems to run out of exciting surprises. And by no means are these gems to be found only in difficult work at an advanced level. All kinds of simple notions are full of ingenuity.   —Ross Honsberger
>   *Mathematical Morsels,* Washington, DC: Mathematical Association of America, 1978, p. vii.

44   Mathematics has elements that are spatial, kinesthetic, elements that are arithmetic or algebraic, elements that are verbal, programmatic. It has elements that are logical, didactic and elements that are intuitive, or even counter-intuitive. It has elements that are related to the exterior world and elements that seem to be self generated. It has elements that are rational and elements that are irrational or mystical. These may be compared to different modes of consciousness.

To place undue emphasis on one element or group of elements upsets a balance. It results in an impoverishment of the science and represents an unfulfilled potential.   —Philip J. Davis and James A. Anderson
"Nonanalytic Aspects of Mathematics and Their Implication for Research and Education," *SIAM Review* 21 (January 1979) 125.

45   Historically, the prime value of mathematics has been that it enables us to answer basic questions about our physical world, to comprehend the complicated operations of nature, and to dissipate much of the mystery that envelops life. The simplest arithmetic, algebra, and geometry suffice to determine the circumference of the earth, the distances to the moon and the planets, the speeds of sound and light, and the reasons for eclipses of the sun and moon. But the supreme value of mathematics, insofar as understanding the world about us is concerned, is that it reveals order and law where mere observation shows chaos. . . .

The understanding we have attained about the physical world is often credited to science. But mathematics provides the dies by which science is formed, and mathematics is the essence of our best scientific theories. . . . Of course, observation and experimentation are indispensable components of the scientific enterprise, but mathematical laws are the essence of our knowledge. Our world is to a large extent what mathematics says it is.   —Morris Kline
Mathematics: An Introduction to Its Spirit and Use, San Francisco: W. H. Freeman, 1979, p. 1.

46   While the extent to which the study of mathematics trains the mind is uncertain, there is no question that mathematics is humanity's most sustained, most enduring, and most powerful achievement. Comprehension of the physical world, intellectual satisfaction, technical utility, and aesthetic values (albeit more esoteric than those offered by music or painting) can be derived from mathematics. In addition, the achievements of mathematics demonstrate the capacity of the human mind, and this exhibition of what human reason can accomplish has given man the courage and confidence to tackle additional seemingly impenetrable mysteries of the cosmos, to seek cures for fatal diseases, and to question and improve the economic and political systems under which people live. Man's success in the difficult realm of mathematics provides one unquenchable source of hope for success in these other areas, whether or not mathematics itself plays a role in the undertakings. The many values described above attest to the assertion that mathematics is a fundamental and integral part of our culture. —Morris Kline

> *Mathematics: An Introduction to Its Spirit and Use,* San Francisco: W. H. Freeman, 1979, p. 4.

47 The ideal mathematician's work is intelligible only to a small group of specialists, numbering a few dozen or at most a few hundred. This group has existed only for a few decades and there is every possibility that it may become extinct in another few decades. However, the mathematician regards his work as part of the very structure of the world, containing truths that are valid forever, from the beginning of time, even in the most remote corner of the universe.

> —Philip Davis and Reuben Hersh
> *The Mathematical Experience,* New York: Birkhäuser, 1981, p. 34.

48 I have absolutely no idea of what paleontology is; and if somebody would spend an hour with me, or an hour a day for a week, or an hour a day for a year, teaching it to me, my soul would be richer. In that sense, I was doing the same thing for my colleague, the paleontologist. I was telling him what mathematics is. That, I think, is important. All educable human beings should know what mathematics is because their souls would grow by that. They would enjoy life more, they would understand life more, they would have greater insight. They should, in that sense, understand all human activity such as paleontology and mathematics. —Paul Halmos

> Donald Albers, "Paul Halmos: Maverick Mathologist," *Two-year Coll. Math. J.* 13 (September 1982) 236.

49 Mathematics is not a book confined within a cover and bound between brazen clasps, whose contents it needs only patience to ransack; it is not a mine whose treasures may take long to reduce into possession, but which fill only a limited number of veins and lodes; it is not a soil, whose fertility can be exhausted by the yield of successive harvests; it is not a continent or an ocean, whose area can be mapped out and its contour defined: it is limitless as that space which it finds too narrow for its aspirations; its possibilities are as infinite as the worlds which are forever crowding in and multiplying upon the astronomer's gaze; it is as incapable of being restricted within assigned boundaries or being reduced to definitions of permanent validity, as the consciousness, the life, which seems to slumber in each monad, in every atom of matter, in each leaf and bud and cell, and is forever ready to burst forth into new forms of vegetable and animal existence.   —James J. Sylvester

> Martin Gardner, *Wheels, Life, and Other Mathematical Amusements,* New York: W. H. Freeman, 1983, p. viii.

50   Mathematicians make natural questions precise.

> —Richard Bellman
> *Eye of the Hurricane,* Singapore: World Scientific, 1984, p. 114.

51   In dealing with academics, it is absolutely superb to be able to say you're a mathematician! Nobody dares to say mathematics is not important or not significant. . . . No discipline surpasses mathematics in purely academic prestige.   —Mina Rees

> Rosamond Dana and Peter J. Hilton, "Mina Rees," in Donald J. Albers and G. L. Alexanderson, editors, *Mathematical People,* Boston: Birkhäuser, 1985, p. 260.

52   Mathematics is a world created by the mind of man, and mathematicians are people who devote their lives to what seems to me a wonderful kind of play!   —Constance Reid

> G. L. Alexanderson, "An Interview with Constance Reid," *Two-Year Coll. Math. J.* 11 (September 1980) 238.

53   Mathematics [is] an array of forms, codifying ideas extracted from human activities and scientific problems and deployed in a network of formal rules, formal definitions, formal axiom systems, explicit theorems with their careful proof and the manifold interconnections of these forms. More briefly, Mathematics aims to understand, to manipulate, to develop, and to apply those aspects of the universe which are formal.   —Saunders Mac Lane

> *Mathematics: Form and Function,* New York: Springer-Verlag, 1986, p. 456.

54   To find the simple in the complex, the finite in the infinite—that is not a bad description of the aim and essence of mathematics.

> —Jacob T. Schwartz
> *Discrete Thoughts: Essays on Mathematics, Science and Philosophy,* Boston: Birkhäuser, 1986, p. 64.

55   What is the strength of mathematics? What makes mathematics possible? It is symbolic reasoning. It is like "canned thought." You have understood something once. You encode it, and then you go on using it without each time having to think about it. Without symbolic reasoning you cannot make a mathematical argument.   —Lipman Bers

> Donald J. Albers and Constance Reid, "An Interview with Lipman Bers," *Coll. Math. J.* 18 (September 1987) 283.

56   The ultimate goal of mathematics is to eliminate all need for intelligent thought.

> —Ronald L. Graham, Donald E. Knuth, and Oren Patashnik
> *Concrete Mathematics,* Reading, MA: Addison-Wesley, 1989, p. 56.

CHAPTER 2

The Development of Mathematics

1   It is useful to reflect from time to time on the character of the [mathematical] structure which is being developed by an ever increasing group of workers. For, while many parts of this structure have become familiar through long acquaintance, it is steadily reaching out in new directions, opening up vistas which stimulate the imagination to envisaging still further extensions and also such as give hitherto unsuspected views of the familiar parts. Ever greater become the distances which separate those who work at different sections of this structure and it is becoming increasingly difficult for them to keep feeling with the fundamental plan which determines its development. The day is long past when unity could be secured through the coordinating agency of a single mind, or even of a group of closely associated minds; and no one can dream of holding together the lines of communication which connect the different parts of the magnificent structure.

—Arnold Dresden
"Some Philosophical Aspects of Mathematics," *Bull. of the Amer. Math. Soc.* 34 (July-August 1928) 438.

2   Mathematical reasoning which seemed quite sound has led to distressing contradictions. As long as one of these is unexplained in a final and conclusive manner there is no guarantee that other forms of reasoning now in good standing may not lead to other contradictions as yet unsuspected. For ages the reasoning employed in mathematics has been regarded as a model of logical perfection; mathematicians have prided themselves that their science is the one science so irrefutably established that never in its long history has it had to take a backward step.

No wonder then, that these paradoxes of Burali-Forti (1897), Russell, and others produced consternation in the camp of the mathematicians; no wonder that the foundations on which mathematics rest are being scrutinized as never before. Elaborate attempts are now in progress to give mathematics a foundation as secure as it was thought to have in the days of Euclid or of Weierstrass. Personally we do not believe that absolute rigor will ever be attained and if a time arrives when this is thought to be the case, it will be a sign the the race of mathematicians has declined. —James Pierpont

"Mathematical Rigor, Past and Present," *Bull. of the Amer. Math. Soc.* 34 (January-February 1928) 23.

3 We have had hitherto prophets of evil. They blithely reiterate that all problems capable of solution have already been solved and that nothing is left but gleaning. Happily the case of the past reassures us. Often it was thought all problems were solved or at least an inventory was made of all admitting solution. And then the sense of the word solution enlarged, and insoluble problems became the most interesting of all, and others unforeseen presented themselves. ... The pessimists thus found themselves always outflanked, always forced to retreat, so that at present I think there are no more. —Henri Poincaré

"Science and Method," in G. B. Halsted (trans.), *The Foundations of Science,* New York: The Science Press, 1929, p. 369.

4 It is well-known that
Scientific knowledge
Is increasing all the time,
That science is a
Living, growing subject.

But one generally thinks of
Mathematics as being
So old and so "finished",
That it cannot grow any more.

Indeed
The mathematics

(Arithmetic, algebra, geometry)
Taught in the schools
Was known
CENTURIES AGO;
And even the
Usual COLLEGE course
Dates back
THREE HUNDRED YEARS,
For analytics was created by Descartes
And calculus by Newton,
Both in the 17th century.

And yet the fact is
That mathematics,
EVEN TO A GREATER EXTENT THAN SCIENCE,
Has moved steadily forward
Since that time.

—Lillian R. Lieber
Galois and the Theory of Groups, Lancaster PA: Science Press, 1932, introduction.

5 We learn more and more to coordinate different mathematical sciences. So, for example, geometry and the theory of numbers, which for long seemed to represent antagonistic tendencies, no longer form an antithesis, but have come in many ways to appear as different aspects of one and the same theory. —Felix Klein

E. T. Bell, "Fifty Years of Algebra in America, 1888-1938," *Semicentennial Addresses of the American Mathematical Society, Vol II,* New York: American Mathematical Society, 1938, p. 12.

6 Banish the infinite process, and mathematics pure and applied is reduced to the state in which it was known to the pre-Pythagoreans.

—Tobias Dantzig
Number the Language of Science, New York: Macmillan, 1939, p. 137.

7 Today we know that possibility and impossibility have each only a relative meaning; that neither is an intrinsic property of the operation but merely a *restriction which human tradition has imposed on the field*

of the operand. Remove the barrier, extend the field, and the impossible becomes possible.   —Tobias Dantzig
> *Number the Language of Science,* New York: Macmillan, 1939, p. 89.

8   A Russian peasant came to Moscow for the first time ... He went to the zoo and saw the giraffes. You may find a moral in his reaction ... "Look," he said, "at what the Bolsheviks have done to our horses." That is what modern mathematics has done to simple geometry and to simple arithmetic.   —Edward Kasner and James Newman
> *Mathematics and the Imagination,* New York: Simon and Schuster, 1940, p. 8.

9   A serious threat to the very life of science is implied in the assertion that mathematics is nothing but a system of conclusions drawn from definitions and postulates that must be consistent but otherwise may be created by the free will of the mathematician. If this description were accurate, mathematics could not attract any intelligent person. It would be a game with definitions, rules and syllogisms, without motivation or goal. The notion that the intellect can create meaningful postulational systems at its whim is a deceptive half-truth. Only under the discipline of responsibility to the organic whole, only guided by intrinsic necessity, can the free mind achieve results of scientific value.
> —Richard Courant and Herbert Robbins
> *What Is Mathematics?,* London: Oxford University Press, 1941, p. xvii.

10   In the opinion of many laymen mathematics is today already a dead science: after having reached an unusually high degree of development, it has become petrified in rigid perfection. This is an entirely erroneous view of the situation; there are but few domains of scientific research which are passing through a phase of such intensive development at present as mathematics. Moreover, this development is extraordinarily manifold: mathematics is expanding its domain in all possible directions, it is growing in height, in width, and in depth. It is growing in height, since, on the soil of its old theories which look back upon hundreds if not thousands of years of development, new problems appear again and again, and ever more perfect results are being achieved. It is growing in width, since its methods permeate other branches of sciences, while its domain of investigation embraces increasingly more comprehensive ranges of phenomena and ever new theories are being included in the large circle of mathematical disciplines. And finally it is growing in depth, since its foundations become more and more firmly established, its methods perfected, and its principles stabilized. —Alfred Tarski

> *Introduction to Logic,* New York: Oxford University Press, 1946, p. xvii.

II From the observation of nature, the ancient Babylonians and Egyptians built up a body of mathematical knowledge which they used in making further observations. Thales perhaps introduced deductive methods; certainly the mathematics of the early Pythagoreans was deductive in character. The Pythagoreans and Plato noted that the conclusions they reached deductively agreed to a remarkable extent with the results of observation and inductive inference. Unable to account otherwise for this agreement, they were led to regard mathematics as the study of ultimate, eternal reality, immanent in nature and the universe, rather than as a branch of logic or a tool of science and technology. An understanding of mathematical principles, they decided, must precede any valid interpretation of experience. This view is reflected in the Pythagorean dictum that all is number, and in the assertion attributed to Plato that God always plays the geometer. —Carl B. Boyer

> *The Concepts of the Calculus,* New York: Hafner, 1949, p. 1.

I2 Brouwer set out to build up a new mathematics which makes no use of that logical principle [the principle of excluded middle]. I think that everybody has to accept Brouwer's critique who wants to hold on to the belief that mathematical propositions tell the sheer truth, truth based on evidence. At least Brouwer's opponent, Hilbert, accepted it tacitly. He tried to save classical mathematics by converting it from a system of meaningful propositions into a game of meaningless formulas, and by showing that this game never leads to two formulas, F and non-F, which are inconsistent. Consistency, not truth, is his aim. His attempts at proving consistency revealed the astonishingly complex logical structure of mathematics. The first steps were promising indeed. But then Gödel's discovery cast a deep shadow over Hilbert's enterprise. Consistency itself may be expressed by a formula. What Gödel showed was this: If the game of mathematics is actually consistent then the formula of consistency cannot be proved within the game.

—Hermann Weyl
"A Half-century of Mathematics," *Amer. Math. Monthly* 58 (October 1951) 552.

13   The axiomatic approach has often revealed inner relations between, and has made for unification of methods within, domains that apparently lie far apart. This tendency of several branches of mathematics to coalesce is another conspicuous feature in the modern development of our science, and one that goes side by side with the apparently opposite tendency of axiomatization. It is as if you took a man out of a milieu in which he had lived not because it fitted him but from ingrained habits and prejudices, and then allowed him, after thus setting him free, to form associations in better accordance with his true inner nature.

—Hermann Weyl
"A Half-century of Mathematics," *Amer. Math. Monthly* 58 (October 1951) 524.

14   Mathematicians create by acts of insight and intuition. Logic then sanctions the conquests of intuition. It is the hygiene that mathematics practices to keep its ideas healthy and strong. Moreover, the whole structure rests fundamentally on uncertain ground, the intuitions of man. Here and there an intuition is scooped out and replaced by a firmly built pillar of thought; however, this pillar is based on some deeper, perhaps less clearly defined intuition. Though the process of replacing intuitions by precise thoughts does not change the nature of the ground on which mathematics ultimately rests, it does add strength and height to the structure.   —Morris Kline
Mathematics in Western Culture, New York: Oxford University Press, 1953, p. 408.

15   If it were possible to weld together the whole of knowledge into two general laws, a mathematician would not be satisfied. He would not be happy until he had shown that these two laws were rooted in a single principle. Nor would he be happy then; indeed he would be miserable, for there would be nothing more for him to do. But there is not the least likelihood of this state of stagnation arising. It is a property of life, a property without which life would be unendurable, that the solution

of one problem always creates another. There always is, there always will be something to learn, something to conquer. —W. W. Sawyer
Prelude to Mathematics, Baltimore: Penguin Books, 1957, p. 29.

16 The history of mathematics therefore consists of alternate expansions and contractions. A problem occupies the attention of mathematicians; hundreds of papers are written, each clarifying one facet of the truth; the subject is growing. Then, helped perhaps by the information so painfully gathered together, some exceptional genius will say, 'All that we know can be seen as almost obvious if you look at it from this viewpoint, and bear this principle in mind'. It then ceases to be necessary to read the hundreds of separate contributions, except for the mathematical historian. The variegated results are welded together into a simple doctrine, the significant facts are separated from the chaff, the straight road to the desired conclusion is open to all. The bulk of what needs to be learnt has contracted. But this is not the end. The new methods having become common property, new problems are found which they are insufficient to solve, new gropings after solutions are made, new papers are published; expansion begins again.

—W. W. Sawyer
Prelude to Mathematics, Baltimore: Penguin Books, 1957, p. 28.

17 Gödel's proof should not be construed as a invitation to despair or as an excuse for mystery-mongering. The discovery that there are arithmetical truths which cannot be demonstrated formally does not mean that there are truths which are forever incapable of becoming known or that a "mystic" intuition (radically different in kind and authority from what is generally operative in intellectual advances) must replace cogent proof. It does not mean, as a recent writer claims, that there are "ineluctable limits to human reason." It does mean that the resources of the human intellect have not been, and cannot be, fully formalized, and that new principles of demonstration forever await invention and discovery. We have seen that mathematical propositions which cannot be established by formal deduction from a given set of axioms may, nevertheless, be established by "informal" meta-mathematical reasoning. It would be irresponsible to claim that these formally indemonstrable truths established by meta-mathematical arguments are based on nothing better than bare appeals to intuition.

Nor do the inherent limitations of calculating machines imply that we cannot hope to explain living matter and human reason in physical and chemical terms. The possibility of such explanations is neither precluded nor affirmed by Gödel's incompleteness theorem. The theorem does indicate that the structure and power of the human mind are far more complex and subtle than any non-living machine yet envisaged. Gödel's own work is a remarkable example of such complexity and subtlety. It is an occasion, not for dejection, but for a renewed appreciation of the powers of creative reason.

—Ernest Nagel and James R. Newman
Gödel's Proof, New York: New York University Press, 1958, p. 101.

18   Poincaré had used the materials of the nineteenth-century mathematics to revolutionize much of mathematics. He had gone so far in mathematics that it is doubtful whether his young colleagues in France could go on in the same sense without introducing essentially new techniques. This was in fact what several of them did. One of the new fields was what is called "set theory," and one of the innovators Lebesgue.

Poincaré criticized the members of the new school rather severely. It is on record that at a Congress in Rome he made this prediction. "Later generations will regard set theory as a malady from which one has recovered." (One may remark parenthetically that the history of art records many maladies from which art has recovered).

The response of Lebesgue to Poincaré was given on his elevation to a Professorship at the Collège de France. An older eminent colleague had praised the school of Lebesgue. Lebesgue made public reference to the "precious encouragement which had largely compensated for the reproaches" which his school had had to suffer. . . .

I am . . . one of the few mathematicians who think that Poincaré as well as Lebesgue was right, in that mathematics will return more completely to the great ideas of Poincaré with full appreciation of the innovations of Lebesgue, but with a truer understanding of the relation of mathematical technique to mathematical art.   —Marston Morse
"Mathematics and the Arts," *Bull. of the Atomic Scientist* 15 (February 1959) 57.

19   It may seem to be a stark paradox that, just when mathematics has been brought close to the ultimate in abstractness, its applications have begun to multiply and proliferate in an extraordinary fashion. ... Far from being paradoxical, however, this conjunction of two apparently opposite trends in the development of mathematics may rightly be viewed as the sign of an essential truth about mathematics itself. For it is only to the extent that mathematics is freed from the bonds which have attached it in the past to particular aspects of reality that it can become the extremely flexible and powerful instrument we need to break paths into areas now beyond our ken.   —Marshall H. Stone

"The Revolution in Mathematics," *Liberal Education* 47 (May 1961) 310.

20   Mathematics is now seen to have no necessary connections with the physical world beyond the vague and mystifying one implicit in the statement that thinking takes place in the brain. The discovery that this is so may be said without exaggeration to mark one of the most significant intellectual advances in the history of mankind, comparable so far as mathematics is concerned with only one other great discovery—the recognition by the Greeks that the empirical facts of geometry fall into logical patterns which can be so amalgamated that the whole subject appears as a coherent logical structure based on a limited number of axioms.   —Marshall H. Stone

"The Revolution in Mathematics," *Liberal Education* 47 (May 1961) 305.

21   What are the distinguishing characteristics of contemporary mathematics? It seems to me that there are four of them which I would describe as follows:

I. Contemporary mathematics is classical mathematics grown mature.

II. Contemporary mathematics is classical mathematics grown self-conscious and self-critical.

III. It is also modern mathematics which developed as a more efficient way of dealing with the content of classical mathematics.

IV. Finally, it is mathematics that is more and more intimately related to man's activities in industry, social life, science, and philosophy.

—Irving Adler

"The Changes Taking Place in Mathematics," *Math. Teacher* 55 (October 1962) 441.

22   Our epoch is the epoch of increasing consciousness; in this field Mathematics has done its bit. It has made us conscious of the limits of its own capabilities.   —Rózsa Péter

> *Playing with Infinity,* New York: Simon and Schuster, 1962, p. 264.

23   The eternal lesson is that Mathematics is not something static, closed, but living and developing. Try as we may to constrain it into a closed form, it finds an outlet somewhere and escapes alive.

—Rózsa Péter

> *Playing with Infinity,* New York: Simon and Schuster, 1962, p. 265.

24   There are and have been, at least since the time of Euclid, two antithetical forces at work in mathematics. These may be viewed in the great periods of mathematical development, one of them moving in the direction of "constructive invention, of directing and motivating intuition," the other adhering to the ideal of precision and rigorous proof that made its appearance in Greek mathematics and has been extensively developed during the nineteenth and twentieth centuries.

—Mina Rees

> "The Nature of Mathematics," *Math. Teacher* 55 (October 1962) 434.

25   Mathematics is the servant as well as the queen of the sciences, and she weaves a rich fabric of creative theory, which is often inspired by observations in the phenomenal world, but is also often inspired by a creative insight that recognizes identical mathematical structures in dissimilar realizations by stripping the realizations of their substance and concerning itself only with undefined objects and the rules governing their relation.   —Mina Rees

> "The Nature of Mathematics," *Math. Teacher* 55 (October 1962) 435.

26   We can see that the development of mathematics is a process of conflict among the many contrasting elements: the concrete and the abstract, the particular and the general, the formal and the material, the finite and the infinite, the discrete and the continuous, and so forth.

—A. D. Aleksandrov

> A. D. Aleksandrov, A. N. Kolmogorov, M. A. Lavrent'ev (eds.), *Mathematics: Its Content, Methods, and Meaning, Vol. I,* Cambridge, MA: MIT Press, 1963, p. 30.

27 Geometers and algebraists perceived almost simultaneously that numbers and number systems are not supernaturally imposed upon human beings from above but are free creations of mortal man.

The progression of ideas is illustrated by the following quotations:

Plato: "God ever geometrizes."

Jacobi: "God ever arithmetizes."

Dedekind: "Man ever arithmetizes."

Cantor: "The essence of mathematics is in its freedom."

—Miriam H. Young
"Number in the Western World—a Bibliography,"
Arithmetic Teacher 11 (May 1964) 339.

28 Postulates and concepts are created not by the common agreement of scientists but by scattered individuals or small groups. At the moment of conception concepts are formless, implications of theories are only partially understood; later, theories produced by specialists in one department of the science are found to conflict with the postulates of other departments, in themselves equally plausible or as firmly established. The necessity of resolving such discords reacts upon the concepts of the science, leads to more exact formulation of the postulates and clearer understanding of the concepts involved. ...

Nowhere have such contradictions been more frequent than in mathematics, nor has progress in any science been more steady. Gauss and Fermat, among scores of other famous names, are sufficient illustrations of famous mathematicians who were able to obtain, by apparently fallacious reasoning, valid results of the highest importance in subsequent mathematical researches.   —Max Black
The Nature of Mathematics, Totowa, NJ: Littlefield,
Adams & Co., 1965, p. 2.

29 When faced with the difficulty of clarifying existing knowledge, the temptation is great to find compensation in admiring the complex structure which represents partial success and to supplement it by unwarranted extrapolation. In the case of one's own philosophic system familiarity or the inertia of habitual thought processes inspires exaggerated respect and tempts the philosopher to bring the technique of theology to the help of the analytic method. God arrives to solve the difficulties of Berkeleian idealism or Bertrand Russell in less ambitious times invokes the Axiom of Reducibility.

In no branch of critical philosophy is this danger greater than in the analysis of mathematics.   —Max Black

> *The Nature of Mathematics,* Totowa, NJ: Littlefield, Adams & Co., 1965, p. 5.

30   The decimal notation is not a heritage from the Greeks. As a result, everything dealing with that notation has been superimposed on Greek teaching and not incorporated into it. *Our teaching does not yet make full use of that historical event, which is perhaps the most important event in the history of science, namely, the invention of the decimal system of numeration.*   — Henri Lebesgue

> *Measure and the Integral,* San Francisco: Holden-Day, 1966, p. 18.

31   Classical mathematics had its roots in the regular geometric structures of Euclid and the continuously evolving dynamics of Newton. Modern mathematics began with Cantor's set theory and Peano's space-filling curve. Historically, the revolution was forced by the discovery of mathematical structures that did not fit the patterns of Euclid and Newton. These new structures were regarded . . . as "pathologica." They were described as a "gallery of monsters," kin to the cubist painting and atonal music that were upsetting established standards of taste in the arts at about the same time. The mathematicians who created the monsters regarded them as important in showing that the world of pure mathematics contains a richness of possibilities going far beyond the simple structures that they saw in nature. Twentieth-century mathematics flowered in the belief that it had transcended completely the limitations imposed by its natural origins. . . .

Nature has played a joke on the mathematicians. The 19th-century mathematicians may have been lacking in imagination, but nature was not. The same pathological structures that the mathematician invented to break loose from 19th-century naturalism turn out to be inherent in familiar objects all around us.   —Freeman Dyson

> "Characterizing Irregularity," *Science* 200 (12 May 1978) 677.

32   Any part of modern mathematics is the end-product of a long history. It has drawn on many other branches of earlier mathematics, it has extracted various essences from them and has been reformulated again and again in increasingly general and abstract forms. Thus a student may not be able to see what it is all about, in much the same way that a caveman confronted with a vitamin pill would not easily recognize it as food.   —W. W. Sawyer

A First Look at Numerical Functional Analysis, Oxford: Clarendon Press, 1978, p. 1.

33   The world of mathematics may be visualized as many concentric layers built on the core of pure mathematics. This core is still red-hot with new ideas, new structures, and new theories. Ideas from the core percolate through the outer layers of the mathematical sciences, providing a constant supply of intellectual fuel for some of the incredibly complex problems of the more applied fields. And, in return, problems arising in the outer layers—in the diffuse boundary where pure mathematics blends with applied science—provide the central core with new structures, new methods, and new concepts.

Core mathematics is the science of significant form. It is nourished both by internal energy, like a self-sustaining atomic reaction, and by new fuel supplied by outer layers that are in closer contact with the surface of human problems. Layers near the core employ sophisticated techniques in the service of external objectives. Theories in these layers are directed more towards solving problems than towards discovering basic form. Layers remote from the core employ mathematics more as a metaphor than as theory: applications blend with technique so thoroughly that a totally different discipline emerges. Theory and problems diffuse through the ill-defined boundaries between these layers, each enriching the other and nourishing both mathematics and science.

—Lynn Arthur Steen

Mathematics Today, New York: Springer-Verlag, 1978, p. 7.

34   Mathematical work does not proceed along the narrow logical path of truth to truth to truth, but bravely or gropingly follows deviations through the surrounding marshland of propositions which are neither simply and wholly true nor simply and wholly false.

—Seymour Papert

Mindstorms, New York: Basic Books, 1980, p. 195.

35   There are original ideas which may, for a while, open up new things, but still they are connected with other important parts of mathematics and interact. The importance of a part of mathematics is

something one can judge roughly by the amount of interaction it has with other parts of the subject. It is a kind of self-consistent definition of importance. —Michael Atiyah
> Robert Minio, "An Interview with Michael Atiyah," *Math. Intell.* 6 (No. 1, 1984) 11.

36   It isn't our sensory and perceptual activity that forces nature into a strait-jacket of mathematics, it is Nature, which, in the process of our evolutionary development, has impressed mathematics into our reason as a real, existing structure, inherent to herself.   —Gert Eilenberger
> "Freedom, Science, and Aesthetics," in H.-O. Peitgen and P. H. Richter, *The Beauty of Fractals,* New York: Springer-Verlag, 1986, p. 178.

37   For the Greeks, Mathematics was geometry, and they formulated real numbers and algebraic operations only in geometric terms. In the 18th century, Mathematics appeared largely in the development of all the aspects of the calculus; this was a natural reflection of the wide opportunities this development offered for formal manipulations and for extensive applications. Subsequently the extraordinary fruitful properties of holomorphic functions made complex variable theory a center about which (much of) Mathematics could revolve. ... In geometry, Felix Klein proposed that the many varieties of space provided by non-Euclidean and other geometries could be classified and hence organized in terms of their groups of symmetries. ...

This variety of proposals for organizations reflects the diversity and richness of Mathematics. —Saunders Mac Lane
> *Mathematics: Form and Function,* New York: Springer-Verlag, 1986, p. 407.

38   Mathematics develops, somehow, by its own inner laws.
> —Lipman Bers
> Donald J. Albers and Constance Reid, "An Interview with Lipman Bers," *Coll. Math. J.* 18 (September 1987) 288.

39   Three shifts can be detected over time in the understanding of mathematics itself. One is a shift from completeness to incompleteness, another from certainty to conjecture, and a third from absolutism to relativity.

—Leone Burton

"Femmes et Mathématiques: Y a-t-il une Intersection?" *Assoc. for Women in Math. Newsletter* 18
(November-December 1988) 17. French version published in Louise Lafortune (ed.), *Femmes et Mathématiques,* Les Editions du remue-ménage, Montréal,
1986.

40   Nowadays if there is an important breakthrough in some area, there is a horde of bright young mathematicians waiting to pounce on it, to exploit all the consequences, and solve all the reasonable problems that are opened up. It is quite possible that after a few years there will be nothing left to do in such an area except to write up a nice expository account, and then wait for another breakthrough.

By contrast, I can imagine that in the early years of this century there would have been very few mathematicians available to work out the consequences of any major breakthrough. Those who did choose to work in the area of such a breakthrough could proceed in a more deliberate manner, without much competition, and they could count on fruitfully spending a substantial portion of their career in this one area.

Obviously this imposes an additional burden on a research mathematician; if he wishes to remain genuinely productive, he may have to change to a new field of research several times during his career.

—W. S. Massey

"Reminiscences of Forty Years as a Mathematician,"
in Peter Duren (ed.), *A Century of Mathematics in
America, Part 1,* Providence, RI: American Mathematical Society, 1988, p. 409.

41   I think mathematics is a vast territory. The outskirts of mathematics are the outskirts of mathematical civilization. There are certain subjects that people learn about and gather together. Then there is a sort of inevitable development in those fields. You get to the point where a certain theorem is bound to be proved, independent of any particular individual, because it is just in the path of development.

—William Thurston

"William P. Thurston," in D. Albers, G. Alexanderson,
C. Reid (eds.), *More Mathematical People,* New York:
Harcourt Brace Jovanovich, 1990, p. 332.

CHAPTER 3

Particular Disciplines in Mathematics

1   In spite of the richness and power of recent geometry, it is noticeable that the geometer himself has become more modest. It was the ambition of Descartes and Leibniz to discover universal methods, applicable to all conceivable questions; later, the Ausdehnungslehre of Grassman and the quaternion theory of Hamilton were believed by their devotees to be ultimate geometric analyses; and Chasles attributed to the principles of duality and homography the same role in the domain of pure space as that of the law of gravitation in celestial mechanics. Today the mathematician admits the existence and the necessity of many theories, many geometries, each appealing to certain interests, each to be developed by the most appropriate methods; and he realizes that, no matter how large his conceptions and how powerful his methods, they will be replaced before long by others larger and more powerful.

—Edward Kasner
"The Present Problems of Geometry," *Bull. of the Amer. Math. Soc.* 11 (February 1905) 283.

2   Modern pure geometry differs from the geometry of earlier times not so much in the subjects dealt with as in the processes employed and the generality of the results obtained. Much of the material is old, but by utilizing the principle of projection and the theory of transversals, facts which were thought of as in no way related, prove to be simply different aspects of the same general truth. This generalizing tendency is the chief characteristic of modern geometry.   —Thomas F. Holgate

"Modern Pure Geometry," in J. W. A. Young (ed.), *Monographs on the Topics of Modern Mathematics Relevant to the Elementary Field,* New York: Longmans, Green, 1911, p. 56.

3   Geometry is a mountain. Vigor is needed for its ascent. The views all along the paths are magnificent. The effort of climbing is stimulating. A guide who points out the beauties, the grandeur, and the special places of interest commands the admiration of his group of pilgrims.

One who fails to do this, who does not know the paths, who puts unnecessary burdens upon the pilgrim, or who blindfolds him in his progress, is unworthy of his position. The pretended guide who says that the painted panorama, seen from the rubber-tired car, is as good as the view from the summit is simply a fakir and is generally recognized as such. The mountain will stand; it will not be used as a mere commercial quarry for building stone; it will not be affected by pellets thrown from the little hillocks about; but its paths will be freed from unnecessary flints, they will be straightened where this can advantageously be done, and new paths on entirely novel plans will be made as time goes on, but these paths will be hewed out of rock, not made out of the dreams of a day. Every worthy guide will assist in all these efforts at betterment, and will urge the pilgrim at least to ascend a little way because of the fact that the same view cannot be obtained from other peaks; but he will not take seriously the efforts of the fakir, nor will he listen with more than passing interest to him who proclaims the sand heap to be a Matterhorn.

—D. E. Smith

The Teaching of Geometry, Boston: Ginn, 1911, p. 333.

4   The struggle between analysis and pure geometry has long since come to an end. Each has its distinct advantages, and the mathematician who cultivates one at the expense of the other will never attain the results that he would attain if both methods were equally ready to his hand. Pure geometry has to its credit some of the finest discoveries in mathematics, and need not apologize for having been born. The day of its usefulness has not passed with the invention of abridged notation and of short methods in analysis. While we may be certain that any geometrical problem may always be stated in analytic form, it does not follow that that statement will be simple or easily interpreted. For many mathematicians the geometric intuitions are weak, and for such the method will have little attraction. On the other hand, there will always be those for whom the subject will have a peculiar glamor—who will follow with delight the curious and unexpected relations between the forms of space. There is a corresponding pleasure, doubtless, for the analyst in tracing the marvelous connections between the various fields in which he wanders, and it is as absurd to shut one's eyes to the beauties in one as it is to ignore those in the other.   —D. N. Lehmer

An Elementary Course in Synthetic Projective Geometry,
New York: Ginn, 1917, p. 119.

5   It was formerly supposed that Geometry was the study of the nature of the space in which we live, and accordingly it was urged, by those who held that what exists can only be known empirically, that Geometry should really be regarded as belonging to applied mathematics. But it has gradually appeared, by the increase of non-Euclidean systems, that Geometry throws no more light upon the nature of space than Arithmetic throws upon the population of the United States.

—Bertrand Russell
"Mathematics and the Metaphysicians," *Mysticism and Logic and Other Essays,* London: George Allen and Unwin, 1917, p. 92.

6   However the formulae [of mathematical probability] may be derived, they frequently prove remarkably trustworthy in practice. The proper attitude is not to reject laws of doubtful origin, but to scrutinize them with care, with a view to reaching the true principles underneath. It seems to me that, in the last analysis, probability is a statistical, that is to say, an experimental science, and the mathematical problem is to establish rules which yield correct and valuable results.

—Julian L. Coolidge
An Introduction to Mathematical Probability, Oxford: Clarendon Press, 1925, p. vi.

7   Our Geometry is an abstract Geometry. The reasoning could be followed by a disembodied spirit who had no idea of a physical point, just as a man blind from birth could understand the Electromagnetic Theory of Light.   —Henry G. Forder

The Foundations of Euclidean Geometry, Cambridge: The University Press, 1927, p. 43.

8   Any mathematical science is a body of theorems deduced from a set of axioms. A geometry is a mathematical science. The question then arises why the name geometry is given to some mathematical sciences and not to others. It is likely that there is no definite answer to this question, but that a branch of mathematics is called a geometry because the name seems good, on emotional and traditional grounds, to a sufficient number of competent people.

—Oswald Veblen and J. H. C. Whitehead
The Foundation of Differential Geometry, Cambridge: University Press, 1932, p. 17.

9   Probably no branch of mathematics has experienced a more surprising growth than has, during the past two decades, that field known variously as Topology or Analysis Situs. Originating in the work of many mathematicians of the past century, including Cantor, Riemann, and Kronecker, it won recognition as a distinct branch of mathematics largely through the writings of Poincaré about the beginning of the present century. Although having many ramifications, it has progressively become a unified subject and due to its foundation in the theory of abstract spaces, has come to collaborate with abstract group theory as a unifying force in mathematics as a whole. It has provided a tool for classification and unification, as well as for extension and generalization, in algebra, analysis, and geometry. Considered as a most specialized and abstract subject in the early 1920's, it is today almost an indispensable equipment for the investigator in modern mathematical theories.

—Raymond L. Wilder
"The Sphere of Topology," *Semicentennial Addresses of the American Mathematical Society, Vol II,* New York: American Mathematical Society, 1938, p. 136.

10   Algebra tends to the study of the explicit structure of postulationally defined systems closed with respect to one or more rational operations.

—George Birkhoff
"Some Recent Advances in Algebra," *Amer. Math. Monthly* 46 (January 1939) 18.

11   There appears a *fundamental principle* which can serve to characterize all possible geometries. .... *Given any group of transformations in space which includes the principal group as a sub-group, then the invariant*

theory of this group gives a definite kind of geometry, and every possible geometry can be obtained in this way. —Felix Klein
Elementary Mathematics from an Advanced Standpoint
—Geometry, New York: Dover, 1939, p. 133.

12 Arithmetic has been the queen and the handmaiden of the sciences from the days of the astrologers of Chaldea and the high priests of Egypt to the present days of relativity, quanta, and the adding machine. Historians may dispute the meaning of ancient papyri, theologians may wrangle over the exegesis of Scripture, philosophers may debate over Pythagorean doctrine, but all will concede that the numbers in the papyri, in the Scriptures and in the writings of Pythagoras are the same as the numbers of today. As arithmetic, mathematics has helped man to cast horoscopes, to make calendars, to predict the risings of the Nile, to measure fields and the height of the Pyramids, to measure the speed of a stone as it fell from a tower in Pisa, the speed of an apple as it fell from a tree in Woolsthorpe, to weigh the stars and the atoms, to mark the passage of time, to find the curvature of space. And although mathematics is also the calculus, the theory of probability, the matrix algebra, the science of the infinite, it is still the art of counting.

—Edward Kasner and James Newman
Mathematics and the Imagination, New York: Simon and Schuster, 1940, p. 28.

13 The function of mathematical logic is to reveal and codify the logical processes employed in mathematical reasoning and to clarify the concepts of mathematics; it is itself a branch of mathematics, employing mathematical symbolism and technique, a branch which has developed in its entirety during the past hundred years and which in its vigour and fecundity and the power and importance of its discoveries may well claim to be in the forefront of modern mathematics.

—Reuben L. Goodstein
Mathematical Logic, Leicester: Leicester University Press, 1957, p. 1.

14 Just as there is an applied mathematics of games, genetics, and mechanics, so there should be an applied mathematics (at least in terms of concepts, perhaps with techniques and operations) of the applications of mathematics. When there is, mathematicians will be able to teach "the applications of mathematics." —John W. Tukey
"The Teaching of Concrete Mathematics," *Amer. Math. Monthly* 65 (January 1958) 8.

15   The intermarriage of traditional analysis with its neighbors has not come about as a rational decision of its practitioners. At first sight, the change seemed to have been largely a matter of semantics; one adopted the terminology of algebra and topology solely as a convenience to describe briefly certain situations which arose frequently. But it soon became evident that the adoption of another viewpoint, another observation platform, gave a clearer vision; the introduction of techniques borrowed from other fields enabled the analyst to achieve both striking economies in proof, and vivid insights into classical phenomena.

—R. C. Buck
Studies in Modern Analysis, Englewood, NJ: Prentice-Hall, 1962, p. 2.

16   The stimulus to the investigations from which the theory of sets grew, was given by problems of analysis, the establishing of the foundations of the theory of irrational numbers, the theory of trigonometric series, etc. However, the further development of set theory went initially in an abstract direction, little connected with other branches of mathematics. This fact, together with a certain strangeness of the methods of set theory which were entirely different from those applied up to that time, caused many mathematicians to regard this new branch of mathematics initially with a certain degree of distrust and reluctance. In the course of years, however, when set theory showed its usefulness in many branches of mathematics such as the theory of analytic functions or theory of measure, and when it became an indispensable basis for new mathematical disciplines (such as topology, the theory of functions of a real variable, the foundations of mathematics), it became an especially important branch and tool of modern mathematics.

—Kazimierz Kuratowski
Introduction to Set Theory and Topology, Reading, MA: Addison-Wesley, 1962, p. 19.

17   The calculus is one of the grandest edifices constructed by mankind.
—Cambridge Conference on School Mathematics
Goals for School Mathematics, Boston: Houghton Mifflin, 1963, p. 9.

18   In 1910 the mathematician Oswald Veblen and the physicist James Jeans were discussing the reform of the mathematical curriculum at Princeton University. "We may as well cut out group theory," said Jeans. "That is a subject which will never be of any use to physics."

It is not recorded whether Veblen disputed Jeans's point, or whether he argued for the retention of group theory on purely mathematical grounds. All we know is that group theory continued to be taught. And Veblen's disregard for Jeans's advice turned out to be of some importance to the history of science at Princeton. By the irony of fate group theory later grew into one of the central themes of physics, and it still dominates the thinking of all of us who are struggling to understand the fundamental particles of nature. —Freeman J. Dyson
"Mathematics in the Physical Sciences," *Scientific American* 211 (September 1964) 129.

19 Geometry today consists of many subdivisions. There are synthetic geometry, analytic geometry, and differential geometry. There are Euclidean geometry, hyperbolic geometry, and elliptic geometry. There are also metric geometry, affine geometry, projective geometry, and other branches besides. The subdivisions of geometry have been compared to the distinguishable regions within a complex landscape. Most of these regions are in a valley. An explorer who is deep within one region can easily lose sight of the fact that the other regions exist. At a boundary where one region touches another he can see the fact that the regions are related to each other. But seeing the regions pair by pair does not suffice to reveal the pattern of this relationship. There is a path from the valley that leads up the side of a mountain to a clearing at the top. The explorer who reaches this clearing suddenly sees the whole valley laid out before his eyes. From his height at the top of he mountain he can see all the regions of the valley and the pattern that they form . . . he can see the grand design of the valley in all its breathtaking splendor.
—Irving Adler
A New Look at Geometry, New York: John Day, 1966, p. 9.

20 The idea of a group was born in the eighteenth century through the study of certain groups that arise in algebra. Later it was found that there are also groups that are important in geometry and other branches of mathematics. Then it was found that groups play an important part in art and science, too. . . . For this reason, group theory is used today in many of the sciences. It is used, for example by crystallographers studying the symmetries of crystals of minerals. It is used by physicists and chemists studying the symmetries of particles and of fields of force.

The importance of group theory was emphasized very dramatically recently when some physicists using group theory predicted the existence of a particle that had never been observed before, and described the properties that it should have. Later experiments proved that this particle really exists and has those properties. —Irving Adler

Groups in the New Mathematics, New York: John Day, 1967, p. 7.

21 In our times, geometers are still exploring those new Wonderlands, partly for the sake of their applications to cosmology and other branches of science but much more for the sheer joy of passing through the looking glass into a land where the familiar lines, planes, triangles, circles, and spheres are seen to behave in strange but precisely determined ways. —H. S. M. Coxeter

"Non-Euclidean Geometry," in COSRIMS, *The Mathematical Sciences,* Cambridge, MA: MIT Press, 1969, p. 58.

22 The basic definitions and facts of this theory [of categories and functors] were so naive that to some it seemed highly unlikely that such a theory could have any impact. Nonetheless, only twenty-five years after the definitions were laid down, it has become clear that the theory is appearing with ever-increasing frequency in many developments of modern mathematics. Sometimes it is helpful only in organizing the formalism, but frequently the contribution is more substantial. One recent application of the theory of categories may be witnessed in the theory of automata, computer languages, and abstract linguistics. There are good reasons to believe that, as a result of research still in progress, these theories will be drastically altered by the use of the theory of categories. —Samuel Eilenberg

"The Algebraization of Mathematics," in COSRIMS, *The Mathematical Sciences,* Cambridge, MA: MIT Press, 1969, p. 159.

23 Modern algebraic geometry has deservedly been considered for a long time as an exceedingly complex part of mathematics, drawing practically on every other part to build up its concepts and methods and increasingly becoming an indispensable tool in many seemingly remote theories. It shares with number theory the distinction of having one of the longest and most intricate histories among all branches of our science, of having always attracted the efforts of the best mathematicians

in each generation, and of still being one of the most active areas of
research.   —Jean Dieudonné
"The Historical Development of Algebraic Geome-
try," *Amer. Math. Monthly* 79 (October 1972) 827.

24 People enjoy inventing slogans which violate basic arithmetic but
which illustrate "deeper" truths, such as "1 and 1 make 1" (for lovers),
or "1 plus 1 plus 1 equals 1" (the Trinity)... Two raindrops running down
a window pane merge; does one plus one make one? A cloud breaks up
into two clouds—more evidence for the same? ... Numbers as realities
misbehave. However, there is an ancient and innate sense in people that
numbers ought not to misbehave. There is something clean and pure in
the abstract notion of number ... and there ought to be a way of talking
about numbers without always having the silliness of reality come in and
intrude. The hard-edged rules that govern "ideal" numbers constitute
arithmetic, and their more advanced consequences constitute number
theory.   —Douglas Hofstadter
Gödel, Escher, Bach: An Eternal Golden Braid, New
York: Basic Books, 1979, p. 56.

25 Why is geometry often described as "cold" and "dry?" One
reason lies in its inability to describe the shape of a cloud, a mountain,
a coastline, or a tree. Clouds are not spheres, mountains are not cones,
coastlines are not circles, and bark is not smooth, nor does lightning
travel in a straight line.

More generally, I claim that many patterns of Nature are so irregular
and fragmented, that, compared with *Euclid,* . . . Nature exhibits not simply a higher degree but an altogether different level of complexity. . . .

The existence of these patterns challenges us to study those forms that
Euclid leaves aside as being "formless," to investigate the morphology
of the "amorphous." Mathematicians have disdained this challenge,
however, and have increasingly chosen to flee from nature by devising
theories unrelated to anything we can see or feel.

Responding to this challenge, I conceived and developed a new geometry of nature and implemented its use in a number of diverse fields.
It describes many of the irregular and fragmented patterns around us,
and leads to full-fledged theories, by identifying a family of shapes I call
fractals.   —Benoit Mandelbrot
The Fractal Geometry of Nature, San Francisco: W. H.
Freeman, 1982, p. 1.

26 On one occasion during World War II ... Lefschetz and I and Oskar Zariski ... traveled into New York together on the train. Lefschetz and Zariski were talking about a certain paper, which had recently appeared in algebraic geometry, which they thought was a very good paper. Lefschetz remarked that he wasn't sure if he would classify the paper as algebra or topology. ... So Zariski, to tease Lefschetz a bit, asked, "How do you draw the line between algebra and topology?" Quick as a flash, Lefschetz came back with, "Well, if it's just turning the crank, it's algebra, but if it's got an idea in it, it's topology!"

—Albert W. Tucker
"Solomon Lefschetz, A Reminiscence," *Two-Year Coll. Math. J.* 14 (June 1983) 227.

27 In mathematics itself abstract algebra plays a dual role: that of a unifying link between disparate parts of mathematics and that of a research subject with a highly active life of its own. ... A subject that was once regarded as esoteric has become considered as fairly down-to-earth for a large cross section of scholars.   —I. N. Herstein

Abstract Algebra, New York: Macmillan, 1986, p. vii.

28 The basic difference between the roles of mathematical probability in 1946 and 1988 is that the subject is now accepted as mathematics whereas in 1946 to most mathematicians mathematical probability was to mathematics as black marketing to marketing; that is, probability was a source of interesting mathematics but examination of the background context was undesirable.   —J. L. Doob
"Commentary on Probability," in Peter Duren (ed.), *A Century of Mathematics in America, Part II,* Providence, RI: American Mathematical Society, 1989, p. 353.

29 [Discrete mathematics is] a subject of great beauty and depth which has gained enormous importance in applications because of the availability of computers. It is mistaken to think that discrete mathematics should compete with or even replace calculus-based applied mathematics in the elementary undergraduate curriculum; this would disregard the explosive growth, thanks to computing, in our ability to bring calculus-based mathematics to bear on applications.

—Peter Lax
"The Flowering of Applied Mathematics in America,"
in Peter Duren (ed.), *A Century of Mathematics in
America, Part II,* Providence, RI: American Mathematical Society, 1989, p. 464.

30   [In statistics] you have the fact that the concepts are not very
clean. The idea of probability, of randomness, is not a clean mathematical idea. You cannot produce random numbers mathematically.
They can only be produced by things like tossing dice or spinning a
roulette wheel. With a formula, any formula, the number you get would
be predictable and therefore not random. So as a statistician you have
to rely on some conception of a world where things happen in some way
at random, a conception which mathematicians don't have.

—Lucien LeCam
"Lucien LeCam," in D. Albers, G. Alexanderson, C.
Reid (eds.), *More Mathematical People,* New York:
Harcourt Brace Jovanovich, 1990, p. 174.

CHAPTER 4

Doing Mathematics

1 It is a remarkable historical fact that there is a branch of science in which there has never been a prolonged dispute concerning the proper objects of that science. It is the mathematics. Mistakes in mathematics occur not infrequently, and not being detected give rise to false doctrine, which may continue a long time. Thus, a mistake in the evaluation of a definite integral by Laplace, in his *Mécanique Céleste,* led to an erroneous doctrine about the motion of the moon which remained undetected for nearly half a century. But after the question had once been raised, all dispute was brought to close within a year. So, several demonstrations in the first book of Euclid, notably that of the 16th proposition, are vitiated by the erroneous assumption that a part is necessarily less than its whole. These remained undetected until after the theory of the non-Euclidean geometry had been completely worked out, but since that time, no mathematician has defended them; nor could any competent mathematician do so, in view of Georg Cantor's, or even of Cauchy's discoveries ... the fact remains that concerning strictly mathematical questions, and among mathematicians who could be considered at all competent, there has never been a single prolonged dispute.

—C. S. Pierce

"The Regenerated Logic," *The Monist,* 7 (October 1896) 21.

2 Many times a scientific truth is placed as it were on a lofty peak, and to reach it we have at our disposal at first only hard paths along

perilous slopes whence it is easy to fall into the abysses where dwells error; only after we have reached the peak by these paths is it possible to lay out safe roads which lead there without peril. Thus it has frequently happened that the first way of obtaining a result has not been quite satisfactory, and that only *afterwards* did the science succeed in completing the demonstration. Certainly also a mathematician can not be really content with a result which he has obtained by non-rigorous methods; he will not feel sure of it until he has rigorously proved it. But he will not reject summarily these imperfect methods in the case of difficult problems when he is unable to substitute better ones, since the history of the science precisely shows what service such methods have always rendered.   —Corrado Serge
"On Some Tendencies in Geometric Investigations,"
Bull. of the Amer. Math. Soc. 10 (June 1904) 453.

3   That mathematics is a difficult subject no one can deny. It demands, among other things, accuracy of thought and statement, definite mental concepts, connected thinking, a fair memory, quickness to recognize relations between forms and numbers, power of generalization, a willingness to work hard. The abstractness of much of the work renders it difficult to most minds, and obnoxious to some. . . .

These are some of the many characteristics that make mathematics hard. Of course it is hardly necessary to say that many of these very characteristics make it attractive and fascinating to some types of mind. The fact that it is abstract and impersonal, that it requires effort and compels concentration has made it a welcome refuge to minds distracted by the perplexities of everyday life. Probably every one of us knows the joy of losing ourselves and our cares completely in a problem that taxes our minds.   —Helen A. Merrill
"Why Students Fail in Mathematics," *Math. Teacher*
11 (December 1918) 46.

4   [Pythagoras] directed attention to number as characterizing the periodicities of notes of music. . . . In the seventeenth century, the birth of modern science required a new mathematics, more fully equipped for the purpose of analyzing the characteristics of vibratory existence. And now in the twentieth century we find physicists largely engaged in analyzing the periodicities of atoms. Truly, Pythagoras in founding European philosophy and European mathematics, endowed them with the

luckiest of lucky guesses—or, was it a flash of divine genius, penetrating to the inmost nature of things?   —Alfred North Whitehead
"Mathematics as an Element in the History of Thought," *Science and the Modern World,* New York: Macmillan, 1925, p. 31.

5 Sufficient unto the day is the precision thereof.   —E. H. Moore
"On the Foundations of Mathematics," in Charles Austin (ed.), *The First Yearbook: A General Survey of Progress in the Last Twenty-five Years,* New York, National Council of Teachers of Mathematics, 1926, p. 48.

6 We seek reality, but what is reality? The physiologists tell us that organisms are formed of cells; the chemists add that cells themselves are formed of atoms. Does this mean that these atoms or these cells constitute reality, or rather the sole reality? ...

Well, there is something analogous to this in mathematics. The logician cuts up, so to speak, each demonstration into a very great number of elementary operations; when we have examined these operations one after the other and ascertained that each is correct, are we to think we have grasped the real meaning of the demonstration? Shall we have understood it even when, by an effort of memory, we have become able to repeat this proof by reproducing all these elementary operations in just the order in which the investor had arranged them? Evidently not; we shall not yet possess the entire reality; that I know not what, which makes the unity of the demonstration, will completely elude us.

—Henri Poincaré
"The Value of Science," in G. B. Halsted (trans.), *The Foundations of Science,* Lancaster PA: Science Press, 1929, p. 217.

7 One can give numerous examples of mathematicians who have discovered theorems of the greatest importance, which they are unable to prove. Should one, then, refuse to recognize this as a great accomplishment and ... insist that this is not mathematics, and that only the successors who supply polished proofs are doing real mathematics?

—Felix Klein
Elementary Mathematics from an Advanced Standpoint —Arithmetic, Algebra, Analysis, New York: Macmillan, 1932, p. 208.

8   Mathematical achievement shall be measured by standards which are peculiar to mathematics. These standards are independent of the crude reality of our senses. They are: freedom from logical contradictions, the generality of the laws governing the created form, the kinship which exists between this new form and those that have preceded it.

—Tobias Dantzig
Number the Language of Science, New York: Macmillan, 1939, p. 231.

9   It was the function of intuition to create new forms; it was the acknowledged right of logic to accept or reject these forms, *in whose birth it had no part.*   —Tobias Dantzig
Number, the Language of Science, New York: Macmillan, 1939, p. 180.

10   No one can possibly carry about in his head the detail of a textbook of 400 pages. At least, not in his conscious mind; there may be a good deal of it lying down in subconscious regions. When a problem comes up for discussion there is a hurried dive into the subconscious to hunt for the necessary material to deal with it. If the subconscious is an untidy mess, it is unlikely that this material will be found. Then the only plan is to let the problem sink down into the subconscious in the hope that sometime a solution will float up to the surface. ... A better plan is to buoy our subconscious by a few conspicuous buoys floating on the surface of the conscious. When a problem presents itself, we see that it belongs to the region of one buoy rather than another, and it may require only comparatively little diving into the subconscious in its neighborhood to bring up the knowledge necessary to solve the problem. ... These buoys are surely familiar to us all—certain formulas or theorems which stand out (for us at least) as so fundamental that we would as soon forget our own names as them.   —J. L. Synge
"Postcards on Applied Mathematics," *Amer. Math. Monthly* 46 (March 1939) 156.

11   The biologist observes the patterns woven by nature; but the mathematician weaves his own patterns—more, he spins out of his own imagination the thread for the cloth which bears the patterns. To most mathematicians aesthetic appreciation of the pattern is begotten only through tedious weaving; in sudden spurts the realization of beauty comes to them. They wade through exhausting pages of detail to find in some hidden corner the formula or idea which reveals the secret of the pattern.

—J. L. Synge
"Postcards on Applied Mathematics," *Amer. Math. Monthly* 46 (March 1939) 153.

12   Important though the general concepts and propositions may be with which the modern industrious passion for axiomatizing and generalizing has presented us, in algebra perhaps more than anywhere else, nevertheless I am convinced that the special problems in all their complexity constitute the stock and core of mathematics; and to master their difficulties requires on the whole the harder labor.

—Hermann Weyl
The Classical Groups, Princeton: Princeton University Press, 1939, p. xi.

13   My experience has seemed to indicate that to meet the danger of a too thorough specialization and technicalization of mathematical research is of particular importance in America. The stringent precision attainable for mathematical thought has led many authors to a mode of writing which must give the reader an impression of being shut up in a brightly illuminated cell where every detail sticks out with the same dazzling clarity, but without relief. I prefer the open landscape under a clear sky with its depth of perspective, where the wealth of sharply defined nearby details gradually fades away towards the horizon.

—Hermann Weyl
The Classical Groups, Princeton: Princeton University Press, 1939, p. viii.

14   Be it strength or weakness, mathematics is not a science that prospers on details, painstakingly collected in the course of a long career, on patient reading, on observations or on filing cards, amassed one by one so as to form a bundle from which an idea will ultimately come forth. Perhaps it is more true in mathematics than in any other branch of knowledge that the idea comes forth in full armor from the brain of the creator. Moreover, mathematical talent usually shows itself at an early age; and the workers of the second rank play a smaller role in it than elsewhere, the role of a sounding board for sounds in whose production they had no part. There are examples to show that in mathematics an old person can do useful work, even inspired work; but they are rare, and each case fills us with wonder and admiration. Therefore, if mathematics is to continue to exist in the way in which it has manifested itself to its votaries until now, the technical complications with which more than one of its subjects is now studded, must be superficial or of only temporary character; in the future, as in the past, the great ideas must be simplifying ideas, the creator must always be one who clarifies, for himself and for others, the most complicated tissues of formulas and concepts. —André Weil

"The Future of Mathematics," *Amer. Math. Monthly* 57 (May 1950) 304.

15   It is certain that few men of our times are as completely free as the mathematician in the exercise of their intellectual activity. Even if some State ideologies sometimes attack his person, they have never yet presumed to judge his theorems. Every time that so-called mathematicians, to please the powers that be, have tried to subject their colleagues to the yoke of some orthodoxy, their only reward has been contempt. Let others besiege the offices of the mighty in the hope of getting the expensive apparatus, without which no Nobel prize comes within reach. Pencil and paper is all the mathematician needs; he can even sometimes get along without these. Neither are there Nobel prizes to tempt him away from slowly maturing work, towards a brilliant but ephemeral result. Mathematics is taught the world over, well here, badly there; the exiled mathematician—and who among us can to-day feel free from the danger of exile—can find everywhere the modest livelihood which allows him to pursue his work to some extent. Even in gaol one can do good mathematics if one's courage fail him not.   —André Weil

"The Future of Mathematics," *Amer. Math. Monthly* 57 (May 1950) 296.

16   If logic is the hygiene of the mathematician, it is not his source of food; the great problems furnish the daily bread on which he thrives.

—André Weil

"The Future of Mathematics," *Amer. Math. Monthly* 57 (May 1950) 297.

17   A theory is the more impressive the greater the simplicity of its premises is, the more different kinds of things it relates, and the more extended is its area of applicability.   —Albert Einstein

"Autobiographical Notes," in Paul A. Schilpp (ed.), *Albert Einstein: Philosopher-Scientist,* New York: Tudor Publishing, 1951, 33.

18 Our mathematics of the last decades has wallowed in generalizations and formalizations. But one misunderstands this tendency if one thinks that generality was sought merely for generality's sake. The real aim is simplicity: every natural generalization simplifies since it reduces the assumptions that have to be taken into account. It is not easy to say what constitutes a natural separation and generalization. For this there is ultimately no other criterion but fruitfulness: the success decides.
—Hermann Weyl
"A Half-century of Mathematics," *Amer. Math. Monthly* 58 (October 1951) 524.

19 In mathematics, as in any scientific research, we find two tendencies present. On the one hand, the tendency toward *abstraction* seeks to crystallize the *logical* relations inherent in the maze of material that is being studied, and to correlate the material in a systematic and orderly manner. On the other hand, the tendency toward *intuitive understanding* fosters a more immediate grasp of the subjects one studies, a live *rapport* with them, so to speak, which stresses the concrete meaning of their relations.
—David Hilbert
D. Hilbert and S. Cohn-Vossen, *Geometry and the Imagination,* New York: Chelsea Publishing Co, 1952, p. iii.

20 The tantalizing and compelling pursuit of mathematical problems offers mental absorption, peace of mind amid endless challenges, repose in activity, battle without conflict, 'refuge from the goading urgency of contingent happenings,' and the sort of beauty changeless mountains present to senses tried by the present-day kaleidoscope of events.
—Morris Kline
Mathematics in Western Culture, New York: Oxford University Press, 1953, p. 470.

21 Rigor is to the mathematician what morality is to man. It does not consist in proving everything, but in maintaining a sharp distinction between what is assumed and what is proved, and in endeavoring to assume as little as possible at every stage.
—André Weil
"Mathematical Teaching in Universities," *Amer. Math. Monthly* 61 (January 1954) 35.

22 It is because the mathematician is expert in analyzing relations, in distinguishing what is essential from what is superficial in the statement of these relations, and in formulating broad and meaningful

problems, that he has come to be an important figure in industrial research teams. —Thornton C. Fry
"Mathematics as a Profession Today in Industry," *Amer. Math. Monthly* 63 (February 1956) 76.

23 I also came to see more definitely than I had before that one of the chief motives driving me to mathematics was the discomfort or even the pain of an unresolved mathematical discord. I became more and more conscious of the need to reduce such a discord to semipermanent and recognizable terms before I could release it and pass on to something else. —Norbert Wiener
I Am a Mathematician, Garden City: Doubleday, 1956, p. 86.

24 We mathematicians who operate with nothing more expensive than paper and possibly printer's ink are quite reconciled to the fact that, if we are working in a very active field, our discoveries will commence to be obsolete at the moment they are written down or even at the moment they are conceived. We know that for a long time everything we do will be nothing more than the jumping off point for those who have the advantage of already being aware of our ultimate results. This is the meaning of the famous apothegm of Newton, when he said, "If I have seen further that other men, it is because I have stood on the shoulders of giants." —Norbert Wiener
I Am a Mathematician, Garden City: Doubleday, 1956, p. 266.

25 Continue in scientific research, you will experience great joy from it. But you must learn to enjoy it alone. You will be a subject of astonishment to those close to you. You will not be much better understood by the scholarly world. Mathematicians have a place apart there, and even they do not always read each other. —Camille Jordan
"Notice sur la Vie et les Travaux de Camille Jordan," *L'enseignement Mathématique* 3, ser. 2 (April-June 1957) 92.

26 A point that should be borne in mind is that, generally speaking, higher mathematics is simpler than elementary mathematics. To explore a thicket on foot is a troublesome business; from an aeroplane the task is easier. —W. W. Sawyer
Prelude to Mathematics, Baltimore: Penguin Books, 1957, p. 11.

27 The *desire to explore* thus marks out the mathematician. This is one of the forces making for the growth of mathematics. The mathematician enjoys what he already knows; he is eager for new knowledge.

—W. W. Sawyer

Prelude to Mathematics, Baltimore: Penguin Books, 1957, p. 19.

28 The peculiar charm of mathematics lies partly in its precision of thought and partly in the fact that it is the only subject which can be remade by each individual who touches it. True, he does not remake it all; life is too short. But it is all open to the remaking. . . . We are the only free creatures in a world of slaves. In that spirit of independence we set off into the world of reason, believing nothing because we are told it on good authority, doubting, questioning in the name of truth, leaving no stone unturned, not even the integers and the fractions!

—J. L. Synge

Kandelman's Krim, London: Jonathan Cape, 1957, p. 84.

29 This pursuit of meaning in mathematics is modern, about a hundred years old. . . .

Do not make the mistake of thinking that the pursuit of meaning is a pleasant recreation to fill an hour of rest. It is a passion that seizes you and will not let go, until in your impotence to lift God's mask you cry out: 'To hell with meaning! Give me some tools and let me do a job of work!'

—J. L. Synge

Kandelman's Krim, London: Jonathan Cape, 1957, p. 15.

30 Usually in mathematics one has to choose between saying more and more about less and less on one hand, and saying less and less about more and more on the other.

—N. G. deBruijn

Asymptotic Methods in Analysis, Amsterdam: North Holland Publishing, 1958, p. v.

31 Mathematicians, at the onset of their creative work, are often confronted by two conflicting motivations: the first is to contribute to the edifice of existing work—it is there that one can be sure of gaining recognition quickly by solving outstanding problems—the second one is a desire to blaze new trails and to create new syntheses. This latter course is the more risky undertaking, the final judgment of value or success appearing only in the future.   —S. M. Ulam

"John von Neumann: 1903–1957," *Bull. of the Amer. Math. Soc.* 64 (May 1958) 8.

32   PRINCIPLE OF BALANCE: *A physically meaningful solution of a mathematical problem arising from a mathematical model of a physical process should never possess a greater degree of complexity than the mathematical model itself.*   —Richard Bellman and Paul Brock

"On the Concepts of a Problem and Problem-Solving," *Amer. Math. Monthly* 67 (January 1960) 124.

33   It has been said that unsolved problems form the very life of mathematics; certainly they can illuminate and, in the best cases, crystallize and summarize the essence of the difficulties inherent in the various fields.   —S. M. Ulam

A Collection of Mathematical Problems, New York: Interscience Publishers, 1960, p. viii.

34   Abel, when asked to what he attributed his great knowledge of mathematics, replied that he read the masters rather than the pupils. Although it must truthfully be stated that following this procedure is no guarantee of producing an Abel, it is, nevertheless, also true that there are many advantages to be gained from pursuing this policy.

In the first place, one can in this way obtain a feeling for what constitutes worthwhile research. It is as difficult to characterize great mathematics in precise terms as it is to attempt to define rigorously artistic and musical excellence. Rather than define a great mathematician as one who produces great mathematics, we shall define great mathematics as that produced by a great mathematician. ...

Watching the intellectual giants of the past construct their theories, reliving with them the labor pains of new results, enjoying with them their victories, and suffering with them their defeats, some of which we know in advance are inevitable, we absorb by a very process of osmosis an intuitive feeling for the essence of creative mathematics. This observing of the birth of theories, this examining of fundamental concepts in their pristine simplicity and elegance cannot fail to illuminate and inspire not only the novice but also the master.   —Richard Bellman

A Collection of Modern Mathematical Classics, New York: Dover, 1961, p. vii.

35 Mathematical abstraction, to be considered significant, must someday pass the test of generality, of applicability, of relatedness. Mathematics too long divorced from reality, it has been said, becomes baroque, decadent, and sterile. —R. A. Rosenbaum
"Mathematics, the Artistic Science," *Math. Teacher* 55 (November 1962) 533.

36 One of the saddest tales in mathematical history concerns the German mathematician Grassmann, who anticipated much of later work in algebra. He published it in his *Ausdehnungslehre* and nobody read it, partly because the exposition was so obscure and partly because he was ahead of his time—mathematicians could not see the significance of what he was doing. He girded up his loins and tried again, revising the *Ausdehnungslehre* to make it more transparent. Still no luck—the exposition remained turgid. So Grassmann turned to philology and made his impact there.

We see in Grassmann's case the two aspects of communication—the exposition must first of all be understandable; and, equally important, the material must strike the reader as *meaningful.* Each mathematician has his own scale of values of "meaningfulness," but I'd guess that two qualities are common to all—generality and relatedness. In a sense these qualities overlap a good deal to ensure that the material under discussion is not *isolated.* —R. A. Rosenbaum
"Mathematics, the Artistic Science," *Math. Teacher* 55 (November 1962) 534.

37 Successes were largely due to forgetting completely about what one ultimately wanted, or whether one wanted anything ultimately; in refusing to investigate things which profit, and in relying solely on guidance by criteria of intellectual elegance, it was by following this rule that one actually got ahead in the long run, much better than any strictly utilitarian course would have permitted. —John von Neumann
"The Role of Mathematics in the Sciences and Society," in A. H. Taub (ed.), *John von Neumann Collected Works, Vol VI,* New York: Pergamon, 1963, p. 489.

38 Mathematics progresses essentially in two different ways. The mathematicians whom I might call the tacticians pounce head on at a problem, using only old and well-tested tools, and they merely rely on their cleverness to give some new twist to traditional arguments, and thus reach the solution which had eluded previous attempts. The strategists, on the other hand, will never be satisfied until the concepts involved in a problem have been so thoroughly analyzed, and their connections put in such a clear light, that the final solution almost appears as a triviality; but of course this may demand lengthy and tedious developments of seemingly unrelated very general theories, which some people will deem out of proportion with the initial question.

I believe, however, that both approaches are essential to the well-being of mathematics.   —Jean Dieudonné
> "Recent Developments in Mathematics," *Amer. Math. Monthly* 71 (March 1964) 239.

39   When a mathematician meets a problem he cannot solve, like any other scientist he tries to solve instead some related problem which seems to contain only part of the difficulties of the original. But the mathematician has far more alternatives in choosing a simpler problem than does the chemist or biologist. Other scientists are restricted by nature, whereas the mathematician is restricted only by logical coherence and somewhat vague considerations of taste.   —Andrew Gleason
> "Evolution of an Active Mathematical Theory," *Science* 145 (31 July 1964) 451.

40   Among mathematicians I have heard a series of discoveries by one person described as follows: The first discovery is like a solitary island in a borderless expanse of sea. Then a second and third island are discovered without any apparent connexion. But gradually it becomes clear that the waters are ebbing away in mass and leaving behind what were at first little isolated islands as the peaks of one great chain of mountains. That is precisely what one would expect to happen if intuition first sensed the fundamental chain of thought, i.e. the mountain range, and consciousness then proceeded to describe it little by little. Actually these unusual processes do not differ in essence from the ordinary event of a hidden chain of mathematical reasoning being discovered by a series of stepwise advances.   —Michael Polanyi
> *Science, Faith, and Society,* Chicago: University of Chicago Press, 1964, p. 31.

41   There are certain emotional difficulties which are intrinsic to the mathematical life, and only a few people are able to live with them all their lives.

First of all, the mathematician must be capable of total involvement in a specific problem. To do mathematics, you must immerse yourself completely in a situation, studying it from all aspects, toying with it day and night, and devoting every scrap of available energy to understanding it. You can permit yourself occasional breaks, and probably should; nevertheless the state of immersion must go on for somewhat extended periods, usually several days or weeks.

Second, the mathematician must risk frustration. Most of the time, in fact, he finds himself, after weeks or months or ceaseless searching, with exactly nothing: no results, no ideas, no energy. SInce some of this time, at least, has been spent in total involvement, the resulting frustration is very nearly total. ... This factor is a more important hindrance than any other, I believe; to risk total frustration, and to be almost certain to lose, is a psychological problem of the first rank.

Next, even the most successful mathematician suffers from lack of appreciation. Naturally his family and his friends have no feeling for the significance of his accomplishments, but it is even worse than this. Other mathematicians don't appreciate the blood, sweat, and tears that have gone into a result that appears simple, straightforward, almost trivial. Mathematical terminology is designed to eliminate extraneous things and focus on fundamental processes, but the method of finding results is far different from these fundamental processes. Mathematical writing doesn't permit any indication of the labor behind the results.

Finally, the mathematician must face the fact that he will almost certainly be dissatisfied with himself. This is partly because he is running head-on into problems which are too vast ever to be solved completely. More importantly, it is because he knows that his own contributions actually have little significance. The history of mathematics makes plain that all the general outlines and most of the major results have been obtained by a few geniuses who are not the ordinary run of mathematicians. These few big men make the long strides forward, then the lesser lights come scurrying in to fill the chinks, make generalizations, and find some new applications; meanwhile the giants are making further strides.
                                                        —Donald R. Weidman
                    "Emotional Perils of Mathematics," *Science* 149 (3 September 1965) 1048.

42 The rules [of the mathematical fraternity] are nowhere explicitly formulated, but they are intuitively felt by everyone in the profession. Mistakes are forgiven and so is obscure exposition—the indispensable requisite is mathematical insight. Sloppy thinking, verbosity without content, and polemics have no role, and—this to me is one of the most wonderful aspects of mathematics—they are much easier to spot than in the non-mathematical fields of human endeavor (much easier than, for instance, in literature among the arts, in art criticism among the humanities, and in your favorite abomination among the social sciences).

—Paul Halmos
"Mathematics as a Creative Art," *Amer. Scientist* 56
(Winter 1968) 381.

43 If you . . . contemplate a career in pure or applied mathematics, whether in industry or research, or in the teaching profession, you should be warned that although there can be one infallible, enduring reward for you in this pursuit—joy in creative activity—there stand certain discouraging hazards, of which four may be noted briefly:

1. The burden of hard mental concentration is a *sine qua non.* You may find that you have to live with a problem day and night for weeks, giving all you have of mental resources in order to solve it: no inspiration without perspiration.

2. Your best efforts may be fruitless. Despite extravagant expenditure of time and skill, the result is nil. Disappointment, frustration and near-despair are common experiences of serious mathematicians.

3. You may be lonely. Scarcely anyone will appreciate your work because few will be capable of understanding it.

4. The results you do obtain will always appear to be disproportionately meager in comparison with the effort you expended to produce them: "The mountain laboured and brought forth a mouse."

The one sure path to satisfaction in a mathematics career is to cultivate assiduously the aesthetic appreciation of the discipline. That pleasure will not fade, it will grow with exercise.   —H. E. Huntley
The Divine Proportion: a Study in Mathematical Beauty,
New York: Dover, 1970, p. 3.

44 An idea which can be used only once is a trick. If you can use it more than once it becomes a method.

—George Pólya and Gábor Szegö
Problems and Theorems in Analysis, Vol I, New York:
Springer-Verlag, 1972, p. viii.

45 Dear Colleague:
. . . I heard lately that [a] lack of understanding and appreciation [of problem solving] led to denying the promotion to a member of your

Department. I feel that there is a serious matter of principle involved, and I wish to write you about it . . .

A faculty member who teaches mainly undergraduate students should have, of course, a good mathematical background and he should not let it get rusty. Yet to extend to his case the 'principle' of 'publish or perish' is unwise and unjust. Under stress—and just for prestige, without real love or interest, the faculty member finally produces a paper that is printed and immediately submerged, unread and unnoticed, in the ocean of the present overproduction—is not such an effort misguided? Another way of not getting rusty is to pose and solve problems—and it is, in my opinion, in many cases a better way: Problem-solving is a perfectly acceptable and respectable professional activity for a mathematician and can favorably influence his teaching . . .

If it is true what I heard that your colleague's promotion was refused, because he 'only' solved problems and did not publish, such a decision is unwise and unfair. —George Pólya

"A Letter by Professor Pólya," *Amer. Math. Monthly* 80 (January 1973) 73.

46 I knew Emmy Noether for many years, although I did not know her well—our mathematical interests were too different. Yet I remember very well a discussion I had with her . . . each of us wanted to defend his or her own mathematical taste. It turned finally into a debate on generalisation and specialisation: Emmy was, of course, all for generalisation and I defended the relatively concrete particular cases. Then once I interrupted Emmy: "Now, look here, a mathematician who can only generalise is like a monkey who can only climb UP a tree." And then Emmy broke off the discussion—she was visibly hurt.

And then I felt sorry. I don't want to hurt anybody and especially I don't want to hurt poor Emmy Noether. I thought about it repeatedly and finally I decided that, after all, it was not one hundred per cent my fault. She should have answered: "And a mathematician who can only specialise is like a monkey who can only climb DOWN a tree."

In fact, neither the up, nor the down, monkey is a viable creature. A real monkey must find food and escape his enemies and so he must incessantly climb up and down, up and down. A real mathematician must be able to generalise and specialise. —George Pólya

"A Story with a Moral," *Math. Gaz.* 57 (June 1973) 86.

47   A good proof is one that makes us wiser.   —Yu I. Manin
A Course in Mathematical Logic, New York: Springer-
Verlag, 1977, p. 51.

48   Why study examples?

Several reasons come to mind. For the mathematician doing research, examples are all but indispensable to his work. To begin with, the
direction of his research is guided by a thorough examination of all the
pertinent examples he can get his hands on. Only after these examples
are analyzed does he attempt to formulate their common properties
into some sort of a theorem, and then attempt to prove the theorem.

For the student of group theory, regardless of his level, examples help
to clarify and justify the definitions and theorems of the subject he is
studying. Take, for instance, the definition of a solvable group. As soon
as the student sees this he will want to know the answers to at least two
questions

(a) Are there such things?

(b) Are there groups that are nonsolvable?

These questions are more than just reasonable, they seem necessary to
an understanding of the concept. Both questions must be answered by
examples.

A third use of examples, related but not identical to the previous
two, is the idea of counterexample. Counterexamples are given, and
rightfully so, a much more honored position in mathematics than the
two kinds of examples previously discussed. Where the examples a
research mathematician uses to formulate a theorem he later proves
take a back seat to the theorem itself, and where the examples a student
(or his instructor) proffers to answer questions such as (a) and (b) are of
a rather personal and short-lived nature, a counterexample is as much
a result in the theory of groups as a theorem is, and occupies a similarly
high position. Theorems and counterexamples are simply results in
opposite directions.   —Michael Weinstein
Examples of Groups, Passaic, NJ: Polygonal Publishing
House, 1977, p. ix.

49   It is convenient to divide conscious mathematics into two categories. The first, possibly more primitive, will be called "analog-
experimental" or analog, for short. The second category will be called

"analytic". Analog mathematizing is sometimes easy, and can be accomplished rapidly, and may make use of none, or very few, of the abstract symbolic structures of "school" mathematics. It can be done to some extent by almost everyone who operates in a world of spacial relationships and everyday technology. Although sometimes it can be easy and almost effortless, sometimes it can be very difficult, as, for example, trying to understand the arrangement and relationships of the parts of a machine, or trying to get an intuitive feeling for a complex system. Results rarely are expressed in words but in "understanding", "intuition", or "feeling".

In analytic mathematics, the symbolic material predominates. It is almost always hard to do. It is time consuming. It is fatiguing. It requires special training. It may require constant verification by the whole mathematical culture to assure reliability. Analytic mathematics is performed only by very few people. Analytic mathematics is elitist and self-critical. The practitioners of its higher manifestations form a "talentocracy". The great virtue of analytic mathematics arises from this, that while it is hard to verify another's intuitions, it is possible, though often difficult, to verify his proofs.

—Philip J. Davis and James A. Anderson
"Nonanalytic Aspects of Mathematics and Their Implication for Research and Education," *SIAM Review* 21 (January 1979) 113.

50 An interesting phenomenon should be noted in connection with difficulties of proof comprehension. A mathematical theorem is popularly called "deep" if its proof is hard. Some of the elements that contribute to deepness are nonintuitiveness of statement or of argument, novelty of ideas, complexity or length of proof material measured from some origin which itself is not deep.

The opposite of "deep" is "trivial" and this word is often used in the sense of a put-down. Some synonyms for "trivial" might be "transparent", "intuitive", "short". It should be noted that although what is trivial is not considered to be on the same intellectual level as what is deep, it does not follow that what is trivial is uninteresting, unuseful, or unimportant.

Now despite this hierarchical ordering, what is deep is frequently suspect and undesirable, so that there is a constant effort on the part of the profession toward simplification, towards the finding of alternative ways of looking at the matter which trivializes what is deep.

—Philip J. Davis and James A. Anderson
"Nonanalytic Aspects of Mathematics and Their Implication for Research and Education," *SIAM Review* 21 (January 1979) 115.

51   A mathematician is usually judged by several criteria. Among these are his ability to solve open problems of importance, his ability to introduce new concepts which clarify existing problems and his ability to develop coherent theories.   —Walter Feit
"Richard D. Brauer," *Bull. of the Amer. Math. Soc. (New series)* 1 (January 1979) 14.

52   [Hilbert] was a most concrete, intuitive mathematician who invented, and very consciously used, a principle; namely, if you want to solve a problem first strip the problem of everything that is not essential. Simplify it, specialize it as much as you can without sacrificing its core. Thus it becomes simple, as simple as it can be made, without losing any of its punch, and then you can solve it.   —Richard Courant
"Reminiscences from Hilbert and Göttingen," *Math. Intell.* 3 (No. 4, 1981) 161.

53   From time to time mathematicians perceive certain similarities of form which elicit an element of surprise. Such a similarity may be called a coincidence. The surprise calls for an explanation. The explanation, if it is forthcoming, serves partially to kill the surprise.

The existence of the coincidence implies the existence of an explanation. If the coincidence is of a high degree of improbability, then there is more to explain and the explanation will be easier in the sense that it involves a more easily accessible theory. If the coincidence is only of a medium order of improbability, the explanation will be more difficult.

A Platonic philosophy of mathematics might say that there are no coincidences in mathematics because all is ordained. In the words of Alexander Pope [Essay on Man]:

All nature is but art unknown to thee

All chance, direction which thou can'st not see.

But for the working mathematician, coincidence exists. He feels it, he identifies it, he uses it as an inductive and constructive element. He

pursues its implications along certain lines. To some extent he even
brings it about.
—Philip J. Davis
"Are There Coincidences in Mathematics?," *Amer.
Math. Monthly* 88 (May 1981) 320.

54   All experience so far seems to show that there are two inexhaustible sources of new mathematical questions. One source is the development of science and technology, which make ever new demands on mathematics for assistance. The other source is mathematics itself. As it becomes more elaborate and complex, each new, completed result becomes the potential starting point for several new investigations. Each pair of seemingly unrelated mathematical specialties pose an implicit challenge to find a fruitful connection between them.
—Philip Davis and Reuben Hersh
The Mathematical Experience, Boston: Birkhäuser,
1981, p. 25.

55   Mathematics often owes more to those who ask questions than to those who answer them. The solution of a problem may stifle interest in the area around it. But "Fermat's Last Theorem", because it is not yet a theorem, has generated a great deal of "good" mathematics, whether goodness is judged by beauty, by depth or by applicability.
—Richard K. Guy
Unsolved Problems in Number Theory, New York:
Springer-Verlag, 1981, p. vii.

56   Here is another thing that has frequently struck me: mathematics (pure mathematics), despite its many subdivisions and their enormous rate of growth (started millennia ago and greater today than ever before), is an amazingly unified intellectual structure. The mathematics that is alive and vigorous today has so many parts, and each is so extensive, that no one can possibly know them all. As a result, we, all of us, often attend colloquium lectures on subjects about which we know much less than an average historian, say, knows about linguistics. It doesn't matter, however, whether the talk is about unbounded operators, commutative groups, or parallelizable surfaces; the interplay between widely separated parts of mathematics always shows up. The

concepts and methods of each one illuminate all others, and the unity of the structure as a whole is there to be marvelled at.   —Paul Halmos
"Applied Mathematics Is Bad Mathematics" in Lynn A. Steen (ed.), *Mathematics Tomorrow,* New York: Springer-Verlag, 1981, p. 15.

57 [At Technische Hochschule I had a] tremendous teaching load, many hours, and I had never taught the courses before so I had to work from morning to night to prepare them. Yet I have never done scientific work more intensely than during that year. It's a general observation of mine that if you have all the time you want for your scientific research, you just end up consulting a psychiatrist. If you have to fight against obstacles, if you have to fight for your time, you do much better. Unless, of course, it goes too far.   —Kurt O. Friedrichs
Constance Reid. "K. O. Friedrichs," *Math. Intell.* 5 (No. 3, 1983) 25.

58 Often graduate students have asked me "How do you get started writing a thesis?" I would say, there are lots of ways, but there is one way I have had good experience with myself. Take something you are interested in, mull it over, and make it your own. There's a good chance that in doing this you will find new ways of looking at the material, and this will turn into something that's publishable.   —Albert W. Tucker
Stephen B. Maurer. "An Interview with Albert W. Tucker," *Two-Year Coll. Math. J.* 14 (June 1983) 227.

59 Why do we do mathematics? We mainly do mathematics because we *enjoy* doing mathematics. But in a deeper sense, why should we be paid to do mathematics? If one asks for the justification for that, then I think one has to take the view that mathematics is part of the general scientific culture. We are contributing to a whole, organic collection of ideas, even if the part of mathematics which I'm doing now is not of direct relevance and usefulness to other people. If mathematics is an integrated body of thought, and every part is potentially useful to every other part, then we are all contributing to a common objective.
—Michael Atiyah
Robert Minio. "An Interview with Michael Atiyah," *Math. Intell.* 6 (No. 1, 1984) 12.

60 [Lefschetz and Einstein] had a running debate for many years. Lefschetz insisted that there was difficult mathematics. Einstein said that there was no difficult mathematics, only stupid mathematicians. I think that the history of mathematics is on the side of Einstein.

—Richard Bellman
Eye of the Hurricane, Singapore: World Scientific, 1984, p. 130.

61 I should have seen the application of dynamic programming to control theory several years before. I should have, but I didn't. ... Scientific developments can always be made logical and rational with sufficient hindsight. It is amazing, however, how clouded the crystal ball looks beforehand. We all wear such intellectual blinders and make such inexplicable blunders that it is amazing that any progress is made at all.

—Richard Bellman
Eye of the Hurricane, Singapore: World Scientific, 1984, p. 182.

62 Mathematicians often argue whether mathematics is discovered or invented. I certainly had the feelings in that case [work on concentration of signals with Dave Slepian and Henry Landau] that I was discovering it and not inventing it. After struggling for years, the insights eventually came to me that made it all fall into place. It all hung together in an incredible way—every loose end had its own natural location. When we looked at the end result, we realized that we had been luckier than we had any right to expect. We couldn't have invented all that. We had discovered a structure that must have been there. At least, that's the feeling I had; it hung together too well.

—Henry O. Pollak
Donald J. Albers and Michael J. Thibodeaux, "A Conversation with Henry Pollak," *Coll. Math. J.* 15 (June 1984) 214.

63 *How have we obtained our conjecture?* In very much the same manner as ordinary people or scientists working in some non-mathematical field obtain theirs. We collected relevant observations, examined and compared them, noticed fragmentary regularities, hesitated, blundered, and eventually succeeded in *combining the scattered details into an apparently meaningful whole.* Quite similarly, an archaeologist may reconstitute a whole inscription from a few scattered letters on a worn-out stone or a palaeontologist may reconstruct the essential features of an extinct animal from a few of its petrified bones.

—George Pólya
"Let Us Teach Guessing" in Gian-Carlo Rota (ed.), *George Pólya, Collected Papers, Vol IV,* Cambridge, MA: MIT Press, 1984, p. 508.

64 The joy of discovering new results ought to be matched by the joy of studying the achievements of others. Unfortunately this latter enjoyment is made difficult by the overwhelming volume of mathematical output and the work involved in absorbing the content of even a single paper. Every mathematician has to compromise on the amount of energy he can devote to literature.   — Fritz John
Jürgen Moser (ed.), *Fritz John, Collected Papers, Vol. I,* Boston: Birkhäuser, 1985, p. 21.

65 [After my year at the Institute for Advanced Study] I was actually glad to go back to the more organized life which academic chores such as teaching and serving on committees provide. Being free from all duties can be quite disconcerting. In research, ideas don't come with great frequency and there are long quiescent periods between bursts of feverish activity. During such periods it is good to have an excuse for not being productive. In a university environment, excuses abound. The students are pestering you, the dean keeps calling, there are too many committee meetings, etc., etc., etc. But at a place like the Institute for Advanced Study all such excuses are removed and if no startling revelation is forthcoming one tends to get depressed.   —Mark Kac
Enigmas of Chance, New York: Harper and Row, 1985, p. 125.

66 I think rather that one does mathematics because one likes to do this sort of thing, and also, much more naturally, because when you have a talent for something, usually you don't have any talent for something else, and you do whatever you have talent for, if you are lucky enough to have it. I must also add that I do mathematics also because it is difficult, and it is a very beautiful challenge for the mind. I do mathematics to prove to myself that I am capable of meeting this challenge, and win it.

—Serge Lang
The Beauty of Doing Mathematics, New York: Springer-Verlag, 1985, p. 5.

67   Of course there is another thing that makes an academic surrounding so different from the civil service. That is the fixed hours of
the civil service. In the evening or during weekends one can hardly
return to one's research. At the University nobody gives you a fixed
time schedule, apart from the fixed teaching schedule. So what happens
is that one works practically all the time! When I wake up during the
night, partially refreshed from a few hours of sleep, my mind goes back
at once to my unsolved problems and I sometimes really make some
progress, but feel worn out the next day. But no doubt more work is
accomplished when fixed hours are removed.   —Olga Taussky-Todd
> "An Autobiographical Essay," in Donald J. Albers
> and G. L. Alexanderson (eds.), *Mathematical People,*
> Boston: Birkhäuser, 1985, p. 332.

68   There are worse things than being wrong, and being dull and
pedantic are surely among them.   —Mark Kac
> *Discrete Thoughts: Essays on Mathematics, Science and
> Philosophy,* Boston: Birkhäuser, 1986, p. 16.

69   G. H. Hardy said he thought on paper ("with my pen"). He
wrote everything out (in his invariably admirable handwriting), scrap-
ping and copying whenever a page got into a mess. When I am thinking
about a difficult problem everything goes onto a single page—all over
the place with odd equations, diagrams, rings. However appalling the
mess, I feel that to scrap this page would somehow break threads in the
unconscious.   —John E. Littlewood
> Béla Bollobás (ed.), *Littlewood's Miscellany,* Cam-
> bridge: Cambridge University Press, 1986, p. 160.

70   It is customary to ask of a piece of Mathematics: "Is it true?"
... this issue of truth is a mistaken question ... [and] the appropriate
questions are different ones:

Is this piece of Mathematics *correct*? That is, do the calculations
follow the formal rules prescribed, and are the theorems deduced from
the stated axioms by rules of inference on which we have agreed?

Is this piece of Mathematics *illuminating*? That is, does it help understand what had gone before, either by further analysis or by abstraction
or otherwise?

Is this piece of Mathematics *promising*? That is, though it is a novel departure from precedent or fashion, is there a reasonable chance that it will subsequently fit into the picture?

Is this piece of Mathematics *relevant*? That is, is it tied to something which is tied to human activities or to science?   —Saunders Mac Lane
         Mathematics: Form and Function, New York: Springer-Verlag, 1986, p. 440.

71   My mother, who taught kindergarten and first grade before her marriage, said that I was the stubbornest child she had ever known. I would say that my stubbornness has been to a great extent responsible for whatever success I have had in mathematics. But then it is a common trait among mathematicians.   —Julia Robinson
         Constance Reid. "The Autobiography of Julia Robinson," *Coll. Math. J.* 17 (January 1986) 4.

72   Throughout the 1960s, while publishing a few papers on other things, I kept working on the Tenth Problem; but I was getting rather discouraged. For a while, I ceased to believe in the Robinson hypothesis although [my husband] Raphael insisted that it was true but just too difficult to prove. I even worked in the opposite direction, trying to show that there was a positive solution to Hilbert's problem; but I never published any of that work. It was a custom in our family to have a get-together for each family member's birthday, and when it came time for me to blow out the candles on my cake, I always wished, year after year, that the Tenth Problem would be solved—not that I would solve it, but just that it would be solved. I felt that I couldn't bear to die without knowing the answer. ...

That year [1970—when the Tenth Problem had been solved] when I went to blow out the candles on my cake, I stopped in mid-breath suddenly realizing that the wish I had made for so many years had actually come true.

I have been told that some people think I was blind not to see the solution myself when I was so close to it. On the other hand, no one else saw it either. There are lots of things, just lying on the beach as it were, that we don't see until someone else picks one of them up. Then we all see that one.   —Julia Robinson
         Constance Reid. "The Autobiography of Julia Robinson," *Coll. Math. J.* 17 (January 1986) 18.

73 Mathematics is an exceedingly cruel profession. You must notice that if somebody has a bachelor's degree in chemistry, he describes himself as a chemist. But if somebody has been a professor of mathematics for ten years and you ask him, "Are you a mathematician?" he may say, "I'm trying to be one!" —Lipman Bers

> Donald J. Albers and Constance Reid. "An Interview with Lipman Bers," *Coll. Math. J.* 18 (September 1987) 282.

74 Mathematics is like a gothic cathedral. If you can build a little part of it, it is there—forever—in some sense. At least I have the illusion that it is so. I feel good about a few things I have done in mathematics. They are not great discoveries, but I experienced great joy when I made them, and other people use them occasionally—it is very pleasant.

—Lipman Bers

> Donald J. Albers and Constance Reid. "An Interview with Lipman Bers," *Coll. Math. J.* 18 (September 1987) 289.

75 A working mathematician is always a Platonist. It doesn't matter what he says. He may not be a Platonist at other times. But I think that in mathematics he always has that feeling of discovery. —Lipman Bers

> Donald J. Albers and Constance Reid. "An Interview with Lipman Bers," *Coll. Math. J.* 18 (September 1987) 286.

76 It would appear that there is a private and public world of mathematics. The private world is where struggle, failure, incomprehension, intuition and creativity dominate. ... The public world is where the results of the private struggle make their appearance in a formal, conventional abstract formulation from which all evidence of false trails, inadequate reasoning or misunderstandings have been eliminated. Unfortunately for our pupils, the majority are given access only to the public world—the pages of text books which present inert knowledge as if it has always been just so. —Leone Burton

> "Femmes et Mathématiques: Y a-t-il une Intersection?" *Assoc. for Women in Math. Newsletter* 18 (November-December 1988) 20. French version published in Louise Lafortune (ed.), *Femmes et Mathématiques,* Les Editions du remue-ménage, Montréal, 1986.

77   Failure, although intrinsically less desirable than success, is often more instructive: It is a lesson to a scientist to determine how one could pass closely to an important discovery without suspecting it. Moreover, this sort of thing occurs frequently in the history of thought.

—Jacques Hadamard
"How I Did Not Discover Relativity," *Math. Intell.* 10 (Spring 1988) 65.

78   I was well aware at the time, like all mathematicians, that there are an infinite number of linear changes of variable that preserve the form of one or the other of the two partial differential equations ... it was very obvious that in general such changes of variables did not preserve the privileged position of Kirchhoff's line, but could make it coincide with any other line that originates at the same point A, and that lies in the interior of the wave cone.

To think that this Kirchhoff line did not have a physical significance—that was a leap too bold for me. ... I had not yet clearly understood that one should be able on occasion to fail to show respect to physics.

And this is how I, a mathematician with an impoverished imagination, found myself totally unable to interpret concretely the conclusion that mathematical theory was irresistibly forcing upon me; I contented myself to bow respectfully before Kirchhoff's point of view. The moral of this story, then, is in one's own field the scholar should respect nothing—one should not heed the word of a Kirchhoff any more than Copernicus respected the work of Aristotle or Ptolemy; that is what we all do ever since Einstein.   —Jacques Hadamard
"How I Did Not Discover Relativity," *Math. Intell.* 10 (Spring 1988) 67.

79   The best seminar I ever belonged to consisted of Allen Shields and me. We met one afternoon a week, for about two hours. We did not prepare for our meetings, and we certainly did not lecture at each other. We were interested in similar things, we got along well, and each of us liked to explain his thoughts and found the other a sympathetic and intelligent listener. We would exchange the elementary puzzles we heard during the week, the crazy questions we were asked in class, the half-baked problems that popped into our heads, the vague ideas for solving last week's problems that occurred to us, the illuminating comments we heard at other seminars—we would shout excitedly, or stare together at the blackboard in bewildered silence—and, whatever we did, we both learned a lot from each other during the year the seminar lasted, and we both enjoyed it. We didn't end up collaborating in the sense of publishing a joint paper as a result of our talks—but we didn't care about that. Through our sessions we grew ... wise? Well, wiser, perhaps.   —Paul Halmos

> *I Want To Be a Mathematician,* Washington, DC:
> Mathematical Association of America, 1988, p. 72.

80   During my first leave I attended Zariski's lectures and I thought I could generalize what he was talking about. I worked very hard, but what I got was a mess. So when the editor of the American Journal of Mathematics came to me and said, "Zariski says you have some work I should publish," I responded, "It's a mess; it's a bad lead." Zariski asked to see what I had done, and of course I had to give it to him. Then he said, "You didn't get what you went in after. But you proved some things. Now back off, and state what you proved. You have to publish what you have to keep other people from going down your dead end. But we don't know; maybe someone will see a fork in the road." That is very hard; if you have a feel for style, you think things should be elegant too.   —Marguerite Lehr

> Patricia Kenschaft, "An Interview with Marguerite Lehr: In Memoriam," *Assoc. for Women in Math. Newsletter* 18 (March-April 1988) 9.

81   The Germans have aptly called *Sitzfleisch* the ability to spend endless hours at a desk doing gruesome work. *Sitzfleisch* is considered by mathematicians to be a better gauge of success than any of the attractive definitions of talent with which psychologists regale us from time to time.   —Gian-Carlo Rota

> "The Lost Cafe," in Necia Grant Cooper (ed.), *From Cardinals to Chaos,* Cambridge: Cambridge University Press, 1988, p. 23.

82   We [as children] had a lot of time to develop games. We had few toys. There was no movie house in town. We listened to things on the radio. That was our only contact with the outside world. But our games were very elaborate and purely in the imagination. I think actually that that is something that contributes to making a mathematician—having some time to think and being in the habit of imagining all sorts of complicated things.   —Mary Ellen Rudin

Donald J. Albers and Constance Reid, "An Interview with Mary Ellen Rudin," *Coll. Math. J.* 19 (March 1988) 117.

83   I lie on the sofa in the living room with my pencil and paper and think and draw little pictures and try this thing and that thing. I'm interested in how ideas fit together. Actually I'm very geometric in my thinking. I'm not good at numbers at all. ... It's a very easy house [Frank Lloyd Wright house] to work in. It has a living room two stories high, and everything else sort of opens onto that. It actually suits the way I've always handled the household. I have never minded doing mathematics lying on the sofa in the middle of the living room with the children climbing all over me. I like to know, even when I am working on mathematics, what is going on. I like to be in the center of things so the house lends itself to my mathematics.   —Mary Ellen Rudin

Donald J. Albers and Constance Reid, "An Interview with Mary Ellen Rudin," *Coll. Math. J.* 19 (March 1988) 133.

84   [I continued] to prove theorems, none of which is very earth-shaking, but each of which conveyed to me the peculiar thrill of briefly knowing a sliver of mathematical truth that *nobody* else knows.

—Louise Hay

"How I Became a Mathematician (or how it was in the bad old days)," *Assoc. for Women in Math. Newsletter* 19 (September-October 1989) 10.

85   In the spring of 1941 Michigan invited me to give a series of five or six lectures, so I talked about group extensions. ... [Sammy] Eilenberg was in the audience, except at the last lecture, and made me give the last lecture to him ahead of time. Then he said, "Well, now that calculation smells like something we do in topology, in a paper of [Norman] Steenrod's." So we stayed up all night trying to figure out what the connection was and we discovered one. We wrote our first joint paper on group extensions in homology, which exploited precisely that connection. It so happened that this was a time when more so-phisticated algebraic techniques were coming into algebraic topology. Sammy knew much more than I did about the topological background, but I knew about the algebraic techniques and had practice in elaborate algebraic calculations. So our talents fitted together. That's how our collaboration got started. And so it went on for fifteen major papers.

—Saunders Mac Lane

G.L. Alexanderson, "A Conversation With Saunders Mac Lane," *Coll. Math. J.* 20 (January 1989) 20.

86 Proofs really aren't there to convince you that something is true—they're there to show you why it is true.   —Andrew Gleason

"Andrew M. Gleason," in D. Albers, G. Alexanderson, C. Reid (eds.), *More Mathematical People,* New York: Harcourt Brace Jovanovich, 1990, p. 86.

87 It is a person's taste in problems that decides what kind of mathematics he does.   —Peter Lax

"Peter D. Lax," in D. Albers, G. Alexanderson, C. Reid (eds.), *More Mathematical People,* New York: Harcourt Brace Jovanovich, 1990, p. 155.

88 Many, many years ago one of the things that made me not want to go into mathematics was the fact that it seemed to me a very lonely life.   —Cathleen S. Morawetz

"Cathleen S. Morawetz," in D. Albers, G. Alexanderson, C. Reid (eds.), *More Mathematical People,* New York: Harcourt Brace Jovanovich, 1990, p. 234.

89 I may have emphasized the need to escape from the devils of mathematics to embark on the pleasures of the real world. But it works both ways, and sometimes the devils of the real world drive one into the pleasures of studying mathematics.   —Cathleen S. Morawetz

"Cathleen S. Morawetz," in D. Albers, G. Alexanderson, C. Reid (eds.), *More Mathematical People,* New York: Harcourt Brace Jovanovich, 1990, p. 238.

CHAPTER 5

Exhortations to Aspiring Mathematicians

I   Only such problems come back improved whose solution we passionately desire, or for which we have worked with great tension; conscious effort and tension seem to be necessary to set the subconscious work going. At any rate, it would be too easy if it were not so; we could solve difficult problems just by sleeping and waiting for a bright idea.

Past ages regarded a sudden good idea as an inspiration, a gift of the gods. You must deserve such a gift by work, or at least by a fervent wish.

—George Pólya
How to Solve It, Princeton: Princeton University Press, 1945, p. 172.

2   First, I should be clear about what the act of discovery entails. It is rarely, on the frontier of knowledge or elsewhere, that new facts are "discovered" in the sense of being encountered, as Newton suggests, in the form of islands of truth in an uncharted sea of ignorance. Or if they appear to be discovered in this way, it is almost always thanks to some happy hypothesis about where to navigate. Discovery, like surprise, favors the well-prepared mind.   —Jerome Bruner
On Knowing—Essays for the Left Hand, Cambridge, MA: Harvard University Press, 1962, p. 82.

3   Solving problems is a practical art, like swimming, or skiing, or playing the piano; you can learn it only by imitation and practice . . . if you wish to learn swimming you have to go into the water, and if you wish to become a problem solver you have to solve problems.

—George Pólya
Mathematical Discovery, Vol I, New York: John Wiley and Sons, 1962, p. v.

4   The best way to learn mathematics is to *do* mathematics. .... The reader is urged to acquire the habit of reading with paper and pencil in hand; in this way mathematics will become increasingly meaningful to him.   —G. Hajós, G. Neukomm, J. Surányi
József Kürschák, compiler, *Hungarian Problem Book I,* Washington, DC: Mathematical Association of America, 1963, note to the reader.

5   How should the reader use this book? All I can say is: without frenzy. With a serious interest and perseverance, everyone will find the way best suited *to him* in order to benefit from the varied material contained in it.   —József Kürschák
Hungarian Problem Book I, Washington, DC: Mathematical Association of America, 1963, p. 4.

6   We should not forget that the solution of many worth-while problems very rarely comes to us easily and without hard work; it is rather the result of intellectual effort of days or weeks or months. Why should the young mind be willing to make this supreme effort? The explanation is probably the instinctive preference for certain values, that is, the attitude which rates intellectual effort and spiritual achievement higher than material advantage. Such a valuation can only be the result of a long cultural development of environment and public spirit which is difficult to accelerate by governmental aid or even by more intensive training in mathematics. The most effective means may consist of transmitting to the young mind the beauty of intellectual work and the feeling of satisfaction following a great and successful mental effort.

—Gábor Szegö
József Kürschák, compiler, *Hungarian Problem Book I,* Washington, DC: Mathematical Association of America, 1963, p. 8.

7   The value of a problem is not so much in coming up with the answer as in the ideas and attempted ideas it forces on the would-be solver.

—I. N. Herstein
Topics in Algebra, Waltham, MA: Ginn, 1964, p. vi.

8   One who has merely looked out from the compartment window of an alpine railway or of a comfortable alpine hotel, will not thereby become a proficient mountaineer. A mathematical work that attempted to glide over all the difficulties of the subject matter would be completely unfit for training a reader in mathematical thinking and giving insight into this special field.   —Heinrich Tietze

Famous Problems of Mathematics, New York: Gray-lock Press, 1965, p. ix.

9   The right way to read mathematics is first to read the definitions of the concepts and the statements of the theorems, and then, putting the book aside, to try to discover the appropriate proofs. If the theorems are not trivial, the attempt might fail, but it is likely to be instructive just the same. To the passive reader a routine computation and a miracle of ingenuity come with equal ease, but later, when he must depend on himself, he will find that they went as easily as they came. The active reader, who has found out what does not work, is in a much better position to understand the reason for the success of the author's method, and, later, to find answers that are not in books.

—Paul Halmos

A Hilbert Space Problem Book, Princeton: Van Nostrand, 1967, p. vii.

IO   The reader who offers solutions in the strict sense only (this is what was asked, and here is how it goes) will miss a lot of the point, and he will miss a lot of the fun. Do not just answer the question, but try to think of related questions, of generalizations (what if the operator is not normal?) and of special cases (what happens in the finite-dimensional case?). What makes an assertion true? What would make it false?

—Paul Halmos

A Hilbert Space Problem Book, Princeton: Van Nostrand, 1967, p. vii.

II   Try to rely on yourself, and try to develop a trust in your own judgment. There is no "right" way to do things.   — Serge Lang

Basic Mathematics, Reading, MA: Addison-Wesley, 1971, p. xii.

I2   Banach used to say "Hope is the mother of fools," a Polish proverb. Nevertheless, it is good to be hopeful and believe that with luck one will succeed . . .

It is most important in creative science not to give up. If you are an optimist you will be willing to "try" more than if you are a pessimist.

—S. M. Ulam
Adventures of a Mathematician, New York: Charles Scribner's Sons, 1976, p. 54.

13 You must never take too much notice of pessimistic comments from your supervisor, or from any other mathematician, however great.

—Hans Heilbronn
J. W. S. Cassels and A. Fröhlich, "Hans Arnold Heilbronn," *Bull. of the London Math. Soc.* 9 (1977) 219.

14 To the young Ph.D's I say: Talk to your friends—the young men and women of your own age in physics, biology, economics, anthropology, psychology. Find out what they are interested in—at some point, you will find a common bond with someone, and from then on, with both of you talking furiously and each learning from the other, you may very well find something of real mathematical interest to you as well as something helpful to them. Remember, they probably know the cut-and-dried mathematics; it's the dreamy, kooky ideas I'm talking about. Next, to the graduate students—if you have the time, or even if you haven't, try to take a graduate course in some field outside of mathematics in which you have some interest and knowledge. I do not mean an introductory survey course—I mean an advanced graduate course where you really find out what the new thinking is in the subject. You may find yourself over your head sometimes, but it will open your eyes to new possibilities; and as you talk to other graduate students, you may give them an idea of what modern mathematics is all about. The undergraduates—well, arrange some joint meetings of your mathematics clubs with clubs in other fields. And, again, talk to your friends. You note there is one group I have left out, the one to which I belong, the senior faculty. We know something of what is going on elsewhere, and some of us ... have been able to bridge the gap between mathematics and applications. But our methods of thought are set, which makes it much harder for us to see new connections and new relations. I believe that young people, starting in the ways I have indicated, can make real progress in established areas by solving new problems, and in new field by defining mathematical problems and beginning to solve them. —Dorothy Bernstein
"The Role Of Applications in Pure Mathematics," *Amer. Math. Monthly* 86 (April 1979) 252.

15 Maturity, it has been said, involves knowing when and how to delay succumbing to an urge, in order by doing so to attain a deeper satisfaction. To be immature is to demand, like a baby, the immediate gratification of every impulse. . . .

What is involved . . . is how we control our natural urge to get to the point. In mathematics, as in serious music or literature, the point sometimes simply cannot be attained immediately, but only by indirection or digression.

The major prerequisite for reading this book is a willingness to cultivate some measure of maturity in mathematics. If you get stuck, be willing to forge ahead, with suspended disbelief, to see where the road is leading. "Go forward, and faith will follow!" was d'Alembert's advice in the eighteenth century to those who would learn the calculus. Your puzzlement may vanish upon turning a page.   —W. M. Priestley

Calculus: An Historical Approach, New York: Springer-Verlag, 1979, p. ix.

16 An obvious suggestion is: generalize; a slightly less obvious one is: specialize; a moderately sophisticated one is: look for a nontrivial specialization of a generalization. Another well-known piece of advice is due to Pólya: make it easier. (Pólya's dictum deserves to be propagated over and over again. In slightly greater detail it says: if you cannot solve a problem, then there is an easier problem that you cannot solve, and your first job is to find it!) The advice I am fondest of is: make it sharp. By that I mean: do not insist immediately on asking the natural question ("what is . . . ?", "when is . . . ?", "how much is . . . ?"), but focus first on an easy (but nontrivial) yes-or-no question ("is it . . . ?").   —Paul Halmos

"The Heart of Mathematics," *Amer. Math. Monthly* 87 (August-September 1980) 524.

17 Be always aware that when the going becomes too difficult in your area of research, there probably lurk ideas in neighboring parts of mathematics, whose consolidation with the concepts with which you are working may hold the key to solving your difficulties. Mathematics has an underlying unity, to which every field of mathematics as it approaches being "worked out" may appeal.   —Raymond L. Wilder

Mathematics as a Cultural System, New York: Pergamon Press, 1981, p. 165.

18   The clearer the teacher makes it, the worse it is for you. You must work things out for yourself and make the ideas your own.
—William F. Osgood
Angus Taylor, "A Life in Mathematics Remembered,"
Amer. Math. Monthly 91 (December 1984) 607.

19   [The first piece of advice to students] is to look at the first case—the easiest case that you don't understand completely. That general theorem down the road—hopefully you'll get to it bye and bye. The second piece of advice: do examples. Do a million examples. I think there are shameful cases of people making (I'll even say) silly and reckless conjectures just because they didn't take the trouble to look at the first few examples. A well-chosen example can teach you so much. . . . Sometimes when you work through an example, you suddenly get an insight which you wouldn't have got if you'd just been working abstractly with the hypothesis of your future theorem. . . . A third piece of advice: if the problem is worthwhile, give it a good try. Take months, maybe years if necessary, before you announce to the world, "This is as far as I can go. I'm quitting." It is disgraceful to give up before you have given it a good college try . . . here's a fourth piece of advice that's especially hard to follow in the years before you have tenure. The advice of Gauss: publish little but make it good. I haven't followed that advice myself. To put it more dramatically, if your problem is a little bit on the obvious side, it's very likely that someone on the planet will do it within the next five years anyway, so don't bother publishing it—turn your attention to other things. Try something that no one else is likely to do for at least twenty years. That's a high ideal but one to keep in mind.
—Irving Kaplansky
D. J. Albers, "Interview with Irving Kaplansky," *Coll. Math. J.* 22 (March 1991) 113.

CHAPTER 6

The Creative Process in Mathematics

I First and foremost [of the non-deductive methods which creative mathematicians really use] there is the use of intuition, whether geometric, mechanical, or physical. The great service which this method has rendered and is still rendering to mathematics both pure and applied is so well known that a mere mention is sufficient.

Then there is the method of experiment; not merely the physical experiments of the laboratory or the geometric experiments ... but also arithmetical experiments, numerous examples of which are found in the theory of numbers and in analysis. ...

Closely allied to this method of experiment is the method of analogy which assumes that something true of a considerable number of cases will probably be true in analogous cases. This is, of course, nothing but the ordinary method of induction. But in mathematics induction may be employed not merely in connection with experimental method, but also to extend results won by deductive methods to other analogous cases. ...

Finally there is what may perhaps be called the method of optimism which leads us either wilfully or instinctively to shut our eyes to the possibilities of evil. Thus the optimist who treats a problem in algebra or analytic geometry will say, if he stops to reflect on what he is doing: "I know that I have no right to divide by zero; but there are so many other values which the expression by which I am dividing might have that I will assume that the Evil One has not thrown a zero in my denominator this time."

This method, if a proceeding often unconscious can be called a method, has been of great service in the rapid development of many branches of mathematics, though it may well be doubted whether in a subject as highly developed as is ordinary algebra it has not now survived its usefulness.

While no one of these methods can in any way compare with that of rigorous deductive reasoning as a method upon which to base mathematical results, it would be merely shutting one's eyes to the facts to deny them their place in the life of the mathematical world, not merely of the past but of today. There is now, and there always will be room in the world for good mathematicians of every grade of logical precision. It is almost equally important that the small band whose chief interest lies in accuracy and rigor should not make the mistake of despising the broader though less accurate work of the great mass of their colleagues; as that the latter should not attempt to shake themselves wholly free from the restraint the former would put upon them. The union of these two tendencies in the same individuals, as it was found, for instance, in Gauss and Cauchy, seems the only sure way of avoiding complete estrangement between mathematicians of these two types.

—Maxime Bôcher
"The Fundamental Conceptions and Methods of Mathematics," *Bull. of the Amer. Math. Soc.* 11, (December 1904) 134.

2 Again and again men have reported that creative ideas came to them suddenly in the night, or at some time when apparently not actively working on the particular subject. However, no man has ever reported that any idea came to him in a field in which he had not previously and even recently been working. No mathematician has reported that the ideas came fully elaborated. Work, work, work; that has been and ever will be the absolutely essential condition for creative thinking.

—Louis C. Karpinski
"The Methods and Aims of Mathematical Science," *School Science and Mathematics* 22 (November 1922) 722.

3   To create consists precisely in not making useless combinations and in making those which are useful and which are only a small minority. Invention is discernment, choice.   —Henri Poincaré
> "Science and Method," in G. B. Halsted (trans.), *The Foundations of Science*, New York: The Science Press, 1929, p. 386.

4   The main sources of mathematical invention seem to be within man rather than outside of him: his own inveterate and insatiable curiosity, his constant itching for intellectual adventure; and likewise the main obstacles to mathematical progress seem to be also within himself; his scandalous inertia and laziness, his fear of adventure, his need of conformity to old standards, and his obsession by mathematical ghosts.   —George Sarton
> *The Study of the History of Mathematics*, Cambridge, MA: Harvard University Press, 1936, p. 16.

5   Some intervention of intuition issuing from the unconscious is necessary at least to initiate the logical work.   —Jacques Hadamard
> *The Psychology of Invention in the Mathematical Field*, Princeton: Princeton University Press, 1945, p. 112.

6   The first rule of discovery is to have brains and good luck. The second rule of discovery is to sit tight and wait till you get a bright idea.
>   —George Pólya
> *How to Solve It*, Princeton: Princeton University Press, 1945, p. 158.

7   Conventional histories take for granted that each fact has been discovered by a natural series of deductions from earlier facts and devote considerable space in the attempt to trace the sequence. But men experienced in research know that at least the germs of many important results are discovered by a sudden and mysterious intuition, perhaps the result of subconscious mental effort, even though such intuitions have to be subject later to the sorting process of the critical faculties.
>   —Leonard E. Dickson
> *History of the Theory of Numbers, Vol 2*, New York: Chelsea, 1952, p. xx.

8   Why should a mathematician care for plausible reasoning? His science is the only one that can rely on demonstrative reasoning alone. The physicist needs inductive evidence, the lawyer has to rely on circumstantial evidence, the historian on documentary evidence, the economist on statistical evidence. These kinds of evidence may carry strong conviction, attain a high level of plausibility, and justly so, but can never attain the force of a strict demonstration. ... Perhaps it is silly to discuss plausible grounds in mathematical matters. Yet I do not think so. Mathematics has two faces. Presented in finished form, mathematics appears as a purely demonstrative science, but mathematics in the making is a sort of experimental science. A correctly written mathematical paper is supposed to contain strict demonstrations only, but the creative work of the mathematician resembles the creative work of the naturalist: observation, analogy, and conjectural generalizations, or mere guesses, if you prefer to say so, play an essential role in both. A mathematical theorem must be guessed before it is proved. The idea of a demonstration must be guessed before the details are carried through.

—George Pólya

"On Plausible Reasoning," in *Proceedings of the International Congress of Mathematicians—1950, Vol 1,* Providence, RI: American Mathematical Society, 1952, p. 739.

9   Granted an urge to create, one creates with what one has.

With me, the particular assets that I have found useful are a memory of a rather wide scope and great permanence and a free-flowing, kaleidoscope-like train of imagination which more or less by itself gives me a consecutive view of the possibilities of a fairly complicated intellectual situation. The great strain on the memory in mathematical work is for me not so much the retention of a vast mass of fact in the literature as of the simultaneous aspects of the particular problem on which I have been working and of the conversion of my fleeting impressions into something permanent enough to have a place in memory. For I have found that if I have been able to cram all my past ideas of what the problem really involves into a single comprehensive impression, the problem is more than half solved. What remains to be done is very often the casting aside of those aspects of the group of ideas that are not germane to the solution of the problem. This rejection of the irrelevant and purification of the relevant I can do best at moments in which I have a minimum of outside impressions. Very often these moments seem to arise on waking up; but probably this really means that sometime during the night I have undergone the process of deconfusion which is necessary to establish my ideas. I am quite certain that at least a part of this process can take place during what one would ordinarily describe as sleep, and in the form of a dream. It is probably more usual for it to take place in the so-called hypnoidal state in which one is awaiting sleep, and it is closely associated with those hypnagogic images which have some of the sensory solidity of hallucinations but which, unlike hallucinations, may be manipulated more or less at the will of the subject.

—Norbert Wiener
Ex-prodigy, New York: Simon and Schuster, 1953, p. 212.

IO There is perhaps not such a gap between mathematical and other forms of thought as exists in popular imagination. Of course, the great in all walks of life have a way of their own, and it would be presumptuous to attempt to penetrate further and say what it is that distinguishes the truly great mathematical mind. Even our own mental processes are largely a mystery to us. We cannot say what happens to us in the moment of enlightenment, or the moment when against probability we notice the clue which turns out to be the essential link in the chain. All we can say is that, if we have thought about a problem, particularly if we have asked ourselves sensible questions about it, the solution will often come to us easily when we return to it after a period of leisure, or even will flash upon us at a moment when we are occupied with other things.

—A. H. Read
"The Mathematician at Work," *A Signpost to Mathematics,* quoted in William L. Schaaf (ed.), "Memorabilia Mathematica," *Math. Teacher* 49 (February 1956) 138.

II Intuition implies the act of grasping the meaning or significance or structure of a problem without explicit reliance on the analytic apparatus of one's craft. It is the intuitive mode that yields hypotheses quickly, that produces interesting combinations of ideas before their worth is known. It precedes proof; indeed, it is what the techniques of analysis and proof are designed to test and check. It is founded on a kind of combinatorial playfulness that is only possible when the consequences of error are not overpowering or sinful. Above all, it is a form of activity that depends upon confidence in the worthwhileness of the process of mathematical activity rather than upon the importance of right answers at all times.

—Jerome Bruner
"On Learning Mathematics," *Math. Teacher* 53 (December 1960) 613.

12 Beginning with nature ... we seek to find as many relationships within it as we can. If we can systematize these we do so, but a lack of organization of our material does not keep us from pushing forward. On the basis of what we have observed, we guess theorems and use these to derive other theorems. Immediately we rush to apply these back again to nature and proceed headlong if our predictions are successful. Axioms, logic, and rigor are thrown to the winds, and we become intoxicated with our success and open to dreadful errors.

This process is called "intuition" and its nature is a matter of the greatest conjecture. ... The products of this intuitive discovery are frequently wrong, usually unorganized, and always speculative. And so there follows the task of sorting them out, weaving them into a proper theory, and proving them on the basis of a set of axioms. It is at this stage that the mathematical model is likely to be constructed. The details of this process go on in our seminars and in our discussions in the corridors of meetings. ... Hence the inner circle of creative mathematicians have a well-kept trade secret that in a great many cases theorems come first and axioms second. This process of justifying a belief by finding premises from which it can be deduced is shockingly similar to much reasoning in our daily lives, and it is somewhat embarrassing to me to realize that mathematicians are experts at this art.
—Carl B. Allendoerfer
"The Narrow Mathematician," *Amer. Math. Monthly* 69 (June-July 1962) 463.

13 My interest in infinitary logic dates back to a February day in 1956 when I remarked to my thesis supervisor, Professor Leon Henkin, that a particularly vexing problem would be so simple if only I could write a formula that would say $x = 0$ or $x = 1$ or $x = 2$ etc. To my surprise he replied, "Well, go ahead." The problem is now long forgotten, but that reply has led to this monograph.   —Carol Karp
Languages with Expressions of Infinite Length, Amsterdam: North-Holland Publishing Co, 1964, p. v.

14 Mathematics—this may surprise you or shock you some—is never deductive in its creation. The mathematician at work makes vague guesses, visualizes broad generalizations, and jumps to unwarranted conclusions. He arranges and rearranges his ideas, and he becomes convinced of their truth long before he can write down a logical proof. The conviction is not likely to come early—it usually comes after many

attempts, many failures, many discouragements, many false starts. It often happens that months of work result in the proof that the method of attack they were based on cannot possibly work, and the process of guessing, visualizing and conclusion-jumping begins again. ... The deductive stage, writing the result down, and writing down its rigorous proof are relatively trivial once the real insight arrives; it is more like the draftsman's work, not the architect's.   —Paul Halmos
"Mathematics as a Creative Art," *Amer. Scientist* 56 (Winter 1968) 380.

15   [When Stefan Banach and his students would gather at the coffee house near the university, t]here would be brief spurts of conversation, a few lines would be written on the table, occasional laughter would come from some of the participants, followed by long periods of silence during which we drank coffee, and stared vacantly at each other. The café clients at neighboring tables must have been puzzled by these strange doings. It is such persistence and habit of concentration which somehow becomes the most important prerequisite for doing genuinely creative mathematical work.   —S. M. Ulam
Adventures of a Mathematician, New York: Charles Scribner's Sons, 1976, p. 34.

16   From him [Stanislaw Mazur] I learned much about the attitudes and psychology of research. Sometimes we would sit for hours in a coffee house. He would write just one symbol like $y = f(x)$ on a piece of paper, or on the marble table top. We would both stare at it as various thoughts were suggested and discussed. These symbols in front of us were like a crystal ball to help us focus our concentration. Years later in America, my friend Everett and I often had similar sessions, but instead of a coffee house they were held in an office with a blackboard.

—S. M. Ulam
Adventures of a Mathematician, New York: Charles Scribner's Sons, 1976, p. 31.

17   Psychologists are not sure but studies of creative thinking suggest some sort of relationship between creative ability and humor. Perhaps there is a connection between hunches and delight in play. ... The spirit of play seems to make him or her more receptive for that flash of insight that solves a problem.   —Martin Gardner
Aha! Insight, New York: W. H. Freeman, 1978, p. vii.

18 Mathematical reasoning may be regarded rather schematically as the exercise of a combination of two faculties, which we may call intuition and ingenuity. .... The activity of the intuition consists in making spontaneous judgments which are not the result of conscious trains of reasoning.   —Alan Turing

> Andrew Hodges, *Alan Turing: The Enigma,* New York: Simon and Schuster, 1983, p. 144.

19 I just move around in the mathematical waters, thinking about things, being curious, interested, talking to people, stirring up ideas; things emerge and I follow them up. Or I see something which connects up with something else I know about and I try to put them together and things develop. I have practically never started off with any idea of what I'm going to be doing or where it's going to go. I'm interested in mathematics; I talk, I learn, I discuss and then interesting questions simply emerge. I have never started off with a particular goal, except the goal of understanding mathematics.   —Michael Atiyah

> Robert Minio, "An Interview with Michael Atiyah," *Math. Intell.* 6 (No. 1, 1984) 10.

20 Creativity in mathematics, a vast and fascinating subject in itself, is, fortunately, not a matter of merely taking "any hypothesis that seems amusing" and deducing its consequences. If it were, it could never generate the kind of fire, despair and triumph that shine through the beautiful letters between Bolyai the elder and his son.

In urging his son to abandon the struggle with the Fifth Postulate, the father, himself a noted and respected mathematician, wrote: "I have traveled past all the reefs of the infernal Dead Sea and have always come back with a broken mast and a torn sail."

To which, some time later, came a reply in triumph and elation: "out of nothing I have created a new and wonderful world!"   —Mark Kac

> *Enigmas of Chance,* New York: Harper and Row, 1985, p. 156.

21 The creative thought processes of a mathematical mind are not easily explained, and it is hard to know what does subconsciously stimulate them.   —Olga Taussky-Todd

> "An Autobiographical Essay," in Donald J. Albers and G. L. Alexanderson (eds.), *Mathematical People,* Boston: Birkhäuser, 1985, p. 321.

22   Most of the best work starts in hopeless muddle and floundering, sustained on the 'smell' that something is there. —John E. Littlewood

> Béla Bollobás (ed.), *Littlewood's Miscellany,* Cambridge: Cambridge University Press, 1986, p. 144.

23   I think in order to do the best work in any area, you have to enjoy it and be intrigued by it. You have to wonder, "Why is this happening?" There are many examples where something slightly out of the ordinary occurs and 99 people notice it yet go on to something else. But one in a hundred—or fewer—is fascinated by that slightly anomalous or even bizarre behavior in one mathematical area or another. They start probing it more deeply and soon find that it's really the tip of a giant iceberg. Once you start to melt it, you have a much deeper understanding about what is really going on.   —Ronald Graham

> Lynn A. Steen (coord. ed.), *For All Practical Purposes,* New York: W. H. Freeman, 1988, p. 55.

24   There are many things you can do with problems besides solving them. First you must define them, pose them. But then of course you can also *refine* them, *depose* them, or *expose* them, even *dissolve* them! A given problem may send you looking for analogies, and some of these may lead you astray, suggesting new and different problems, related or not to the original. Ends and means can get reversed. You had a goal, but the means you found didn't lead to it, so you found a new goal they did lead to. It's called play. Creative mathematicians play a lot; around any problem really interesting they develop a whole cluster of analogies, of playthings.   —David Hawkins

> "The Spirit of Play," in Necia Grant Cooper (ed.), *From Cardinals to Chaos,* Cambridge: Cambridge University Press, 1988, p. 44.

CHAPTER 7

Moments of Mathematical Insight

I [When I cease working and seek sleep, it] is not in my power to pass the sponge over my poor brain even as I pass it over the blackboard. The network of ideas remains and forms as it were a moving cobweb in which repose wriggles and tosses, incapable of finding a stable equilibrium. When sleep does come at last, it is often but a state of somnolence which, far from suspending the activity of the mind, actually maintains and quickens it more than waking would. During this torpor, in which night has not yet closed upon the brain, I sometimes solve mathematical difficulties with which I struggled unsuccessfully the day before. A brilliant beacon, of which I am hardly conscious, flares in my brain. Then I jump out of bed, light my lamp again and hasten to jot down my solutions, the recollection of which I should have lost on awakening. Like lightning-flashes, those gleams vanish as suddenly as they appear.

Whence do they come? Probably from a habit which I acquired very early in life: to have food always there for my mind, to pour the never-failing oil constantly into the lamp of thought. Would you succeed in the things of the mind? The infallible method is to be always thinking of them.
—Jean Henri Fabre
The Life of the Fly, New York: Dodd, Mead and Co, 1915, p. 301.

2 For fifteen days I strove to prove that there could not be any functions like those I have since called Fuchsian functions. I was then very ignorant; every day I seated myself at my work table, stayed an hour or two, tried a great number of combinations and reached no results. One evening, contrary to my custom, I drank black coffee and could not sleep. Ideas rose in crowds; I felt them collide until pairs interlocked, so to speak, making a stable combination. By the next morning I had established the existence of a class of Fuchsian functions, those which come from the hypergeometric series; I had only to write out the results, which took but a few hours. . . .

Just at this time I left Caen, where I was then living, to go on a geologic excursion under the auspices of the school of mines. The changes of travel made me forget my mathematical work. Having reached Coutances, we entered an omnibus to go some place or other. At the moment when I put my foot on the step the idea came to me, without anything in my former thoughts seeming to have paved the way for it, that the transformations I had used to define the Fuchsian function were identical to those of non-Euclidean geometry. I did not verify the data . . . but I felt a perfect certainty. —Henri Poincaré
"Science and Method," in G. B. Halsted (trans.), *The Foundations of Science,* New York: The Science Press, 1929, p. 387.

3 Then I turned my attention to the study of some arithmetical questions apparently without much success and without a suspicion of any connection with my preceding researches. Disgusted with my failure, I went to spend a few days at the seaside, and thought of something else. One morning, walking on the bluff, the idea came to me, with just the same characteristics of brevity, suddenness and immediate certainty, that the arithmetic transformations of indeterminate ternary quadratic forms were identical with those of non-Euclidean geometry.

—Henri Poincaré
"Science and Method," in G. B. Halsted (trans.), *The Foundations of Science,* New York: The Science Press, 1929, p. 388.

4 What is progress toward the solution? Advancing mobilization and organization of our knowledge, evolution of our conception of the problem, increasing prevision of the steps which will constitute the final argument. We may advance steadily, by small imperceptible steps, but now and then we advance abruptly, by leaps and bounds. A sudden advance toward the solution is called a BRIGHT IDEA, a good idea, a happy thought, a brain wave (in German there is a more technical term, Einfall). What is a bright idea? An abrupt and momentous change in our outlook, a sudden reorganization of our mode of conceiving the problem, a just emerging confident prevision of the steps we have to take in order to attain the solution. —George Pólya

How to Solve It, Princeton: Princeton University Press, 1945, p. 146.

5 One time when I was visiting the show at the old Copley Theatre, an idea came into my mind which simply distracted all my attention from the performance. It was the notion of an optical computing machine for harmonic analysis. I had already learned not to disregard these stray ideas, no matter when they came to my attention, and I promptly left the theatre to work out some of the details of my new plan. ... The idea was valid. —Norbert Wiener

I Am a Mathematician, Garden City: Doubleday, 1956, p. 112.

6 The American accent took me by surprise, and I missed most of what was being said. Then after a week I understood everything. This is a common experience, not only in language but also with mathematics— a discontinuous process—nothing, nothing, at first, and suddenly one gets the hang of it. —S. M. Ulam

Adventures of a Mathematician, New York: Charles Scribner's Sons, 1976, p. 70.

7 It is usually more difficult to discover than to demonstrate any proposition; for the latter process we may have rules, but for the former we have none. The traces of those ideas which, in the mind of the discoverer of any new truth, connect the unknown with the known, are so faint, and his attention is so much more intensely directed to the object, than to the means by which he attains it, that it not unfrequently happens, that while we admire the happiness of the discovery we are totally at a loss to conceive the steps by which its author ascended to it. —Charles Babbage

J. M. Dubbey, The Mathematical Work of Charles Babbage, Cambridge: Cambridge University Press, 1978, p. 197.

8 I recently had an odd and vivid experience. I had been struggling for two months to prove a result I was pretty sure was true. When I was walking up a Swiss mountain, fully occupied by the effort, a very odd device emerged—so odd that, though it worked, I could not grasp the resulting proof as a whole. But not only so; I had the sense that my subconscious was saying, "Are you never going to do it, confound you; try this." —J. E. Littlewood

"The Mathematicians's Art of Work," *Math. Intell.* 1 (No. 2, 1978) 114.

9 I spent August in Batz. ... Here, among the rocks on the seashore ... the idea came to me of the nerve of a family of sets, a fundamental idea in all my later work in topology. It was then that I realized that the nerves of infinitely refining finite covers of a compactum approximate indefinitely closely to this conpactum and enable us to reduce the investigation of its topology to that of a sequence of finite simplicial complexes. When I realized this, I immediately settled down to write a new paper. —P. S. Aleksandrov

"Pages from an Autobiography, Part 2," *Russian Mathematical Surveys* 35 (May-June 1980) 323.

IO At the computing center, [Richard] Strauss showed me how all these controls could be used to get various views of three-dimensional projections of a hypercube. I watched, and tried my best to grasp what I was looking at. Then he stood up and offered me the chair at the control.

I tried turning the hypercube around, moving it away, bringing it up close, turning it around another way. Suddenly I could *feel* it! The hypercube had leaped into palpable reality, as I learned how to manipulate it, feeling in my fingertips the power to change what I saw and change it back again. The active control at the computer console created a union of kinesthetics and visual thinking which brought the hypercube up to the level of intuitive understanding.

—Philip Davis and Reuben Hersh

The Mathematical Experience, Boston: Birkhäuser, 1981, p. 404.

II As a first year graduate student, I took a course from Pierce Ketchum on complex function theory. I had absolutely no idea of what was going on. I didn't know what epsilons were, and when he said take the unit circle, and some other guy in class said "open or closed", I thought that silly guy was hair-splitting, and what was he fussing about. ...

Then one afternoon something happened. I remember standing at the blackboard in Room 213 of the mathematics building talking to Warren Ambrose and suddenly I understood epsilons. I understood what limits were, and all of the stuff that people had been drilling into me became clear. I could prove the theorems. That afternoon I became a mathematician.
                                                           —Paul Halmos
> Donald J. Albers, "Paul Halmos: Maverick Matholo-
> gist," *Two-Year Coll. Math. J.* 13 (September 1982) 230.

12   I will be thinking about something and suddenly it will dawn on me that this is related to something else I heard about last week, last month, talking to somebody. Much of my work has come that way. I go around shopping, talking to people, I get their ideas, half understood, pigeon-holed in the back of my mind. I have this vast card-index of bits of mathematics from all of those areas.   —Michael Atiyah
> Robert Minio, "An Interview with Michael Atiyah,"
> *Math. Intell.* 6 (No. 1, 1984) 16.

13   The sages who had designed the mathematics curriculum for secondary schools in Poland had stopped at solving quadratic equations. Questions by curious students about cubic and higher-order equations were deflected with answers such as "This is too advanced for you" or "You will learn this when you study higher mathematics," thereby creating a forbidden-fruit aura about the subject. But I wasn't having any of this and was determined to find out how one goes about solving cubic equations. ...

I announced that I was going to find a different derivation which would be more satisfactory. My father's skepticism can best be measured by his offering an award of five Polish zlotys ... if I succeeded.

Throughout my life I have had a number of bouts with the virus of obsession and a number of the problems causing the infection turned out to be of some significance in mathematics and science, but at no time after the summer of 1930 have I worked as hard or as feverishly. I rose early and, hardly taking time out for meals, I spent the day filling reams of paper with formulas before I collapsed into bed late at night. Conversation with me was useless since I replied only in monosyllabic grunts. I stopped seeing friends; I even gave up dating. Devoid of a strategy, I struck out in random directions, often repeating futile attempts and wedging myself into blind alleys.

Then one morning—there they were! Cardano's formulas on the

page in front of me. It took the rest of the day and more to pick out the thread of the argument from the mountain of paper. In the end, the whole derivation could be condensed into three or four pages. My father glanced at the result of my labors and paid up.   —Mark Kac
Enigmas of Chance, New York: Harper and Row, 1985, p. 2.

14   George [Uhlenbeck] ... who keeps wonderfully orderly notebooks, loaned me the one which contained his abortive attempt to solve the [Paul Ehrenfest's dog-flea] problem. It ended with an intractable differential equation which I checked, but I was unable to proceed any further.

In the fall of 1946 George asked for his notebook back. I mailed it to him and this proved to be an unexpected blessing. One evening I decided to take one more look at the problem.

Without going into technicalities, let me say that there are two seemingly equivalent ways of seeking the solution. George tried one and ran into a cul-de-sac. Not having his notes to guide me, I accidentally chose the second and it worked. In a couple of hours, I had the complete solution. Sheer serendipity!   —Mark Kac
Enigmas of Chance, New York: Harper and Row, 1985, p. 120.

15   One day I was playing round with this [derivates theorem], and a ghost of an idea entered my mind of making r, the number of differentiations, *large.* At that moment the spring cleaning that was in progress reached the room I was working in, and there was nothing for it but to go walking for 2 hours, in pouring rain. The problem seethed violently in my mind: the material was disordered and cluttered up with irrelevant complications cleared away in the final version, and the 'idea' was vague and elusive. Finally I stopped, in the rain, gazing blankly for minutes on end over a little bridge into a stream (near Kenwith wood), and presently a flooding certainty came into my mind that the thing was done. The 40 minutes before I got back and could verify were none the less tense.   —John E. Littlewood
Béla Bollobás (ed.), *Littlewood's Miscellany,* Cambridge: Cambridge University Press, 1986, p. 93.

16   Two rats fell into a can of milk. After swimming for a time one of them realized his hopeless fate and drowned. The other persisted, and at last the milk was turned into butter and he could get out.

In the first part of the war, Miss [Mary] Cartwright and I got drawn into van der Pol's equation. For something to do we went on and on at the thing with no earthly prospect of "results": suddenly the entire vista of the dramatic fine structure of solutions stared us in the face.

—John E. Littlewood
Béla Bollobás (ed.), *Littlewood's Miscellany,* Cambridge: Cambridge University Press, 1986, p. 13.

17   Often, half the battle in trying to solve a difficult problem is knowing the right question to ask. If you know what it is you are trying to look for, you can often be very far along in finding the solution. It's useful for me, and for many others who are working on a difficult problem to look at a special case first. You can work your way up to the full problem by trying easier special cases that you still can't do. You may be bouncing the idea around a bit and not forcing it, and it's amazing how often it happens that the next day or next week something will seem obvious that was very hard to imagine even a week earlier.

—Ronald Graham
Lynn A. Steen (coord. ed.), *For All Practical Purposes,* New York: W. H. Freeman, 1988, p. 55.

18   I like to understand mathematics, and to clarify it for myself and for the world, more even than to discover it. The joy of suddenly learning a former secret and the joy of suddenly discovering a hitherto unknown truth are the same to me—both have the flash of enlightenment, the almost incredibly enhanced vision, and the ecstacy and euphoria of released tension. At the same time, discovering a new truth, similar in subjective pleasure to understanding an old one, is in one way quite different. The difference is the pride, the feeling of victory, the almost malicious satisfaction that comes from being first. "First" implies that someone is second; to want to be first is asking to be "graded on the curve". I seem to be saying, almost, that clarifying old mathematics is more moral than finding new, and that's obviously silly—but let me say instead that insight is better without an accompanying gloat than with.

—Paul Halmos
I Want To Be a Mathematician, Washington, DC: Mathematical Association of America, 1988, p. 3.

CHAPTER 8

The Love of Mathematics

I [describing his first encounter with an algebra book] And now we are together, O mysterious tome, whose Arab name breathes a strange mustiness of occult lore and claims kindred with the sciences of almagest and alchemy. What will you show me? Let us turn the leaves at random. Before fixing one's eyes on a definite point in the landscape it is well to take a summary view of the whole. Page follows swiftly upon page, telling me nothing. A chapter catches my attention in the middle of the volume; it is headed, Newton's Binomial Theorem.

The title allures me. What can a binomial theorem be, especially, one whose author is Newton, the great English mathematician who weighed the worlds? What has the mechanism of the sky to do with this? Let us read and seek for enlightenment. With my elbows on the table and my thumbs behind my ears, I concentrate all my attention.

I am seized with astonishment, for I understand! There are a certain number of letters, general symbols which are grouped in all manner of ways, taking their places here, there and elsewhere by turns; there are, as the text tells me, arrangements, permutations and combinations. Pen in hand, I arrange, permute and combine. ... What a delightful afternoon that was, before my grate, amid my permutations and combinations! By the evening, I had nearly mastered my subject. When the bell rang, at seven, to summon me to the common meal at the principal's table, I went downstairs puffed up with the joys of the newly initiated

neophyte. I was escorted on my way by a,b,c, intertwined in cunning
garlands.   —Jean Henri Fabre
          The Life of the Fly, New York: Dodd, Mead and Co.,
          1915, p. 282.

2   Our science, which we loved above everything, had brought us
[Hilbert and Klein] together. It appeared to us as a flowering garden. In
this garden there are beaten paths where one may look around at leisure
and enjoy oneself without effort, especially at the side of a congenial
companion. But we also liked to seek out hidden trails and discovered
many a novel view, beautiful to behold, so we thought, and when we
pointed them out to one another our joy was perfect. —David Hilbert
          Hermann Weyl, "David Hilbert and His Mathematical
          Work," *Bull. of the Amer. Math. Soc.* 50 (September
          1944) 614.

3   I came to Göttingen as a country lad of eighteen, having chosen
that university mainly because the director of my high school happened
to be a cousin of Hilbert's and had given me a letter of recommendation
to him. In the fullness of my innocence and ignorance I made bold to
take the course Hilbert had announced for that term, on the notion of
number and the quadrature of the circle. Most of it went straight over
my head. But the new world swung open for me, and I had not sat long at
Hilbert's feet before the resolution formed itself in my young heart that
I must by all means read and study whatever this man had written. And
after the first year I went home with Hilbert's *Zahlbericht* under my arm,
and during the summer vacation I worked my way though it—without
any previous knowledge of elementary number theory or Galois theory.
These were the happiest months of my life, whose shine, across years
burdened with our common share of doubt and failure, still comforts
my soul.   —Hermann Weyl
          "David Hilbert and His Mathematical Work," *Bull. of
          the Amer. Math. Soc.* 50 (September 1944) 614.

4   [The mathematician believes] that he will be able to slake his thirst
at the very sources of knowledge, convinced as he is that they will always
continue to pour forth, pure and abundant, while others have to have
recourse to the muddy streams of a sordid reality. If he be reproached
with the haughtiness of his attitude, if he be asked why he persists on

the high glaciers whither no one but his own kind can follow him, he will answer, with Jacobi: For the honor of the human spirit.   —André Weil
"The Future of Mathematics," *Amer. Math. Monthly* 57 (May 1950) 306.

5   At the age of 12 I experienced a second wonder . . . in a little book dealing with Euclidean plane geometry, which came into my hands at the beginning of a schoolyear. Here were assertions, as for example the intersection of the three altitudes of a triangle in one point, which— though by no means evident—could nevertheless be proved with such certainty that any doubt appeared to be out of the question.   This lucidity and certainty made an indescribable impression upon me. . . .

If thus it appeared that it was possible to get certain knowledge of the objects of experience by means of pure thinking, this "wonder" rested upon an error. Nevertheless, for anyone who experiences it for the first time, it is marvelous enough that man is capable at all to reach such a degree of certainty and purity in pure thinking as the Greeks showed us for the first time to be possible in geometry.   —Albert Einstein
"Autobiographical Notes" in Paul A. Schilpp (ed.), *Albert Einstein: Philosopher-Scientist,* New York: Tudor Publishing, 1951, p. 9.

6   What induced the author to interrupt his own investigations for the greater part of the past nine years to write this history? Because it fitted in with his convictions that every person should aim to perform at some time in his life some serious, useful work for which it is highly improbable that there will be any reward whatever other than his satisfaction therefrom.   —Leonard E. Dickson
History of the Theory of Numbers, Vol 2, New York: Chelsea, 1952, p. xx.

7   To make mathematics you must be interested in mathematics. The fascination of pattern and the logical classification of pattern must have taken hold of you. It need not be the only emotion in your mind; you may pursue other aims, respond to other duties; but if it is not there, you will contribute nothing to mathematics.   —W. W. Sawyer
Prelude to Mathematics, Baltimore: Penguin Books, 1957, p. 17.

8   Beautiful in its hard cold austerity is the art of arithmetical calculation. . . . The northern ocean is beautiful, and beautiful the delicate intricacy of the snowflake before it melts and perishes, but such beauties are as nothing to him who delights in numbers, spurning alike the wild irrationality of life and baffling complexity of nature's laws.

—J. L. Synge

Kandelman's Krim, London: Jonathan Cape, 1957, p. 101.

9   If you should ask me as a student of the thought processes what produces the most fundamental form of pleasure in man's intellectual life, I think I would reply that it is the reduction of surprise and complexity to predictability and simplicity. Indeed, it is when a person has confidence in his ability to bring off this feat that he comes to enjoy surprise, to enjoy the process of imposing puzzle forms upon difficulties in order to convert them into problems.   —Jerome Bruner

"On Learning Mathematics," *Math. Teacher* 53 (December 1960) 618.

10   The theory of elliptic functions is the fairyland of mathematics. The mathematician who once gazes upon this enchanting and wondrous domain crowded with the most beautiful relations and concepts is forever captivated.   —Richard Bellman

A Brief Introduction to Theta Functions, New York: Holt, Rinehart and Winston, 1961, p. vii.

11   I love mathematics not only for its technical applications, but principally because it is beautiful; because man has breathed his spirit of play into it, and because it has given him his greatest game—the encompassing of the infinite.   —Rózsa Péter

Playing with Infinity, New York: Simon and Schuster, 1962, p. v.

12   I remember vividly the time when I participated in this phase of the [Hungarian Mathematics] Journal [for students] (in the years between 1908 and 1912); I would wait eagerly for the arrival of the monthly issue and my first concern was to look at the problem section, almost breathlessly, and to start grappling with the problems without delay. The names of the others who were in the same business were quickly known to me and frequently I read with considerable envy how they had succeeded with some problems which I could not handle with complete success, or how they had found a better solution (that is, simpler, more elegant or wittier) than the one I had sent in. The following story may not be accurate in all details but it is certainly revealing:

"The time is about 1940, the scene is one of the infamous labor camps of fascist Hungary just at the beginning of its pathetic transformation from semi-dictatorship to the cannibalism of the Nazi pattern. These camps were populated mostly by Jewish youth forced to carry out some perfectly useless tasks. One young man (at present one of the leading mathematicians of Hungary) was in the camp; let us call him Mr. X. He was panting under the load of a heavy beam when the sargeant shouted at him in a not too complimentary manner, addressing him by his last name. The supervising officer stood nearby, just a few steps away, and said: 'Say, did I hear right, your name is X?' 'Yes,' was the answer. 'Are you by chance the same X who worked years ago in the High School Journal?' 'Yes,' was again the answer. 'You know, you solved more, and more difficult problems than any one of us and we were very envious of you.' The end of the story is that Mr. X received more lenient treatment in the camp and later even had some mathematical contact with the all-powerful officer."

The profound interest which these young men took in the Journal was decisive in many of their lives. The intensive preoccupation with interesting problems of simple and elementary character and the effort of finding clear and complete answers gave them a new experience, the taste of creative intellectual adventure. Thus they were bound finally and unalterably to the jealous mistress that mathematics is. There remained still the question of what special studies to undertake, whether it should be mathematics or physics or engineering; but this was after all a secondary matter; the main road was charted for life. We may think of the adage of Kronecker who compares mathematicians with lotus eaters: "He who has once tasted of this fruit can never more foreswear it."

—Gábor Szegö

József Kürschák, compiler, *Hungarian Problem Book I*, Washington, DC: Mathematical Association of America, 1963, p. 7.

13 [Archimedes speaking to King Hieron] ... mathematics rewards only those who are interested in it not only for its rewards but also for itself. Mathematics is like your daughter, Helena, who suspects every time a suitor appears that he is not really in love with her, but is only interested in her because he wants to be the king's son-in-law. She wants a husband who loves her for her own beauty, wit and charm, and not for the wealth and power he can get by marrying her. Similarly,

mathematics reveals its secrets only to those who approach it with pure love, for its own beauty. Of course, those who do this are also rewarded with results of practical importance. But if somebody asks at each step, 'what can I get out of this?' he will not get far. 　　　　—Alfréd Rényi
Dialogues on Mathematics, San Francisco: Holden-Day, 1967, p. 46.

14　　At the age of eleven, I began Euclid with my brother as my tutor. This was one of the great events of my life, as dazzling as first love. I had not imagined that there was anything so delicious in the world.

After I learned the fifth proposition, my brother told me that it was generally considered difficult, but I had no difficulty whatever. This was the first time it had dawned on me that I might have some intelligence. From that moment until Whitehead and I finished *Principia Mathematica,* when I was thirty-eight, mathematics was my chief interest, and my chief source of happiness. 　　　　—Bertrand Russell
The Autobiography of Bertrand Russell 1872–1914, London: George Allen and Unwin, 1967, p. 36.

15　　Just before my 16th birthday, I was sent to an Army crammer at Old Southgate. ... I remained, however, profoundly unhappy. There was a footpath leading across fields to New Southgate and I used to go there alone to watch the sunset and contemplate suicide. I did not, however, commit suicide because I wished to know more of mathematics.
　　　　—Bertrand Russell
The Autobiography of Bertrand Russell 1872–1914, London: George Allen and Unwin, 1967, p. 43.

16　　I could not resist the obsession that through unrestrained preoccupation with mathematics my life would become worthwhile.
　　　　—Constantin Carathéodory
Constance Reid, *Hilbert,* New York: Springer-Verlag, 1970, p. 87.

17　　Paul Erdős is really a prophet, a missionary, of combinatorics. Traveling frequently, lecturing at many places on appealing combinatorical problems which may be understood without learning a mass of definitions, Paul Erdős has acquired an always growing army of new followers. His prophetical activity is facilitated by the fact that he has not to entertain the uninitiated with hopes of other-worldly rewards: The intellectual pleasures offered by dealing with combinatorial problems can be felt and understood even after working unsuccessfully on such problems.   —Paul Turán

"Forward," in Joel Spencer (ed.), *Paul Erdős: The Art of Counting, Selected Writings,* Cambridge, MA: MIT Press, 1973, p. xviii.

18 Somehow under his [Lee Lorch's] prodding, I gradually became aware of the beauty and power of mathematics. . . . Dr. Lorch truly loved mathematics, and it was impossible to listen to him without acquiring some of this love.   —Etta Zuber Falconer

Vivienne Mayes, "Lee Lorch at Fisk: a Tribute," *Amer. Math. Monthly* 83 (November 1976) p. 709.

19 I gave my own little talk [at the Congress in Zurich in 1932] feeling only moderately nervous. The reason for this comparative lack of nervousness, I think, in retrospect, was due to my attitude, compounded of a certain drunkenness with mathematics and a constant preoccupation with it.   —S. M. Ulam

Adventures of a Mathematician, New York: Charles Scribner's Sons, 1976, p. 45.

20 It was arithmetic which Malevich taught best and most innovatively. I have to confess, however, that when I first began to study with him, arithmetic held little interest for me. Probably because of Uncle Pyotr's influence, I was much more taken with abstract considerations— infinity for example. And, as a matter of fact, it is the philosophical aspects of mathematics which has attracted me all through my life. Mathematics has always seemed to me a science which opens up completely new horizons.

Besides arithmetic, Malevich taught me elementary geometry and algebra. Not until I grew somewhat more familiar with this latter field did I begin to feel an attraction to mathematics so intense that I started to neglect my other studies.   —Sofya Kovalevskaya

A Russian Childhood, New York: Springer-Verlag, 1978, p. 216.

21 When we came to the theory of parallel lines, Eiges began with amazing pedagogical tact and skill to tell us about Lobachevskii's geometry. The very statement of the problem astounded me. Never before had anything aroused my interest and enthusiasm to that extent.

Geometry became an enchanted kingdom for me, and I dreamed of that alone.   —P. S. Aleksandrov
"Pages from an Autobiography," *Russian Mathematical Surveys* 34 (November-December 1979) 275.

22   My idea of a joyful Christmas vacation was different [from my father's]. I arrived at the cottage on the coast with my precious [copy of] Piaggio's [*Differential Equations*] book and did not intend to be parted from him. I soon discovered that Piaggio's book was ideally suited to a solitary student. It was a serious book, and went rapidly enough ahead into advanced territory. But unlike most advanced texts, it was liberally sprinkled with "Examples for Solution." There were more than seven hundred of these problems. The difference between a text without problems and a text with problems is like the difference between learning to read a language and learning to speak it. ... I started at six in the morning and stopped at ten in the evening, with short breaks for meals. ... Never have I enjoyed a vacation more.   —Freeman Dyson
Disturbing the Universe, New York: Harper and Row, 1979, p. 13.

23   In those days, mathematics was for me a half-understood welter of formulas that had to be endured for physics' sake. Things began to change with a famous course at the University of Michigan under R. L. Wilder, on the Foundations of Mathematics. Even so, the formal switch to mathematics that I made in my senior year was made as a tactful detour to theoretical physics. That is, it was intended to get me out of the examination in the laboratory course on heat. But it was perhaps a bad thing to do. The hook was set, and by the next year becoming a mathematician seemed to me the most desirable and most unattainable thing in the world.   —Jimmie Savage
The Writings of Leonard Jimmie Savage, a Memorial Selection, Washington, DC: American Statistical Association, 1981, p. 18.

24   But his [Galois'] first contact with mathematics early in 1827 aroused in him an irresistible passion, a vocation which put him even more openly in opposition to the school authorities. The report by his director of studies is particularly suggestive:
"It is the passion of mathematics which dominates him; I think it would be best for him if his parents would allow him to study nothing

but this; he is wasting his time here and does nothing but torment his teachers and overwhelm himself with punishments." —René Taton
"Évariste Galois and His Contemporaries," *Bull. of the London Math. Soc.* 15 (1983) 107.

25 When it was suggested to me that an article of reminiscences might be welcomed by the *Monthly*, I found that I could not resist the opportunity to review my love affair with mathematics. —Angus Taylor
"A Life in Mathematics Remembered," *Amer. Math. Monthly* 91 (December 1984) 605.

26 In my sophomore year I got acquainted with Garrett Birkhoff, one year ahead of me as an undergraduate, and far more knowledgeable. We both lived in Lowell House, then brand new. Garrett impressed on me that, to succeed as a mathematician, one had to be utterly dedicated to the subject. I had no reservations about my commitment to mathematics, even though I had as yet little understanding of what would be involved in making a successful career as a mathematician on a university faculty. —Angus Taylor
"A Life in Mathematics Remembered," *Amer. Math. Monthly* 91 (December 1984) 606.

27 The next year I really fell in love with mathematics. I had a course in elementary analysis. We used Hardy's *Pure Mathematics* as a text. That's the first time I knew that serious mathematics was for me. I became clear that it was not simply a few things that I liked. The whole subject was just beautiful. —David Blackwell
Donald J. Albers, "David Blackwell," in D. Albers and G. Alexanderson (eds.), *Mathematical People*, Boston: Birkhäuser, 1985, p. 21.

28 In spite of his misgivings, Father succumbed and started to give me informal lessons in geometry. In no time I had a firm grasp of the subject and was able to solve quite difficult problems. . . . What I enjoyed most were challenging problems. Among my father's books there were several collections of especially tough ones taken from competitive entrance examinations to various engineering schools in tsarist Russia. Oh, what a pleasure it was to crack one of those toughies! —Mark Kac
Enigmas of Chance, New York: Harper and Row, 1985, p. 14.

29   The syllabus [of Analysis with Differential and Integral Calculus] included Dedekind cuts and also suggested books to read to prepare for the examination. But I wanted to learn calculus now and I didn't fully understand the system. In distress, I ran to Marceli [a junior assistant at the Institute]. He showed surprisingly little sympathy or understanding of my predicament. "But I never heard of Dedekind cuts," I pleaded. "Then you should read about them," he said and as the only concession he recommended a book. So I went home and read, and as I read, the beauty of the concept hit me with a force that sent me into a state of euphoria. When, a few days later, I rhapsodized to Marceli about Dedekind cuts—in fact, I acted as if I had discovered them—his only comment was that perhaps I had the makings of a mathematician after all.   —Mark Kac

Enigmas of Chance, New York: Harper and Row, 1985, p. 31.

30   [After my father's death] I worked all through the summer after school was over, but was burdened by the fact that my future in mathematics was at stake. ... My family thought that I would do better to study chemistry, and to join up with my sister [in running the family business]. In any case, what was I to do with mathematics? There did not seem a prosperous future in it. ... I spent the whole summer worrying. One day I met a lady, a friend of my family, who had heard of my dreams. She was decades older and mentioned that she too had hoped to study mathematics. That was more than I could take. In a flash, I saw myself decades older saying exactly the same words to a young woman. It seemed unbearable. I cannot say that this created the final decision. However, when the summer was over it was decided to let me begin studies in mathematics at the University of Vienna, taking also a major in chemistry, a truly wonderful subject.

—Olga Taussky-Todd

"An Autobiographical Essay," in Donald J. Albers and G. L. Alexanderson (eds.), *Mathematical People*, Boston: Birkhäuser, 1985, p. 315.

31   The real inspiration, however, I got from my father. He showed me a few mathematical things when I came back from Berlin. He showed me mathematical induction, for instance. ... And then he showed me how to represent equations by lines and how to solve two linear equations by seeing where the lines intersect. And this seemed to me the most beautiful thing in the world. —Lipman Bers

Donald J. Albers and Constance Reid, "An Interview with Lipman Bers," *Coll. Math. J.* 18 (September 1987) 271.

32 The most exhilarating experience that summer was my introduction to set theory. I would sit on the swing on the front porch, drink iced tea, and devour Hausdorff's *Grundzüge der Mengenlehre*. I was like a child with a new toy: I thought it was beautiful and astonishing.

The most elementary ideas took me by surprise, and yet I was sufficiently prepared for them to be able to appreciate their significance when they came. I loved cardinal arithmetic, and I eagerly computed the number of elements of every set I could think of. Ordinal numbers were another revelation, and the strange order types, the non-well-ordered ones, were like music: intricate, but just right.

—Paul Halmos

I Want To Be a Mathematician, Washington, DC: Mathematical Association of America, 1988, p. 57.

33 Someone asked me if I was ever sorry I had chosen mathematics. I said, "I didn't choose! Mathematics is an addiction with me!"

—Marguerite Lehr

Patricia Kenschaft, "An Interview with Marguerite Lehr: In Memoriam," *Assoc. for Women in Math. Newsletter* 18 (March-April 1988) 9.

34 Of all escapes from reality, mathematics is the most successful ever. It is a fantasy that becomes all the more addictive because it works back to improve the same reality we are trying to evade. All other escapes—love, drugs, hobbies, whatever—are ephemeral by comparison. The mathematician's feeling of triumph, as he forces the world to obey the laws his imagination has freely created, feeds on its own success. The world is permanently changed by the workings of his mind, and the certainty that his creations will endure renews his confidence as no other pursuit. The mathematician becomes totally committed, a monster like Nabokov's chess player, who eventually sees all life as subordinate to the game of chess. —Gian-Carlo Rota

"The Lost Cafe," in Necia Grant Cooper (ed.), *From Cardinals to Chaos,* Cambridge: Cambridge University Press, 1988, p. 26.

35 [When I went to study in Zurich, the] outside world had suddenly opened up to me, and I was thrilled. Never mind that I was on short rations and had to become a vegetarian to make ends meet. Never mind that the luxury around me was completely out of my reach. I had found what I wanted. For the first time I could listen to live lectures on contemporary mathematics. . . . From that point on I knew that I was a mathematician.   —L. V. Ahlfors
"The Joy of Function Theory," in Peter Duren (ed.), *A Century of Mathematics in America, Part III,* Providence, RI: American Mathematical Society, 1989, p. 444.

36 Some people think that mathematics is a serious business that must always be cold and dry; but we think mathematics is fun, and we aren't ashamed to admit the fact. Why should a strict boundary line be drawn between work and play? Concrete mathematics is full of appealing patterns; the manipulations are not always easy, but the answers can be astonishingly attractive. The joys and sorrows of mathematical work are . . . part of our lives.
—Ronald L. Graham, Donald E. Knuth, Oren Patashnik
Concrete Mathematics, Reading, MA: Addison- Wesley, 1989, p. vii.

37 The following year I took my last high school mathematics course, geometry. It was a traditional course, very near to Euclid; it talked about axioms and postulates, defined lines and points in utterly confusing ways. . . . It was the loveliest course, the most beautiful stuff that I've ever seen. I thought so then; I think so now.   —J. L. Kelley
"Once Over Lightly," in Peter Duren (ed.), *A Century of Mathematics in America, Part III,* Providence, RI: American Mathematical Society, 1989, p. 473.

38 Some years ago, after I had given a talk, somebody said, "You seem to make mathematics sound like so much fun." I was inspired to reply, "If it isn't fun, why do it?" I am proud of the sentiment, even if it is overstated.   —Ralph P. Boas
"Ralph P. Boas, Jr.," in D. Albers, G. Alexanderson, C. Reid (eds.), *More Mathematical People,* New York: Harcourt Brace Jovanovich, 1990, p. 41.

39 [Edwin Olds] showed me a generating function. It was the most marvelous thing I had ever seen in mathematics. It used mathematics that up to that time, in my heart of hearts, I had thought was something that mathematicians just did to create homework problems for innocent students in high school and college. . . . I was stunned when I saw how Olds used this mathematics that I hadn't believed in. He used it in such an unusually outrageous way. It was a total retranslation of the meaning of the numbers.   —Frederick Mosteller

> "Frederick Mosteller," in D. Albers, G. Alexanderson, C. Reid (eds.), *More Mathematical People,* New York: Harcourt Brace Jovanovich, 1990, p. 246.

40   No other field can offer, to such an extent as mathematics, the joy of discovery, which is perhaps the greatest human joy.

—Rósza Péter

> "Mathematics is Beautiful," *Math. Intell.* 12 (Winter 1990) 62.

41   Individually [mathematicians] are very different in their mathematical personalities, the kind of mathematics they like, and the way that they do mathematics, but they are alike in one respect. Almost without exception, they love their subject, are happy in their choice of a career, and consider that they are exceptionally lucky in being able to do for a living what they would do for fun.   —Constance Reid

> "Becoming a Mathematician," in D. Albers, G. Alexanderson, C. Reid (eds.), *More Mathematical People,* New York: Harcourt Brace Jovanovich, 1990, p. xvii.

CHAPTER 9

Pure and Applied Mathematics:
Comparison, Controversy, Collaboration

I   During the last two centuries and a half, physical knowledge has been gradually made to rest upon a basis which it had not before. It has become *mathematical.* ... Even in those sciences which are not yet under the dominion of mathematics, and perhaps never will be, a working copy of the mathematical process has been made. This is not known to the followers of those sciences who are not themselves mathematicians and who very often exalt their horns against the mathematics in consequence.   —Augustus de Morgan
> *A Budget of Paradoxes, Vol. I* Chicago: Open Court, 1915, p. 2.

2   When it was decided that we must enter the World War, it was natural that mathematicians, along with other loyal citizens, should volunteer to assist in their special capacity, but they were told by the Secretary of War that there seemed to be nothing needed in their line. It was not long, however, before the Government found that it *did* need the mathematicians, in fact, that it could not "carry on" without them in so important a matter as the effective development of the ordnance department. In a short time a corps of workers was organized under the leadership of a number of outstanding mathematicians and they speedily applied modern and powerful mathematical methods, both theoretical and practical, to those problems of ballistics which needed to be solved in order to properly equip our army. So effective had this service become at the time of the armistice, that the American forces were undoubtedly supplied with the best data of any of the armies for determining the effectiveness of gun fire. Other groups of mathematicians rendered similar effective service in developing submarine detection appliances. These two achievements were of vital importance in determining the outcome of the war and they revealed the power of mathematics in a most emphatic manner to the unsuspecting public.

It came as a revelation to thousands of young men, many of whom had deliberately side-stepped all mathematical courses which they could possibly avoid in their school days, to find that those very courses were prerequisite to appointment or advancement as officers in either the army or the navy. It was a common experience to hear such men begging for the opportunity to enter classes in mathematics which they had previously ignored—and bragged about it too. The war served to elevate mathematics to a position of prominence not previously recognized by the casual public. This fact undoubtedly helped to swell the courses in mathematics in colleges in the immediately succeeding years.

—H. E. Slaught
"Mathematics and the Public," in Charles Austin, (ed.), *The First Yearbook: A General Survey of Progress in the Last Twenty-five Years,* New York: National Council of Teachers of Mathematics, 1926, p. 189.

3   Nothing is more impressive than the fact that as mathematics withdrew increasingly into the upper regions of ever greater extremes of abstract thought, it returned back to earth with a corresponding growth of importance for the analysis of concrete fact . . .

The paradox is now fully established that the utmost abstractions are the true weapons with which to control our thought of concrete fact.

—Alfred North Whitehead
"Mathematics as an Element in the History of Thought," *Science and the Modern World,* New York: Macmillan, 1928, p. 48.

4   A simple abstraction without present application is [not] to be regarded as without value. All abstractions are significant if they possess beauty; and the experience of the race shows that such abstractions are almost certain sooner or later to prove useful.   —George Birkhoff
"Mathematics: Quantity and Order," in J. G. Crowther (ed.), *Science Today,* London: Eyre & Spottiswoode, 1934, p. 315.

5   Everybody knows that being able to chatter in several foreign languages is not a sign of great social intelligence. Neither is being able to chatter in the language of size [mathematics]. Real social intelligence lies in the use of a language, in applying the right words in the right context. It is important to know the language of size, because entrusting the laws of human society, social statistics, population, man's hereditary make-up, the balance of trade, to the isolated mathematician without checking his conclusions is like letting a committee of philologists manufacture the truths of human, animal, or plant anatomy from the resources of their own imaginations.   —Lancelot Hogben

> *Mathematics for the Million,* New York: W. W. Norton, 1937, p. 28.

6   The evolution of this theory [of matrices] from its almost accidental beginning in Cayley's work, of about eighty years ago, into one of the most useful tools of algebra, suggests that there is but little rhyme and less reason in the historical development of algebra. It also suggests that other apparent trivia may be the germs of equally significant and useful theories. Now that the theory of matrices is full-blown before us, it is easy for any empirical historian to see the inevitability of the growth from seed to flower. But the familiar historical explanation through linear transformations, etc., explains precisely nothing, unless the explainer is able to validate himself and his explanations by making a prediction from the present phenomena of algebra for observers half a century hence to confirm or refute. The like applies to a good deal of the rest of algebra during the past fifty years.   —E. T. Bell

> "Fifty Years of Algebra in America, 1888–1938," *Semicentennial Addresses of the American Mathematical Society, Vol II,* New York: American Mathematical Society, 1938, p. 25.

7   In default of a better term we use the designation of applied mathematics for that large part of mathematics which seems to be closely connected with physics or some other branch of science. Inasmuch as most of the so-called "pure" mathematics of the present day was at one time "applied," the term is a very vague one. Nevertheless, the field of applied mathematics always will remain of the first order of importance

inasmuch as it indicates those directions of mathematical effort to which
nature herself has given approval.   —George Birkhoff
> "Fifty Years of American Mathematics," *Semicenten-*
> *nial Addresses of the American Mathematical Society,*
> *Vol II,* New York: American Mathematical Society,
> 1938, p. 313.

8   It is a falsification of the history of mathematics to represent pure
mathematics as a self-contained science drawing inspiration from itself
alone and morally taking in its own washing. Even the most abstract
ideas of the present time have something of a physical history. The
somewhat snobbish point of view of the purely abstract mathematician
would draw but little support from mathematical history. On the other
hand, whenever applied mathematics has been merely a technical em-
ployment of methods already traditional and jejune, it has been very
poor applied mathematics. The desideratum in mathematical as well as
physical work is an attitude which is not indifferent to the extremely instructive nature of actual physical situations, yet which is not dominated
by these to the dwarfing and paralyzing of its intellectual originality.
> —Norbert Wiener
> "The Historical Background of Harmonic Analysis,"
> *Semicentennial Addresses of the American Mathemati-*
> *cal Society, Vol II,* New York: American Mathematical
> Society, 1938, p. 68.

9   Logic is the railway track along which the mind glides easily. It
is the axioms that determine our destination by setting us on this track
or the other, and it is in the matter of choice of axioms that applied
mathematics differs most fundamentally from pure. Pure mathematics
is controlled (or should we say "uncontrolled"?) by a principle of ideo-
logical isotropy: any line of thought is as good as another, provided that
it is logically smooth. Applied mathematics on the other hand follows
only those tracks which offer a view of natural scenery; if sometimes the
track dives into a tunnel it is because there is prospect of scenery at the
far end.   —J. L. Synge
> "Postcards on Applied Mathematics," *Amer. Math.*
> *Monthly* 46 (March 1939) 156.

IO   If useful knowledge is, as we agreed provisionally to say, knowledge which is likely, now or in the comparatively near future, to contribute to the material comfort of mankind, so that mere intellectual

satisfaction is irrelevant, then the great bulk of higher mathematics is useless. Modern geometry and algebra, the theory of numbers, the theory of aggregates and functions, relativity, quantum mechanics—no one of them stands the test much better than another, and there is no real mathematician whose life can be justified on this ground. If this be the test, then Abel, Riemann, and Poincaré wasted their lives; their contribution to human comfort was negligible, and the world would have been as happy a place without them.   —G. H. Hardy
A Mathematician's Apology, Cambridge: University Press, 1940, p. 75.

II I have never done anything 'useful'. No discovery of mine has made, or is likely to make, directly or indirectly, for good or ill, the least difference to the amenity of the world. I have just one chance of escaping a verdict of complete triviality, that I may be judged to have created something worth creating. And that I have created something is undeniable: the question is about its value.

The case for my life, then, or for that of any one else who has been a mathematician in the same sense in which I have been one, is this: that I have added something to knowledge, and helped others to add more; and that these somethings have a value which differs in degree only, and not in kind, from that of the creations of the great mathematicians, or of any of the other artists, great or small, who have left some kind of memorial behind them.   —G. H. Hardy
A Mathematician's Apology, Cambridge: University Press, 1940, p. 90.

I2 Concerning the fruitlessness of the future results, about which strictly speaking, we most often do not know anything in advance, that sense of beauty can inform us and I cannot see anything else allowing us to foresee. At least, without knowing anything further, we *feel* that such a direction of investigation is worth following; we feel that the question *in itself* deserves interest; that its solution will be of some value for science, whether it permits further applications or not.
—Jacques Hadamard
The Psychology of Invention in the Mathematical Field, Princeton: Princeton University Press, 1945, p. 127.

I3 [My thesis is that] much of the best mathematical inspiration comes from experience and that it is hardly possible to believe in the existence of an absolute, immutable concept of mathematical rigor, dissociated from all human experience.   —John von Neumann

> "The Mathematician," in Robert B. Heywood (ed.), *The Works of the Mind,* Chicago: University of Chicago Press, 1947, p. 190.

I4   Since the seventeenth century, physical intuition has served as a vital source for mathematical problems and methods. Recent trends and fashions have, however, weakened the connection between mathematics and physics; mathematicians, turning away from the roots of mathematics in intuition, have concentrated on refinement and emphasized the postulational side of mathematics, and at times have overlooked the unity of their science with physics and other fields. In many cases, physicists have ceased to appreciate the attitudes of mathematicians. This rift is unquestionably a serious threat to science as a whole; the broad stream of scientific development may split into smaller and smaller rivulets and dry out. It seems therefore important to direct our efforts toward reuniting divergent trends by clarifying the common features and interconnections of many distinct and diverse scientific facts.   —Richard Courant

> R. Courant and D. Hilbert, *Methods of Mathematical Physics,* New York: Interscience, 1953, p. v.

I5   The basic requirements for a mathematical consultant are threefold. In addition to the research training and the broad mathematical background, the mathematical consultant needs, as do consultants based on any scientific field, above all else an interest in the other man's problems—in these problems as wholes, not just in their mathematical aspects.   —John W. Tukey

> "Mathematical Consultants, Computational Mathematics and Mathematical Engineering," *Amer. Math. Monthly* 62 (October 1955) 565.

I6   The school buildings [at MIT] overlook the River Charles and command a never changing skyline of much beauty. The moods of the waters of the river were always delightful to watch. To me, as a mathematician and a physicist they had another meaning as well. How could one bring to a mathematical regularity the study of the mass of ever shifting ripples and waves, for was not the highest destiny of mathematics the discovery of order among disorder? At one time the waves ran high, flecked with patches of foam, while at another they were barely noticeable ripples. Sometimes the lengths of the waves were to

be measured in inches, and again they might be many yards long. What descriptive language could I use that would portray these clearly visible facts without involving me in the inextricable complexity of a complete description of the water surface? This problem of the waves was clearly one of averaging and statistics, and in this way was closely related to the Lebesgue integral, which I was studying at the time. —Norbert Wiener
> *I Am a Mathematician,* Garden City: Doubleday, 1956, p. 33.

17 I hold ... that utility alone is not a proper measure of value, and would even go so far as to say that it is, when strictly and short-sightedly applied, a dangerously false measure of value. For mathematics which is at once the pure and untrammelled creation of the mind and the indispensable tool of science and modern technology, the adoption of a strictly utilitarian standard could lead only to disaster; it would first bring about the drying up of the sources of new mathematical knowledge and would thereby eventually cause the suspension of significant new activity in applied mathematics as well. In mathematics we need rather to aim at a proper balance between pure theory and practical applications ... —Marshall H. Stone
> "Mathematics and the Future of Science," *Bull. of the Amer. Math. Soc.* 63 (March 1957) 66.

18 My interests as a mathematician have been directed toward pure mathematics; and I have never entertained the ambition of contributing explicitly to the advancement of applied mathematics or cherished the illusion that I might have such a contribution to make. I have not, however, been one of those mathematicians whose joy in their mathematical achievements is intensified by the belief that these are to remain forever useless and unused outside the happy realm of pure mathematics. On the contrary, the satisfaction which I have derived from working in mathematics has been increased by the knowledge that what I have done could be seen, with few exceptions, to have some bearing upon mathematical physics or upon some other branch of applied mathematics. I have taken much pleasure in acquainting myself with the ways in which the results of pure mathematics could be turned to good account in probing Nature's secrets and rendering them intelligible—and, eventually, useful. —Marshall H. Stone
> "Mathematics and the Future of Science," *Bull. of the Amer. Math. Soc.* 63 (March 1957) 61.

I9　　The enormous usefulness of mathematics in the natural sciences is something bordering on the mysterious . . .　　—Eugene Wigner
"The Unreasonable Effectiveness of Mathematics in the Natural Sciences," *Comm. on Pure and Appl. Math.* 13 (February 1960) 2.

20　　The miracle of the appropriateness of the language of mathematics for the formulation of the laws of physics is a wonderful gift which we neither understand nor deserve. We should be grateful for it and hope that it will remain valid in future research and that it will extend, for better or for worse, to our pleasure even though perhaps also to our bafflement, to wide branches of learning. —Eugene Wigner
"The Unreasonable Effectiveness of Mathematics in the Natural Sciences," *Comm. on Pure and Appl. Math.* 13 (February 1960) 14.

2I　　There are those who believe that mathematics can sustain itself and grow without any further contact with anything outside itself, and those who believe that nature is still and always will be one of the main (if not the main) sources of mathematical inspiration. The first group is identified as "pure mathematicians" (though "purist" would be more adequate) while the second is, with equal inadequacy, referred to as "applied".　　　　　　　　　　　　　　　　—Mark Kac
Robert W. Ritchie (ed.), *New Directions in Mathematics,* Englewood Cliffs, NJ: Prentice-Hall, 1963, p. 60.

22　　Applied mathematics is mathematics for which I happen to know an application. This, I think, includes almost everything in mathematics.
—Henry O. Pollak
Robert W. Ritchie (ed.), *New Directions in Mathematics,* Englewood Cliffs, NJ: Prentice-Hall, 1963, p. 69.

23　　I surely don't insist that mathematics is an art rather than a science. Its unique appeal, I think, comes from the fact that it draws so heavily on both art and science. What can be more satisfying, more exhilarating, than to perceive an elegant mathematical solution of a significant practical problem? Nothing—nothing can surpass this—but one experience can equal it: to find an unsuspected practical application of a elegant mathematical system.　　　　　　—R. A. Rosenbaum
"Mathematics, the Artistic Science," *Math. Teacher* 55 (November 1962) 534.

24   In the final analysis the vitality of mathematics arises from the fact that its concepts and results, for all their abstractness, originate, as we shall see, in the actual world and find widely varied application in the other sciences, in engineering, and in all the practical affairs of daily life: to realize this is the most important prerequisite for understanding mathematics.   —A. D. Aleksandrov

> A. D. Aleksandrov, A. N. Kolmogorov, M. A. Lavrent'ev (eds.), *Mathematics: Its Content, Methods, and Meaning, Vol. I,* Cambridge, MA: MIT Press, 1963, p. 3.

25   But still a large part of mathematics which became useful developed with absolutely no desire to be useful, and in a situation where nobody could possibly know in what area it would become useful; and there were no general indications that it ever would be so. By and large it is uniformly true in mathematics that there is a time lapse between a mathematical discovery and the moment when it is useful; and that this lapse of time can be anything from 30 to 100 years, in some cases even more; and that the whole system seems to function without any direction, without any reference to usefulness, and without any desire to do things which are useful.   —John von Neumann

> "The Role of Mathematics in the Sciences and Society," in A. H. Taub (ed.), *John von Neumann Collected Works, Vol VI,* New York: Pergamon, 1963, p. 489.

26   There is a strange mixture of attitudes towards the usefulness of mathematics. Men both overestimate and underestimate it. Most men feel that although mathematics is very useful in physics and engineering, it has no place in medicine, sociology, or business (other than business arithmetic). Yet there is no inherent reason why mathematics should, in the long run, be more useful in physics than in medicine. It is only that problems in medicine are more difficult to solve than in physics, and hence the use of mathematics will take a longer time to develop.

However, the same men are under the impression that the very act of formulating a problem as mathematics solves it. They have implicit faith in mathematical proofs of the existence of God, in quack formulas for winning at roulette, and in anything statistical.

It is time that we learned as part of our basic education that mathematics is simply a language, distinguished by its ability for clarity, and particularly well suited to develop logical arguments. The power of mathematics is no more and no less than the power of pure reason.

> —John G. Kemeny
> *Random Essays on Mathematics, Education and Computers,* Englewood Cliffs, NJ: Prentice-Hall, 1964, p. 4.

27 Applied mathematics is not a definable scientific field but a human attitude. The attitude of the applied scientist is directed toward finding clear cut answers which can stand the test of empirical observation. To obtain the answers to theoretically often insuperably difficult problems, he must be willing to make compromises regarding rigorous mathematical completeness; he must supplement theoretical reasoning by numerical work, plausibility considerations and so on.

> —Richard Courant
> "Professor Richard Courant's Acceptance Speech for the Association's Distinguished Service Award," *Amer. Math. Monthly* 72 (April 1965) 378.

28 In view of the fact that the power and utility of mathematics have increased as its conceptual patterns have become more and more abstract, it seems justifiable to formulate what might be termed the Magna Charta of the creative worker in the field:

There shall be established no limit to the "intrinsic" character or nature of conceptualization, other than what may be imposed by the scientific merit of its consequences. The judgment regarding scientific merit is to be post facto. In particular, a concept will not be rejected because of such vague criteria as "unreality" or because of the manner in which it has been devised. 　　—Raymond L. Wilder

> *Evolution of Mathematical Concepts,* New York: John Wiley, 1968, p. 211.

29 People who read *The Elements* for the first time often get a feeling that things are missing: it has no preface or introduction, no statement of objectives, and it offers no motivation or commentary. Most strikingly, there is no mention of the scientific and technological uses to which many of the theorems can be put, nor any warning that large sections of the work have no practical use at all. Euclid was certainly aware of applications, but for him they were not an issue. To Euclid a theorem was significant, or not, in and of itself; it did not become more significant if applications were discovered, or less so if none were discovered. He saw applications as external factors having no bearing on a theorem's inherent quality. The theorems are included *for their own sake*, because they are interesting in themselves. This attitude of self-sufficiency is the hallmark of pure mathematics.

—Richard Trudeau
Dots and Lines, Kent, OH: Kent State University Press, 1976, p. 2.

30 It took me considerable time and effort to forge the link between mathematics and my professional work [with the Indian railroad]. The first obstacle was a mental block that prevented me from even thinking that the two could be connected at all. The whole of my previous scientific education and training had led me to hold in contempt any utilitarian application of science and knowledge. This attitude arose not merely from youth and inexperience—and I had then plenty of both— but from the profound conviction that mathematics like art ought to be pursued for its own sake... Higher learning in our universities in my time, nearly fifty years ago, was supposed to be an exploration of knowledge for its own sake and nothing else.   —Jagjit Singh
Memoirs of a Mathematician Manqué, New Delhi: Vikas House, 1980, p. 3.

31 The motivation of the applied mathematician is to understand the world and perhaps to change it; the requisite attitude (or, in any event, a customary one) is one of sharp focus (keep your eye on the problem); the techniques are chosen for and judged for their effectiveness (the end is what is important); and the satisfaction comes from the way the answer checks against reality and can be used to make predictions . . .

The motivation of the pure mathematician is frequently just curiosity; the attitude is more that of a wide angle lens than a telescopic one (is there a more interesting and perhaps deeper question nearby?); the choice of technique is dictated at least in part by its harmony with the context (half the fun is getting there); and the satisfaction comes from the way the answer illuminates unsuspected connections between ideas that had once seemed to be far apart. For the pure mathematician, his subject is an inexhaustible source of artistic pleasure: not only the excitement of the puzzle and the satisfaction of the victory (if it ever comes!), but mostly the joy of contemplation. The challenge doesn't come from our opponent who can win only if we lose, and victory doesn't disappear as soon as it's achieved (as in tennis, say); the challenge is

the breathtakingly complicated logical structure of the universe, and the victory is permanent (more like recovering precious metal from a sunken ship).   —Paul Halmos
"Applied Mathematics Is Bad Mathematics," in Lynn A. Steen (ed.), *Mathematics Tomorrow*, New York: Springer-Verlag, 1981, p. 14.

32   Between pure mathematicians and theoretical physics the thinking process bears many similarities. . . . Mathematicians start with certain facts—which we call axioms—and deduce consequences, theorems. In physics, in a sense, it is the other way around; The physicists have a lot of facts, lots of relations, formal expressions, which are the result of experiments; and they search for a small number of simple laws—we could call them axioms in this case—from which these results can be deduced. So in some ways it is an inverse process, but the course of thinking about it and the intuitions have great resemblance in both cases. And the question of habits, so-called rigor, which mathematicians require is often absent in physics. If one is tolerant, however, you could say that what physicists do is quite rigorous, but with different primitive notions than the ones too naively pursued.   —S. M. Ulam
Anthony Barcellos, "An interview with Stan Ulam," *Two-Year Coll. Math. J.* 12 (June 1981) 183.

33   Scientists will (I am sure) be surprised and delighted to find that not a few shapes they had to call *grainy, hydralike, in between, pimply, pocky, ramified, seaweedy, strange, tangled, tortuous, wiggly, wispy, wrinkled,* and the like, can henceforth be approached in rigorous and vigorous quantitative fashion.
    Mathematicians will (I hope) be surprised to find that sets thus far reputed exceptional . . . should in a sense be the rule, that constructions deemed pathological should evolve naturally from very concrete problems, and that the study of Nature should help solve old problems and yield so many new ones.   —Benoit Mandelbrot
The Fractal Geometry of Nature, San Francisco: W. H. Freeman, 1982, p. 5.

34   Von Kármán continually stressed the difference between mathematical physics and applied mathematics. Once to make his point, he compared working in applied mathematics to shopping in "a warehouse of mathematical knowledge." The scientist could live in the warehouse and find uses for the equations on the shelf, or he could visit the place from time to time with a shopping list.

> —John L Greenberg and Judith R. Goodstein
> "Theodore von Kármán and Applied Mathematics in
> America," *Science* 222 (23 December 1983) 1303.

35   Kenneth Harrison was also acquainted with some of [Bertrand] Russell's ideas, and he and Alan [Turing] would spend hours discussing them. Rather to Alan's annoyance, however, he would ask 'but what use is it?' Alan would say quite happily that of course it was completely useless.

> —Andrew Hodges
> *Alan Turing: The Enigma,* New York: Simon and
> Schuster, 1983, p. 85.

36   The specialist who wishes to accomplish work of the highest excellence must be learned in the resources of science and have constantly in mind its unity and its grandeur.

> —Percy A. MacMahon
> "Presidential Address," in George E. Andrews (ed.),
> *Percy Alexander MacMahon, Collected Papers, Vol II,*
> Cambridge MA: MIT Press, 1986, p. 893.

37   That form of wisdom which is the opposite of single-mindedness, the ability to keep many threads in hand, to draw for an argument from disparate sources, is quite foreign to mathematics. This inability accounts for much of the difficulty which mathematics experiences in attempting to penetrate the social sciences.

> —Jacob T. Schwartz
> *Discrete Thoughts: Essays on Mathematics, Science and
> Philosophy,* Boston: Birkhäuser, 1986, p. 22.

38   [These are] the satisfactions of the life devoted to doing useful mathematics. First, you are apt to learn much more mathematics than the pure mathematician who tends to research only a few fields or even a single one. . . .

Second, because of the importance of the work there are often implicit deadlines that tend to push you forward. Hence over a lifetime you learn more mathematics than you would otherwise.

Third, you often find that some long forgotten (by current teachers) field needs to be examined again. And because your interests are different from those of your predecessors you often find new results!

Fourth, new fields of mathematics, such as Information Theory and Coding Theory, arise from the "use of mathematics" view, and one finds oneself in on the ground floor as it were.

Fifth, because the same mathematics tends to arise in many different fields you get alternate, and often fruitful, versions of it, and may thereby be led to new discoveries, or at least cross fertilization.

Sixth, as you look around the world in which you live you see many consequences of your work. . . .

Lastly, the material rewards tend to be greater, not only in money, but in opportunities to travel to interesting places, to meet other people doing important and exciting things, to see new developments as they are being created in the laboratories, and to get a broad education beyond mathematics . . . Doing useful mathematics can be an exciting, rewarding life!   —R. W. Hamming
> "The Use of Mathematics," in Peter Duren (ed.), *A
> Century of Mathematics in America, Part I,* Providence,
> RI: American Mathematical Society, 1988, p. 436.

39   Abstract mathematics is a wonderful subject, and there's nothing wrong with it: It's beautiful, general, and useful. But its adherents had become deluded that the rest of mathematics was inferior and no longer worthy of attention. The goal of generalization had become so fashionable [by the 1960s] that a generation of mathematicians had become unable to relish beauty in the particular, to enjoy the challenge of solving quantitative problems, or to appreciate the value of technique. Abstract mathematics was becoming inbred and losing touch with reality; mathematical education needed a concrete counterweight in order to restore a healthy balance.
> —Ronald L. Graham, Donald E. Knuth, Oren Patashnik
> *Concrete Mathematics,* Reading, MA: Addison-Wes-
> ley, 1989, p. v.

40   [During] the late 1930s through the early 1950s, the predominant view in American mathematical circles was the same as Bourbaki's: mathematics is an autonomous abstract subject, with no need of any input from the real world, with its own criteria of depth and beauty, and with the internal compass for guiding further growth. Applications come later by accident; mathematical ideas filter down to the sciences and engineering. ... Today we can safely say that the tide of purity has turned; most mathematicians are keenly aware that mathematics

does not trickle down to the applications, but that mathematics and the sciences ... are equal partners, feeding ideas, concepts, problems, and solutions to each other. —Peter Lax
"The Flowering of Applied Mathematics in America," in Peter Duren (ed.), *A Century of Mathematics in America, Part II,* Providence, RI: American Mathematical Society, 1989, p. 456.

41 I myself work in a field that was created for purposes internal to mathematics. This is the theory of the so-called recursive functions—I would not have dreamed that this theory could also be applied practically. And today? My book on recursive functions was the second Hungarian mathematical book to be published in the Soviet Union, and precisely on the practical grounds that its subject matter has become indispensable to the theory of computers. And so it goes, sooner or later, for all branches of so-called pure mathematics ... one never has to worry that one is working on something useless. —Rósza Péter
"Mathematics Is Beautiful," *Math. Intell.* 12 (Winter 1990) 64.

CHAPTER 10

Mathematics and the Arts

I   We study music because music gives us pleasure, not necessarily our own music, but good music, whether ours, or, as is more probable, that of others. We study literature because we derive pleasure from books; the better the book, the more subtle and lasting the pleasure. We study art because we receive pleasure from the great works of the masters, and probably we appreciate them the more because we have dabbled a little in pigments or in clay. We do not expect to be composers, or poets, or sculptors, but we wish to appreciate music and letters and the fine arts, and to derive pleasure from them and to be uplifted by them. At any rate these are the nobler reasons for their study.

So it is with geometry. We study it because we derive pleasure from contact with a great and an ancient body of learning that has occupied the attention of master minds during the thousands of years in which it has been perfected, and we are uplifted by it. ... This enjoyment is partly that of the game,—the playing of a game that can always be won, but that cannot be won too easily. It is partly that of the aesthetic, the pleasure of symmetry of form, the delight of fitting things together. But probably it lies chiefly in the mental uplift that geometry brings, the contact with absolute truth, and the approach that one makes to the Infinite. ... The uplift of this contact with absolute truth, with truth eternal, gives pleasure to humanity to a greater or less degree, depending upon the mental equipment of the particular individual; but

it probably gives an appreciable amount of pleasure to every student
who has a teacher worthy of the name.   —D. E. Smith
> *The Teaching of Geometry,* New York: Ginn, 1911, p.
> 15.

2   The rules of logic are to mathematics what those of structure are
to architecture. In the most beautiful work, a chain of argument is
presented in which every line is important on its own account, in which
there is an air of ease and lucidity throughout, and the premises achieve
more than would have been thought possible, by means which appear
natural and inevitable.   —Bertrand Russell
> "The Study of Mathematics," *Mysticism and Logic
> and Other Essays,* London: George Allen and Unwin,
> 1917, p. 61.

3   Mathematics and Music, the most sharply contrasted fields of
intellectual activity which one can discover, and yet bound together,
supporting one another as if they would demonstrate the hidden bond
which draws together all activities of our mind, and which also in the rev-
elations of artistic genius leads us to surmise unconscious expressions
of a mysteriously active intelligence.   —H. Helmholtz
> R. C. Archibald, "Mathematicians and Music," *Amer.
> Math. Monthly,* 31 (January 1924) 1.

4   Voltaire remarked that "one merit of poetry few persons will
deny; it says more in fewer words than prose"; and why may we not
with perfect truth continue,—"one merit of mathematics no one can
deny,—it says more in fewer words than any other science in the world"?
                                                    —D. E. Smith
> "Mathematics in the Training for Citizenship," *Se-
> lected Topics in the Teaching of Mathematics,* NCTM
> Third Yearbook, New York: Teachers College Press,
> 1928, p. 15.

5   Mathematics and poetry lie, if not on, at least not far from the
extremes, the one of systematic and the other of unsystematic thought,
and thus are about as far removed as possible one from the other. And
yet they have a very striking common property, namely, the property of
permanence. No other large domains of thought than mathematics and
literature have acquired large bodies of truth retaining their values essentially unimpaired for two thousand years, not in a stagnant state, but
in a state of vitality and effectiveness. It is a matter of great inspiration
to see the Greek geometry and the Greek tragedy surviving through

the ages and retaining the active power to excite our admiration and increase our happiness today.   —R. D. Carmichael
> *The Logic of Discovery,* Chicago: Open Court, 1930, p. 244.

6   It is contact with the infinite that has been the dream of the sage as seer, as poet, and as mathematician since the days when the world was young, and this will endure until the world is old, for it is an instinct of the race, the instinct that separates it from the brute. —D. E. Smith
> *The Poetry of Mathematics and Other Essays,* New York: Scripta Mathematica, 1934, p. 2.

7   Pure mathematics is, in its way, the poetry of logical ideas. One seeks the most general ideas of operation which will bring together in simple, logical and unified form the largest possible circle of formal relationships. In this effort toward logical beauty spiritual formulae are discovered necessary for the deeper penetration into the laws of nature.
> —Albert Einstein
> "Letter to the Editor," *New York Times,* May 5, 1935.

8   Abstract mathematics is a work of invention—*a free creation of the human spirit,* as truly a work of art as the Moonlight Sonata or the Sistine Madonna, but on a much vaster scale than the entire library of great symphonies, the whole gallery of famous paintings, or, indeed, the total assemblage of celebrated cathedrals.   —F. L. Griffin
> *Introduction to Mathematical Analysis,* Boston: Houghton Mifflin, 1936, p. 512.

9   As to sheer abstract beauty the logarithmic spiral may well be considered to stand unsurpassed among the objects of human contemplation.   —Robert E. Moritz
> "On the Beauty of Geometrical Forms," *Scripta Mathematica* 4 (1936) 34.

10   The mathematician's patterns, like the painter's or the poet's must be *beautiful*; the ideas, like the colours or the words, must fit together in a harmonious way.   Beauty is the first test; there is no permanent place in the world for ugly mathematics.   —G. H. Hardy
> *A Mathematician's Apology,* Cambridge: University Press, 1940, p. 25.

11   A mathematician, like a painter or a poet, is a maker of patterns.
                                                                —G. H. Hardy
                    A Mathematician's Apology, Cambridge: University
                    Press, 1940, p. 24.

12   Mathematics is an activity governed by the same rules imposed
upon the symphonies of Beethoven, the paintings of DaVinci, and the
poetry of Homer. Just as scales, as the laws of perspective, as the rules of
metre seem to lack fire, the formal rules of mathematics may appear to
be without lustre. Yet ultimately, mathematics reaches pinnacles as high
as those attained by the imagination in its most daring reconnoiters.
And this conceals, perhaps, the ultimate paradox of science. For in
their prosaic plodding both logic and mathematics often outstrip their
advance guard and show that the world of pure reason is stranger than
the world of pure fancy.   —Edward Kasner and James Newman
                    Mathematics and the Imagination, New York: Simon
                    and Schuster, 1940, p. 362.

13   The ideas chosen by my unconscious are those which reach my
consciousness, and I see that they are those which agree with my aesthetic sense.   —Jacques Hadamard
                    The Psychology of Invention in the Mathematical Field,
                    Princeton: Princeton University Press, 1945, p. 39.

14   One expects a mathematical theorem or a mathematical theory
not only to describe and to classify in a simple and elegant way numerous
and a priori disparate special cases. One also expects "elegance" in its
"architectural," structural makeup. Ease in stating the problem, great
difficulty in getting hold of it and in all attempts at approaching it, then
again some very surprising twist by which the approach, or some part of
the approach, becomes easy, etc. Also, if the deductions are lengthy or
complicated, there should be some simple general principle involved,
which "explains" the complications and detours, reduces the apparent
arbitrariness to a few simple guiding motivations, etc. These criteria
are clearly those of any creative art, and the existence of some underlying empirical, worldly motif in the background—overgrown by aes-
theticizing developments and followed into a multitude of labyrinthine

variants—all this is much more akin to the atmosphere of art pure and simple than to that of the empirical sciences.   —John von Neumann
"The Mathematician," in Robert B. Heywood (ed.), *The Works of the Mind,* Chicago: University of Chicago Press, 1947, p. 195.

15   I think that it is a relatively good approximation to truth … that mathematical ideas originate in empirics, although the genealogy is sometimes long and obscure. But, once they are conceived, the subject begins to live a peculiar life of its own and is better compared to a creative one, governed by almost entirely aesthetical motivations, than to anything else and, in particular, to an empirical science.

—John von Neumann
"The Mathematician," in Robert B. Heywood (ed.), *The Works of the Mind,* Chicago: University of Chicago Press, 1947, p. 195.

16   Mathematics is, on the artistic side, a creation of new rhythms, orders, designs and harmonies, and on the knowledge side, is a systematic study of the various rhythms, orders, designs and harmonies. We may condense this into the statement that mathematics is, on the one side, the qualitative study of the structure of beauty, and on the other side is the creator of new artistic forms of beauty. The mathematician is at once creator and critic.   —James B. Shaw
"Mathematics—the Subtle Fine Art," in W. L. Schaaf (ed.), *Mathematics: Our Great Heritage,* New York: Harper, 1948, p. 50.

17   Symmetry, as wide or as narrow as you may define its meaning, is one idea by which man through the ages has tried to comprehend and create order, beauty, and perfection.   —Hermann Weyl
Symmetry, Princeton: Princeton University Press, 1952, p. 5.

18   Much research for new proofs of theorems already correctly established is undertaken simply because the existing proofs have no aesthetic appeal. There are mathematical demonstrations that are merely convincing; to use a phrase of the famous mathematical physicist, Lord Rayleigh, they 'command assent.' There are other proofs 'which woo and charm the intellect. They evoke delight and an overpowering desire

to say, Amen, Amen.' An elegantly executed proof is a poem in all but
the form in which it is written.   —Morris Kline
> Mathematics in Western Culture, New York: Oxford
> University Press, 1953, p. 470.

19   Mathematics is too arduous and uninviting a field to appeal to
those to whom it does not give great rewards. These rewards are of
exactly the same character as those of the artist. To see a difficult,
uncompromising material take living shape and meaning is to be Pyg-
malion, whether the material is stone or hard, stonelike logic. To see
meaning and understanding come where there has been no meaning
and no understanding is to share the work of a demiurge. No amount
of technical correctness and no amount of labor can replace this creative
moment, whether in the life of a mathematician or in that of a painter
or musician. Bound up with it is a judgment of values, quite parallel
to the judgment of values that belongs to the painter or the musician.
Neither the artist nor the mathematician may be able to tell you what
constitutes the difference between a significant piece of work and an
inflated trifle; but if he is never able to recognize this in his own heart,
he is no artist and no mathematician.   —Norbert Wiener
> Ex-prodigy, New York: Simon and Schuster, 1953, p.
> 212.

20   In other arts, if we see a pattern we can admire its beauty; we may
feel that it has significant form, but we cannot say what the significance
is. And it is much better not to try . . .
    But in mathematics it is not so. In mathematics, if a pattern occurs,
we can go on to ask, Why does it occur? What does it signify? And
we can find answers to these questions. In fact, for every pattern that
appears, a mathematician feels he ought to know why it appears.
                    —W. W. Sawyer
> Prelude to Mathematics, Baltimore: Penguin Books,
> 1957, p. 23.

21   There is not much difference between the delight a novice experiences in cracking a clever brain teaser and the delight a mathematician
experiences in mastering a more advanced problem. Both look on
beauty bare—that clean, sharply defined, mysterious, entrancing order
that underlies all structure.   —Martin Gardner
> Mathematical Puzzles and Diversions, New York: Si-
> mon and Schuster, 1959, p. ix.

22   The basic affinity between mathematics and the arts is psychological and spiritual and not metrical or geometrical.

The first essential bond between mathematics and the arts is found
in the fact that discovery in mathematics is not a matter of logic. It is
rather the result of mysterious powers which no one understands, and in
which unconscious recognition of beauty must play an important part.
Out of an infinity of designs a mathematician chooses one pattern for
beauty's sake, and pulls it down to earth, no one knows how. Afterwards
the logic of words and of forms sets the pattern right. Only then can
one tell someone else. The first pattern remains in the shadows of the
mind. . . .

A second affinity between mathematicians and other artists lies in
a psychological necessity under which both labor. Artists are distinguished from their fellows who are not artists by their overriding instinct
of self-preservation as creators of art. This is not an economic urge as
everyone knows who has a variety of artist friends. . . .

The third type of evidence of the affinity of mathematics with the arts
is found in the comparative history of the arts. The history of the arts
is the history of recurring cycles and sharp antitheses. These antitheses
set pure art against mixed art, restraint against lack of restraint, the
transient against the permanent, the abstract against the nonabstract.
These antitheses are found in all of the arts, including mathematics.

—Marston Morse
"Mathematics and the Arts," *Bull. of the Atomic Scientist,* 15 (February 1959) 56.

23   Consider a sculptor—not one particular man, but a generic
sculptor. He begins by fashioning in clay or wood an image of his
subject—the bust of his model, say. At first he may attempt to make
a replica of his model, so that the beholder is moved to remark, "Why
that's the spit and image of Alexander." Later, with more sophistication,
he may modify the replica, by altering the set of the mouth, or the size
of the eyes, so as to express traits which everyone sees in Alexander or,
perhaps, that the sculptor alone sees in Alexander, or, if he needs the
money, that Alexander would like to see in himself. Later still, he may
make a bust which emphasizes some fundamental traits of man rather
than Alexander: "Ecce homo!" or "Behold the king-philosopher" or
"Behold the hero-with-feet-of-clay." And finally, he may be a Henry
Moore whose sculptures, in the form of rounded mounds full of holes,

are reminiscent of Al Capp's spoofing of Dick Tracy and cause the casual viewer to approach close enough to read the card on which the title of the sculpture is printed, shrugging his shoulders and shaking his head as he proceeds to the next (meaningless) abstraction.

Do we not have here a parallel with the work of the generic mathematician? The mathematician begins with a replica of the physical situation—he makes a mathematical model, to use the current jargon, which helps him to solve a practical problem—surveying a field in Egypt, or navigating the Mediterranean. Having solved the problem, he doesn't throw the model away, but looks at it carefully to see whether, if it's modified somewhat, the model may apply to other, perhaps subtler problems. And then he may become interested in the model for its own sake, and may pursue the delightful suggestions of his imagination with no immediate interpretation in mind—an abstract game, if you will.

—R. A. Rosenbaum
"Mathematics, the Artistic Science," *Math. Teacher,*
55 (November 1962) 533.

24   Perhaps the closest analogy is between mathematics and painting. The origin of painting is physical reality, and so is the origin of mathematics—but the painter is not a camera and the mathematician is not an engineer . . . How close to reality painting (and mathematics) should be is a delicate matter of judgment. Asking a painter to "tell a concrete story" is like asking a mathematician to "solve a real problem." Modern painting and modern mathematics are far out—too far in the judgment of some. Perhaps the ideal is to have a spice of reality always present, but not to crowd it the way descriptive geometry, say, does in mathematics, and medical illustration, say, does in painting.

Talk to a painter (I did) and talk to a mathematician, and you'll be amazed at how similarly they react. Almost every aspect of the life and of the art of a mathematician has its counterpart in painting, and vice versa. Every time a mathematician hears "I could never make my check book balance" a painter hears "I could never draw a straight line" . . . The invention of perspective gave the painter a useful technique, as did the invention of 0 to the mathematician. Old art is as good as new; old mathematics is as good as new. Tastes change, to be sure, in both subjects, but a twentieth century painter has sympathy for cave paintings and a twentieth century mathematician for the fraction juggling of the Babylonians. A painting must be painted and then looked at; a theorem must be printed and then read. The painter who thinks good pictures and the mathematician who dreams beautiful theorems are dilettantes; an unseen work of art is incomplete. In painting and mathematics there are some objective standards of good—the painter speaks of structure, line, shape, and texture, where the mathematician speaks of truth, validity, novelty, generality—but they are relatively the easiest to satisfy. Both painters and mathematicians debate among themselves whether these objective standards should even be told to the young—the beginner may misunderstand and overemphasize them and at the same time lose sight of the more important subjective standards of goodness. Painting and mathematics have a history, a tradition, a growth.   —Paul Halmos

> "Mathematics as a Creative Art," *Amer. Scientist* 56
> (Winter 1968) 388.

25   Although the acquisition of skill in mathematics and the sense of increased mathematical power contribute to the enjoyment of mathematical pursuits, neither can exceed the joy of the creation of beauty, remembering that even appreciation is a reenactment of creative activity, so that creating new mathematics and reading old mathematics produced by someone else result in very similar types of aesthetic feeling.   —H. E. Huntley

> *The Divine Proportion, a Study in Mathematical Beauty,*
> New York: Dover, 1970, p. 3.

26   To the aesthetically minded mathematician much mathematics reads like poetry.   —H. E. Huntley

> *The Divine Proportion, a Study in Mathematical Beauty,*
> New York: Dover, 1970, p. vii.

27   The comparison of mathematics and music is often particularly apt. The most attractive music is spoiled by a bad performance. So it is that many an admirable mathematical thought languishes amid the colorless rigor of a formal exposition.   —Ross Honsberger

> *Mathematical Gems,* Washington, DC: Mathematical
> Association of America, 1973, p. ix.

28   To Steinhaus mathematics was a mirror of reality and life much in the same way as poetry is such a mirror, and he liked to "play" with numbers, sets, and curves, the way a poet plays with words, phrases, and sounds.   —Mark Kac

> "Hugo Steinhaus–A Reminiscence and a Tribute,"
> *Amer. Math. Monthly,* 81 (June-July 1974) 580.

29   I understand your surprise at my being able to busy myself simultaneously with literature and mathematics. Many who have never had an opportunity of knowing any more about mathematics confound it with arithmetic, and consider it an arid science. In reality, however, it is a science which requires a great amount of imagination, and one of the leading mathematicians of our century states the case quite correctly when he says that it is impossible to be a mathematician without being a poet in soul. Only, of course, in order to comprehend the accuracy of this definition, one must renounce the ancient prejudice that a poet must invent something which does not exist, that imagination and invention are identical. It seems to me that the poet has only to perceive that which others do not perceive, to look deeper than others look. And the mathematician must do the same thing.   —Sonya Kovalevsky
Lynn M. Osen, *Women in Mathematics,* Cambridge, MA: MIT Press, 1974, p. 136.

30   Freeman Dyson has quoted Weyl as having told him: "My work always tried to unite the true with the beautiful; but when I had to choose one or the other, I usually chose the beautiful." I inquired of Dyson whether Weyl had given an example of his having sacrificed truth for beauty. I learned that the example which Weyl gave was his gauge theory of gravitation, which he had worked out in his *Raum-Zeit-Materie.* Apparently, Weyl became convinced that this theory was not true as a theory of gravitation; but still it was so beautiful that he did not wish to abandon it and so he kept it alive for the sake of its beauty. But much later, it did turn out that Weyl's instinct was right after all, when the formalism of gauge invariance was incorporated into quantum electrodynamics. ... We have evidence, then, that a theory developed by a scientist, with an exceptionally well-developed aesthetic sensibility, can turn out to be true even if, at the time of its formulation, it appeared not to be so. As Keats wrote a long time ago, "What the imagination seizes as beauty must be truth—whether it existed before or not."
—S. Chandrasekhar
"Beauty and the Quest for Beauty in Science," *Physics Today* 32 (July 1979) 27.

31   It is hard to overestimate the value of appropriate symbolism. Of all creatures, only human beings have much ability to name things and to coin phrases. Poets do this best of all.

   ... as imagination bodies forth

The forms of things unknown, the poet's pen
Turns them to shapes and gives to airy nothing
A local habitation and a name.
>Shakespeare

It can be contended that Leibniz's way of writing the calculus approaches the poetic. One can be borne up and carried along purely by his symbolism, while his symbols themselves may appear to take on a life of their own. Mathematics and poetry are different, but they are not so far apart as one might think. —W. M. Priestley
Calculus: An Historical Approach, New York: Springer-Verlag, 1979, p. 110.

32 When I was sufficiently mature to think about my career ... I knew that I was dedicated to an intellectual life, with science, in particular mathematics, my main interest. However, from early childhood on, poetry and writing came to me in a natural way. But it seems to me that both in the work of others and in my own I look for beauty, and not only for achievement. Only an expert will understand what I mean by this. —Olga Taussky-Todd
"An Autobiographical Essay," in Donald J. Albers and G. L. Alexanderson (eds.), *Mathematical People,* Boston: Birkhäuser, 1985, p. 336.

33 Perhaps the most convincing argument in favor of the study of fractals is their sheer beauty.
—Heinz-Otto Peitgen and Peter H. Richter
The Beauty of Fractals, New York: Springer-Verlag, 1986, p. vi.

34 But I think that mathematics is very much like poetry. I think that what makes a good poem—a great poem—is that there is a large amount of thought expressed in very few words. In this sense formulas are like poems. Now you can tell somebody what poetry is. Then you want to give him an example. If he doesn't know English, you can't give him a poem in English. That won't work. My son, who is a classicist, told me that Pindar was one of the greatest poets ever. I said, "What is a good translation?" He said, "There is no good translation. Either you read it in Greek, or you just forget it!" As far as mathematics is concerned, something similar may be true. Either you can use symbols, or just forget it!   —Lipman Bers

Donald J. Albers and Constance Reid, "An Interview with Lipman Bers," *Coll. Math. J.* 18 (September 1987) 288.

35   [Hilbert] once had a student in mathematics who stopped coming to his lectures, and Hilbert was finally told that the young man had gone off to become a poet. Hilbert is reported to have remarked: "I never thought he had enough imagination to be a mathematician."

—George Pólya

G. L. Alexanderson, (ed.), *A Pólya Picture Album,* Boston: Birkhäuser, 1987, p. 30.

36   I like to think of mathematics as a vast musical instrument on which one can play a great variety of beautiful melodies. Many generations of mathematicians have provided us with rich tonal resources that offer limitless possibilities for harmonious combination.

A great performance of mathematics can be as exciting to the audience as it is to the person controlling the instrument. Whether we are replaying a classic theme, or improvising a new one, or just fooling around, we experience deep pleasure when we encounter patterns that fit together just right, or when we can pull out all the stops in order to unify independent voices and timbres.

This analogy isn't perfect, because mathematics is the music as well as the organ for its creation.   —Donald E. Knuth

"Algorithmic Themes," in Peter Duren (ed.), *A Century of Mathematics in America, Part I,* Providence, RI: American Mathematical Society, 1988, p. 439.

37   Mathematics and poetry are head-tail of the same coin. Both are an attempt to discern pattern—because you refuse the idea of a chaotic universe—and to develop language which has to be metaphoric, or you'll drown in jargon.   —Marguerite Lehr

Patricia Kenschaft, "An Interview with Marguerite Lehr: In Memoriam," *Assoc. for Women in Math. Newsletter* 18 (March-April 1988) 9.

38   Stan Ulam's best work is a game played in the farthest reaches of abstraction, where the cares of the world cannot intrude: in set theory, in measure theory, and in the foundations of mathematics. He used to

refer to his volume of collected papers as a slim volume of poems. It is just that.
—Gian-Carlo Rota
"The Lost Cafe," in Necia Grant Cooper (ed.), *From Cardinals to Chaos,* Cambridge: Cambridge University Press, 1988, p. 31.

39 After passing through several rooms in a museum filled with the paintings of a rather well-known modern painter, [Antoni Zygmund] mused, "Mathematics and art are quite different. We could not publish so many papers that used repeatedly, the same idea and still command the respect of our colleagues."
—Ronald R. Coifman and Robert S. Strichartz
"The School of Antoni Zygmund," in Peter Duren (ed.), *A Century of Mathematics in America, Part III,* Providence, RI: American Mathematical Society, 1989, p. 348.

40 I think there certainly is a link [between mathematics and music], for various reasons. One is that they are both creative arts. When you're sitting with a bit of paper creating mathematics, it is very like sitting with a sheet of music paper creating music. Both have rules which you must follow. They are also both languages. A page of mathematics and a page of music are both meaningless unless you happen to know what the various symbols mean and how they relate to each other and you understand the rules that they satisfy. But there's obviously a difference, in the sense that a piece of mathematics is superseded by a better, or more general, bit of mathematics, whereas Mozart was not superseded by Beethoven. You still enjoy listening to Mozart.
—Robin Wilson
D. J. Albers and G. L. Alexanderson, "A Conversation with Robin Wilson," *Coll. Math. J.* 21 (May 1990) 193.

CHAPTER II

Mathematics and Matters of the Spirit

I   Geometry, that is to say, the science of harmony in space, presides over everything. We find it in the arrangement of the scales of a fir-cone, as in the arrangement of an Epeira's lime-snare; we find it in the spiral of a snail-shell, in the chaplet of a spider's thread, as in the orbit of a planet; it is everywhere, as perfect in the world of atoms as in the world of immensities.

And this universal geometry tells us of an Universal Geometrician, whose divine compasses have measured all things. —Jean Henri Fabre
> *The Life of the Spider,* New York: Dodd, Mead and
> Co., 1915, p. 399.

2   The humble mollusc [the snail] coils its shell according to the laws of a curve known as the logarithmic spiral. . . .

Did the Snail even invent this cunning curve himself? No, for all the molluscs with turbinate shells, those which dwell in the sea and those which live in fresh water or on the land, obey the same laws, with variations of detail as to the conoid on which the typical spiral is projected. Did the present-day builders accomplish it by gradually improving on an ancient and less exact curve? No, for the spiral of abstract science has presided over the scrollwork of their shells ever since the earliest ages of the globe . . .

The logarithmic spiral of the mollusc is as old as the centuries. It proceeds from the sovran Geometry Which rules the world attentive alike to the Wasp's cell and to the Snail's spiral.   —Jean Henri Fabre
> *The Mason-Wasps,* New York: Dodd, Mead and Co., 1919, p. 237.

3   Any dynamic subdivision of a dynamic rectangle is like a seed endowed with the eternal principle of growth. It possesses the property of expanding or dividing until it includes the entire dynamic system. Like an osier twig planted in congenial soil which soon develops into a beautiful tree, dynamic shapes have in them a life impulse which causes design to grow.   —Jay Hambidge
> *The Elements of Dynamic Symmetry,* New York: Brentano's, 1926, p. 72.

4   [Parallels between mathematics and religion]

MATHEMATICS	RELIGION
1. The Infinite exists.	1. God exists.
2. Eternal laws exist.	2. Eternal laws exist.
3. The laws relating to finite magnitudes do not hold respecting the infinitely large or the infinitely small.	3. God's laws are so different from ours as to be absolutely non-understandable by us.
4. The existence of hyperspace with gradations is entirely reasonable.	4. The existence of a heaven, with gradations, is entirely reasonable.
5. No factor is ever lost.	5. The soul is eternal.
6. Time may be a closed curve.	6. God looks at time as a whole.
7. Time may be a fourth dimension.	7. In the next world, the direction of time may actually be seen.
8. Positive infinity may physically coincide with negative infinity, if lines curve through four-space.	8. In God's sight the infinite past and the infinite future are the same.

9. A Flatlander has enough of the third dimension in his being to give him some feeling of that dimension; and so this may explain the fact that we have some feeling for the fourth dimension.

9. The human soul has enough of the divine within it to have some feeling of the reality of divinity and of the world beyond.

10. Mathematics is a vast storehouse of the discoveries of the human intellect. We cannot afford to discard this material.

10. Religion is a vast storehouse of the discoveries of the human spirit. We cannot afford to discard this material.

11. It is not necessary that the solution of a problem, by limited means—say, the trisection of an angle—should be found in order that we may feel certain that the problem can be solved by *some* means.

11. It is not necessary that the solution of a problem of religion, by our limited human means, should be found in order that we may feel certain that the problem can be solved by *some* means.

12. Every term in an infinite sequence is in a small way a part of infinity.

12. Lucretius spoke wisely when he said, "Every one is in a small way the image of God."

—D. E. Smith
"Religio Mathematici," *Amer. Math. Monthly* 28 (October 1921) 347.

5 The whole hearted and unreserved acceptance of some formulated code of values and ideals, which transcends immediate self-interest and to which our vital energies can be devoted, forms the essential ingredient of individual salvation in the only genuinely important sense. Unhappy indeed is he who lives without a code of this kind. The scientific attitude should enable us to choose our personal code with increased enlightenment.

In this sense there is no spiritual loss attendant upon the unreserved adoption of the scientific attitude, unless it be the loss of placidity to him who would dream. On the contrary, there is gained an infinitely larger vision of the whole, a growth in ideals, and a deep realization

that we are part of a world whose dramatic qualities and evolutionary possibilities in all directions are beyond our powers to fathom.
—George Birkhoff
"Science and Spiritual Perspective," *Century Magazine* 118 (June 1929) 165.

6   Our remote ancestors tried to interpret nature in terms of anthropomorphic concepts of their own creation and failed. The efforts of our nearer ancestors to interpret nature on engineering lines proved equally inadequate. Nature has refused to accommodate herself to either of these man-made moulds. On the other hand, our efforts to interpret nature in terms of the concepts of pure mathematics have, so far, proved brilliantly successful ... from the intrinsic evidence of His creation, the Great Architect of the Universe now begins to appear as a pure mathematician.   —James H. Jeans
The Mysterious Universe, Cambridge: University Press, 1931, p. 143.

7   First, mathematics soon leads us to a feeling that the Infinite exists. The inquisitive child shows this when he asks his teacher what is the largest number; and the teacher shows it in her inability to reply. This feeling grows more impressive when the child becomes the youth and studies any elementary series, even the summation of n terms of the geometric or any other type. It increases when he studies geometry and wonders what happens to the sum of the angles of a triangle when the vertex is "carried to infinity," and when he asks the teacher what infinity means.

It increases when he studies simple trigonometry and finds that, as an angle approaches 90° the tangent approaches infinity, suddenly becoming minus infinity when it passes through the right angle. ... And finally, when he measures the known universe, or universe of universes, and thinks in light years ... and finds that the distance across explored space may be 400,000,000 of these light years, and lets his imagination carry him to the verge of this space and leads him to wonder about that which lies beyond—then the mystery becomes overpowering. He has pushed back the clouds of ignorance only to see that his own ignorance has become more and more hopeless, and that science leaves him helpless in the presence of a new infinity. The childish boast that we will believe only what we see, the most childish of all our feeble assertions of our faith in our puerile strength, avails us not. Mathematics has lured us on, and at the last we feel more helpless than ever, because we have come to see how full of awe we are in the presence of the awful Infinite.

> —D. E. Smith
> "Mathematics and Religion," in W. D. Reeve (ed.),
> *Mathematics in Modern Life,* NCTM Sixth Yearbook,
> New York: Bureau of Publications, Columbia University, 1931, p. 55.

8   He is taught in mathematics that certain postulates are sacred and that he must not question them. In religious instruction he is taught the same. ... In general, many teachers in each domain display a kind of fear of honest inquiry, a fear based either upon ignorance, or upon faith in tradition. No field of mathematics need fear searching inquiry, and no religion or sect need fear the scientific study of its essential nature, however much it may fear a study of the nonessentials which have accumulated through the ages ... the bases of geometry have been more firmly fixed through a search into its fundamentals. ... It is the nonessentials that go; the essentials stand. Modern religious thinking leads to the same conclusion—that it has nothing to fear from honest study; if its nonessentials go, the essentials stand the more firmly.

> —D. E. Smith
> "Mathematics and Religion," in W. D. Reeve, (ed.),
> *Mathematics in Modern Life,* NCTM Sixth Yearbook,
> New York: Bureau of Publications, Columbia University, 1931, 55.

9   Mathematics is the one area of human enterprise where the motivation to deceive has been practically eliminated. Not because mathematicians are necessarily virtuous people, but because the nature of mathematical ability is such that deception can be immediately determined by other mathematicians. This requirement of honesty soon affects the character of the continuous student of mathematics.

> —Howard F. Fehr
> "Reorientation in Mathematics Education," *Teachers College Record* 54 (May 1953) 433.

10   The study of science and mathematics involved a process of discerning order, system, balance and law in the wonderful phenomena of the biological, chemical and physical world. Scientists and mathematicians conceive of the universe as a logical, orderly, predictable place. The vastness and the splendor of the heavens, the order and precision of the sun, planets, stars and comets, the marvels of the human body and mind, the beauty of nature, the mystery of photosynthesis, the mathematical structure of the universe, the concept of infinity cannot do other than lead to humbleness before God's handiwork. ...

Both science and mathematics, by their very methods, lay the groundwork for developing a devotion to truth. They develop ability to examine facts and evaluate evidence, to maintain open-mindedness, intellectual honesty, and suspended judgment, and to reach unbiased conclusions. —Board of Education of the City of New York

The Development of Moral and Spiritual Ideals in the Public Schools, quoted in William L. Schaaf (ed.), "Memorabilia Mathematica," *Math. Teacher* 50 (April 1957) 295.

II In the common opinion certainty is to be found in two places and only two—religion and mathematics. In religion you believe by faith, in mathematics you prove what you want to prove. Outside these cosy domains, life is full of doubt and uncertainty and that is what people prefer because it is what they are used to. But it is a comfort to feel that, if the doubt and uncertainty become excessive, one can fall back on the eternal verities of religion or mathematics. —J. L. Synge

Kandelman's Krim, London: Jonathan Cape, 1957, p. 13.

I2 [Whether] his interest is focused on the golden cuboid, or the dodecahedron, or the logarithmic spiral or the genealogy of the drone bee, [he] should realize that, in the act of appreciation, he is re-enacting the creative act and, attracted by beauty, is experiencing himself the joy of creative activity. He is in fact, in Kepler's phrase, "thinking God's thoughts after Him." —H. E. Huntley

The Divine Proportion, a Study in Mathematical Beauty, New York: Dover, 1970, p. 22.

I3 At a reception in his [Einstein's] honor at Princeton, when asked to comment on some dubious experiments that conflicted with both relativistic and prerelativistic concepts, he responded with a famous remark—a scientific credo—that was overhead by the American geometer, Professor Oswald Veblen, who must have jotted it down. Years later, in 1930, when Princeton University constructed a special building for mathematics, Veblen requested and received Einstein's permission to have the remark inscribed in marble above the fireplace of the faculty lounge. It was engraved there in the original German: "Raffiniert ist

der Herrgott, aber boshaft ist er nicht," which may be translated "God is subtle, but he is not malicious." In his reply to Veblen, Einstein explained that he meant that Nature conceals her secrets by her sublimity and not by trickery.   —Banesh Hoffmann and Helen Dukas
> *Albert Einstein, Creator and Rebel,* New York: Viking
> Press, 1972, p. 146.

14   If we concentrate our attention on trying to solve a problem in geometry, and if at the end of an hour we are no nearer to doing so than at the beginning, we have nevertheless been making progress each minute of that hour in another more mysterious dimension. Without our knowing or feeling it, this apparently barren effort has brought more light into the soul. The result will one day be discovered in prayer.
> —Simone Weil
> "Reflections on the Right Use of School Studies with
> a View to the Love of God," in George A. Panichas
> (ed.), *A Simone Weil Reader,* New York: David McKay,
> 1977, p. 45.

15   I am so in favor of the actual infinite that instead of admitting that Nature abhors it, as is commonly said, I hold that Nature makes frequent use of it everywhere, in order to show more effectively the perfections of its Author. Thus I believe that there is no part of matter which is not—I do not say divisible—but actually divisible; and consequently the least particle ought to be considered as a world full of an infinity of different creatures.   —Georg Cantor
> Joseph Dauben, *Georg Cantor, His Mathematics and
> Philosophy of the Infinite,* Cambridge, MA: Harvard
> University Press, 1979, p. 124.

16   The study of infinity is much more than a dry, academic game. The intellectual pursuit of the absolute infinity is, as Georg Cantor realized, a form of the soul's quest for God. Whether or not the goal is ever reached, an awareness of the process brings enlightenment.
> —Rudy Rucker
> *Infinity and the Mind,* Boston: Birkhäuser, 1982, p. ix.

17   Just as the man on the street is unaware of the difficulties that lie below the surface of his everyday arithmetic, so there are those who are untroubled by the utter incomprehensibility of the content of the traditional catechism. Contemporary theologians, however, as well as

mathematicians, are more aware than ever that the area of certainty in
their discipline is limited.   —Mary Coughlin
> "Mathematics Rooted in Mystery," *Math. Intell.* 5
> (No. 1, 1983) 51.

I8   Mathematics, like theology and all free creations of the Mind,
obeys the inexorable laws of the imaginary . . .   —Gian-Carlo Rota
> *Discrete Thoughts: Essays on Mathematics, Science and*
> *Philosophy,* Boston: Birkhäuser, 1986, p. 154.

I9   The occupation of natural science can be compared to the construction of a monumental building, say the cathedral of Cologne. We
scientists are working on the cathedral of the scientific view of the
universe. Though this cathedral, like the Cologne cathedral, has its
practical uses, our reason for working on it is really, as it was expressed
in the middle ages, for the glory of God. Only with *this* goal in mind
does it indeed become a cathedral instead of a factory. And just as
the workers in the construction-shack of the medieval cathedral are
anonymous today, for it was the edifice itself that mattered not they,
the contributions of most scientists will also remain anonymous. The
cathedral is a communal work, and the scientists are the journeymen of
a huge construction team, or, considering the worldwide extension of
their activity, they are brothers in a worldwise order where the individual ought to retreat behind the great common work.
>   —Gert Eilenberger
> "Freedom, Science, and Aesthetics," in H.-O. Peitgen
> and P. H. Richter, *The Beauty of Fractals,* New York:
> Springer-Verlag, 1986, p. 175.

CHAPTER 12

Mathematics and the Computer

1 To obtain a result of real value, it is not enough to grind out calculations or to have a machine to put things in order; it is not order alone, it is unexpected order, which is worth while. The machine may gnaw on the crude fact, the soul of the fact will always escape it.

—Henri Poincaré
"Science and Method," in G. B. Halsted, (trans.), *The Foundations of Science*, New York: The Science Press, 1929, p. 373.

2 If the activity of a science can be supplied by a machine, that science cannot amount to much, so it is said; and hence it deserves a subordinate place. The answer to such arguments, however, is that the mathematician, even when he is himself operating with numbers and formulas, is by no means an inferior counterpart of the errorless machine, "thoughtless thinker" of Thomae; but rather, he sets for himself his problems with definite, interesting, and valuable ends in view, and carries them to solution in appropriate and original manner. He turns over to the machine only certain operations which recur frequently in the same way, and it is precisely the mathematician—one must not forget this—who invented the machine for his own relief, and who, for his own intelligent ends, designates the tasks which it shall perform.

—Felix Klein
Elementary Mathematics from an Advanced Standpoint—Arithmetic, Algebra, Analysis, New York: Macmillan, 1932, p. 22.

3 Computers do not decrease the need for mathematical analysis, but rather greatly increase this need. They actually extend the use of analysis into the fields of computers and computation, the former area being almost unknown until recently, the latter never having been as intensively investigated as its importance warrants. Finally, it is up to the user of computational equipment to define his needs in terms of his problems. In any case, computers can never eliminate the need for problem-solving through human ingenuity and intelligence.
> —Richard Bellman and Paul Brock
> "On the Concepts of a Problem and Problem-Solving," *Amer. Math. Monthly* 67 (January 1960) 133.

4 There is . . . the very real danger that a number of problems which could profitably be subjected to analysis, and so treated by simpler and more revealing techniques, will instead be routinely shunted to the computing machines. . . . The role of computing machines as a mathematical tool is not that of a panacea for all computational ills.
> —Richard Bellman and Paul Brock
> "On the Concepts of a Problem and Problem-Solving," *Amer. Math. Monthly* 67 (January 1960) 122.

5 I think everyone would agree that the computer just makes the mathematician all the more necessary, because it can't decide what to do, and can't think out what the problem should be. As a result the more computing help is available, the more we'll need the mathematician to tell us what to do.
> —Donald C. May
> "Professional Mathematicians in Government and Industry," *SIAM Review* 2 (January 1960) 9.

6 Roughly speaking, there are two kinds of human thinking. There is creative thinking, based on imagination and insight. . . . This kind of thinking follows unpredictable channels, and follows no fixed rules. There is also routine thinking, that requires no special talent to carry it out. It proceeds according to fixed rules along a course that is easily foreseen. . . . It is only this kind of routine thinking that a so-called "thinking machine" can do. The fact that it is routine thinking, however, does not make it unimportant. A large part of the thinking we do in our daily lives is of this routine type. And often, while it is routine, it is also complex and time-consuming. We save a lot of time and energy, and avoid many errors, by letting the machine take this thinking off our hands, or rather, off our minds. Moreover, it is no routine matter to design a machine that can do routine thinking. Behind the routine thinking of the machine is the creative thinking of the men who invented it.

—Irving Adler

Thinking Machines, New York: John Day, 1961, p. 13.

7 The computer is really very much more than a super slide rule. Our whole intellectual horizons are going to increase a great deal because computers exist and they are going to imply something like a new way of life in many respects. You could, of course, go back and look at some historical analogues. An automobile is not just a super horse. It is true that, given enough time and given enough horses, you can get a group of horses to do just about everything that an automobile can do, but still the automobile has changed our entire way of life. I think that a computer may well do the same.

—Henry O. Pollak

Robert W. Ritchie (ed.), *New Directions in Mathematics,* Englewood Cliffs, NJ: Prentice-Hall, 1963, p. 40.

8 Many of the most able people in computing were attracted there from mathematics and probably represent a loss to mathematics. On the other hand, the glamor and money in computing probably have attracted some people to mathematics. The net balance would be hard to measure.

—R. W. Hamming

"Impact of Computers," *Amer. Math. Monthly* 72 (February 1965, Part II) 7.

9 We use computers in a rather inhibited fashion. . . . In practice we care surprisingly little for a rigorous mathematical proof of convergence so long as we get an answer we like; on the other hand, mathematical rigor based on an inappropriate model does not impress us much.

In a way, we have gone back to the classical mathematicians who created the mathematics they felt was appropriate to the physical situation at hand, who ignored the mathematics they did not like, and in the absence of rigorous proof went ahead anyway.

I happen to believe that this uninhibited approach to mathematics will eventually enrich mathematics by giving it many new fruitful and useful models to explore.

—R. W. Hamming

"Impact of Computers," *Amer. Math. Monthly* 72 (February 1965, Part II) 6.

IO   I must emphasize that the amount of computing done for applied mathematics is an almost invisible fraction of the total amount of computing today.   —George E. Forsythe
"What to Do till the Computer Scientist Comes,"
Amer. Math. Monthly 75 (April 1968) 455.

II   In the past fifteen years many numerical analysts have progressed from being queer people in the mathematics departments to being queer people in the computer science departments!
—George E. Forsythe
"What to Do till the Computer Scientist Comes,"
Amer. Math. Monthly 75 (April 1968) 456.

I2   For three years I taught a sophomore course in abstract algebra, for mathematics majors at Caltech, and the most difficult topic was always the study of "Jordan canonical form" for matrices. The third year I tried a new approach by looking at the subject algorithmically, and suddenly it became quite clear. The same thing happened with the discussion of finite groups defined by generators and relations; and in another course, with the reduction theory of binary quadratic forms. By presenting the subject in terms of algorithms, the purpose and meaning of the mathematical theorems became transparent.

Later, while writing a book on computer arithmetic, I found that virtually every theorem in elementary number theory arises in a natural, motivated way in connection with the problem of making computers do high-speed numerical calculations. Therefore I believe that the traditional courses in elementary number theory might well be changed to adopt this point of view, adding a practical motivation to the already beautiful theory.   —Donald E. Knuth
"Computer Science and Its Relation to Mathematics,"
Amer. Math. Monthly 81 (April 1974) 327.

I3   Like mathematics, computer science will be a subject which is considered basic to a general education. Like mathematics and other sciences, computer science will continue to be vaguely divided into two areas, which might be called "theoretical" and "applied." Like mathematics, computer science will be somewhat different from the other sciences, in that it deals with man-made laws which can be proved, instead of natural laws which are never known with certainty. Thus, the two subjects will be like each other in many ways. The difference is in the subject matter and approach—mathematics dealing more or less with

theorems, infinite processes, static relationships, and computer science dealing more or less with algorithms, finitary constructions, dynamic relationships.   —Donald E. Knuth
"Computer Science and Its Relation to Mathematics,"
Amer. Math. Monthly 81 (April 1974) 326.

14   The most significant thing [impact of computer science on mathematics] is that the study of algorithms themselves has opened up a fertile vein of interesting new mathematical problems; it provides a breath of life for many areas of mathematics which had been suffering from a lack of new ideas. Charles Babbage, one of the "fathers" of computing machines, predicted this already in 1864: "As soon as an Analytical Engine [i.e., a general purpose computer] exists, it will necessarily guide the future course of the science. Whenever any result is sought by its aid, the question will then arise—By what course of calculation can these results be arrived at by the machine in the shortest time?" And again, George Forsythe in 1958: "The use of practically any computing technique itself raises a number of mathematical problems. There is thus a very considerable impact of computation on mathematics itself, and this may be expected to influence mathematical research to an increasing degree." Garrett Birkhoff has observed that such influences are not a new phenomenon, they were already significant in the early Greek development of mathematics.   —Donald E. Knuth
"Computer Science and Its Relation to Mathematics,"
Amer. Math. Monthly 81 (April 1974) 328.

15   Whereas in the past, with applied mathematics, statistics and mathematical logic, problem areas developed slowly, and ignoring them or general procrastination in the face of them, was not disastrous to the service side of mathematics teaching, in the case of computing, problem areas could develop very quickly, well within the next ten years, and to ignore them could be disastrous.   —Ronald Harrop
"Computing and Mathematics Departments—The Years Ahead," *Amer. Math. Monthly* 82 (January 1975) 70.

16   Early in the history of computing the great von Neumann preached that the many numerical solutions of particular cases we could compute would shed a great deal of light on many parts of mathematics, and would prove to be a significant stimulus to the whole of mathematics. ... But we found that most mathematicians simply ignored computers, if they did not deliberately flee from them! . . . Computers have had a great deal less influence [on mathematics] than we had hoped.

—R. W. Hamming
"The History of Computing in the United States,"
in Dalton Tarwater (ed.), *The Bicentennial Tribute to American Mathematics,* Washington, DC: Mathematical Association of America, 1977, p. 125.

I7   Most mathematicians who were educated prior to the development of fast computers tend not to think of the computer as a routine tool to be used in conjunction with other older and more theoretical tools in advancing mathematical knowledge. Thus they intuitively feel that if an argument contains parts that are not verifiable by hand calculations it is on rather insecure ground. There is a tendency to feel that verification of computer results by independent computer programs is not as certain to be correct as independent hand checking of the proof of theorems proved in the standard way.

This point of view is reasonable for those theorems whose proofs are of moderate length and highly theoretical. When proofs are long and highly computational, it may be argued that even when hand checking is possible, the probability of human error is considerably higher than that of machine error; moreover, if the computations are sufficiently routine, the validity of programs themselves is easier to verify than the correctness of hand computations.

In any event, even if the Four-Color Theorem turns out to have a simpler proof, mathematicians might be well advised to consider more carefully other problems that might have solutions of this new type, requiring computation or analysis of a type not possible for humans alone. There is every reason to believe that there are a large number of such problems. After all, the argument that almost all known proofs are reasonably short can be answered by the argument that if one only employs tools which will yield short proofs, that is all one is likely to get.

—Kenneth Appel and Wolfgang Haken.
"The Four-Color Problem," in Lynn A. Steen (ed.),
Mathematics Today, New York: Springer-Verlag, 1978, p. 178.

I8   Calculation was just a chore that had a rather narrow scope, an uninteresting matter of calculating numerical answers. But now, the electronic computer has not only increased the capacity and speed of

calculation but also enlarged the whole concept of what computing is. It is all of organized information handling, all algorithmic handling of data. ... We are developing the most general, most abstract, and most effective methods of handling information. —Kenneth O. May
"Historiography: A Perspective for Computer Scientists," in N. Metropolis, J. Howlett, G. Rota (eds.), *A History of Computing in the Twentieth Century*, New York: Academic Press, 1980, p. 17.

19   The relationship of computers to mathematics has been far more complex than the layman might suspect. Most people assume that anyone who calls himself a professional mathematician uses computing machines. In truth, compared to engineers, physicists, chemists, and economists, most mathematicians have been indifferent to and ignorant of the use of computers. Indeed the notion that creative mathematical work could ever be mechanized seems, to many mathematicians, demeaning of their professional self-esteem.
—Philip Davis and Reuben Hersh
The Mathematical Experience, New York: Birkhäuser, 1981, p. 15.

20   I must admit that for a number of my friends, mostly number theorists and topologists, who fool around with small numbers and low-dimensional spaces, the computer is a tremendous scratch pad. But those same friends, perhaps in other bodies, got along just fine twenty-five years ago, before the computer became a scratch pad, using a different scratch pad. Maybe they weren't as efficient but mathematics isn't in a hurry. Efficiency is meaningless. Understanding is what counts. So, is the computer important to mathematics? My answer is no. It is important, but not to mathematics.   —Paul Halmos
Donald Albers, "Paul Halmos: Maverick Mathologist," *Two-year Coll. Math. J.* 13 (September 1982) 240.

21   Machines do not supersede Simpson's rule for the approximate calculation of definite integrals; on the contrary, they use it.
   The same is true of Gaussian elimination for solving systems of linear equations. The primary effect of computer science on mathematics has

been to make various mathematical ideas more important than they were before by making them usable.   —Edwin E. Moise
> "Mathematics, Computation, and Psychic Intelligence," in Viggo P. Hansen (ed.), *Computers in Mathematics Education*, Reston, VA: National Council of Teachers of Mathematics, 1984, p. 38.

22   I think that our world is much too bound by scientific standards of thinking. We have fostered the attitude in our schools that everything can be "figured out". Even if we use computers to teach young children the "logical" way of thinking, I'm not sure we should.

Let me explain further: I think that children have a power to imagine that is almost magical when compared to the adult imagination, and this is something irrevocable that a child loses when he or she becomes bound by logic. We adults continue to have our children's power of imagination only in our dreams. .... Of course it's awfully necessary that children not run their entire lives on the basis of such thinking; they do need to learn how to think logically. But the world will soon teach that to them. And in overabundance. I think we should do everything we can to make it possible for children to hang onto the power to imagine in the almost magical sense for as long as possible.

—Joseph Weizenbaum
> Holly Brady, "Hang on to the Power to Imagine," *Classroom Comp. Learning* 6 (November/December 1985) 26.

23   In the quest for simplification, mathematics stands to computer science as diamond mining to coal mining. The former is a search for gems. .... The latter is permanently involved with bulldozing large masses of ore—extremely useful bulk material.   —Jacob T. Schwartz
> *Discrete Thoughts: Essays on Mathematics, Science and Philosophy*, Boston: Birkhäuser, 1986, p. 64.

24   People have noted, with irony, that we mathematicians are the most computer-phobic of scientists; most of us stick to pencil and paper, while our colleagues in various scientific disciplines have come to rely on high-powered computational tools and techniques. .... If you expand the notion of computer use to include tools that make life easier, such as text processors, mathematics faculty may be among the most computer-phobic of college and university faculty. .... To put things simply, the vast majority of us mathematics faculty haven't yet become comfortable with the idea of computer as tool.

As a community, we are even less familiar with computers as tools for teaching than we are with computers as tools in our professional lives. ... Indeed, this problem is far more severe at the college level than it is at the elementary and secondary levels.   —Alan Schoenfeld

"Uses of Computers in Mathematics Instruction," in David A. Smith et al. (eds.), *Computers and Mathematics,* Washington, DC: Mathematical Association of America, 1988, p. 1.

25   I believe computer science has made and will continue to make important contributions to mathematics primarily because it provides an inspiration for new themes and rhythms by which the delicious modulations of mathematics can be enjoyed and enriched. ... Computer science is now enriching mathematics ... by asking new sorts of questions, whose answers shed new light on mathematical structures. In this way computer science makes fundamental improvements to the mathematical ensemble.   When good music is played, it influences the builders of musical instruments; my claim is that the cadences of computer science are having a profound and beneficial influence on the inner structure of mathematics.   —Donald E. Knuth

"Algorithmic Themes," in Peter Duren (ed.), *A Century of Mathematics in America, Part I,* Providence, RI: American Mathematical Society, 1988, p. 439.

26   It is impossible to exaggerate the extent to which modern applied mathematics has been shaped and fueled by the general availability of fast computers with large memories.   Their impact on mathematics, both applied and pure, is comparable to the role of telescopes in astronomy and microscopes in biology.   —Peter Lax

"The Flowering of Applied Mathematics in America," in Peter Duren (ed.), *A Century of Mathematics in America, Part II,* Providence, RI: American Mathematical Society, 1989, p. 463.

27   The computer has made it so that the sort of things that in the past we could not do on our own are now feasible, so we are trying all sorts of procedures, but we don't really know at all what they do. I don't think that's going to last. Somehow, sometime, somebody will have to find out what are the properties of these procedures. It's not going to be easy to do, mathematically, but somebody will have to try because, even though computers are very efficient, it's impossible for them to try all procedures under all possible circumstances. We will have to decide on other grounds what's good and what's not good. —Lucien LeCam

"Lucien LeCam," in D. Albers, G. Alexanderson, C. Reid (eds.), *More Mathematical People,* New York: Harcourt Brace Jovanovich, 1990, p. 177.

28   [Using a computer] has been very time-consuming for me, and it's not clear that the benefit is worth it when I have to spend all this time personally just maintaining the computer, let alone programming it. Programming is one of the most discouraging things. The rate of translation of ideas into working programs can be very slow, so you tend to lower your sights quite a bit. On the other hand, a lot of these things could be done pretty efficiently by programmers. So if there were money to hire staff to maintain computer systems and programmers to write interesting programs and to be informed about what is available . . . then I think mathematicians would find computers much more useful. The payoff would be quicker. One wouldn't have the sense of being stuck in the muck.   —William Thurston

"William P. Thurston," in D. Albers, G. Alexanderson, C. Reid (eds.), *More Mathematical People,* New York: Harcourt Brace Jovanovich, 1990, p. 342.

CHAPTER 13

About Mathematicians, A–L

1 Mathematics was Albert's great enthusiasm. It was impossible to associate with him for any length of time without feeling the vigor with which he pursued his theorems. He was always willing to talk about his latest mathematical exploits. When his son, Alan, was still very young, Albert insisted on explaining even to him his latest theorems, patiently describing the necessary ingredients to the intrigued schoolboy who had not yet formally seen any real mathematics. —D. Zelinsky
"A. A. Albert," *Amer. Math. Monthly* 80 (June-July 1973) 664.

2 It is characteristic of [P.S.] Aleksandrov's originality that once he had found the central, fundamental results in a new field he never tried to exhaust it since he regarded his work as a starting-point for the work of his own pupils and other research workers. And this quality is undoubtedly connected with the breadth of his scientific interests. —A. V. Arkhangel'skii, A. N. Kolmogorov, A. A. Mal'tsev, O. A. Oleinik
"Pavel Sergecvich Aleksandrov," *Russian Math. Surveys* 31 (September-October 1976) 6.

3 [R.] Nevanlinna introduced the class to Denjoy's conjecture on the number of asymptotic values of an entire function, including Carleman's partial proof. I had the incredible luck of hitting upon a new approach, based on conformal mapping, which with very considerable help from Nevanlinna and Pólya led to a proof of the full conjecture.

With unparalleled generosity they forbade me to mention the part they had played, and Pólya, who rightly did not trust my French, wrote the *Comptes Rendus* note. For my part I have tried to repay my debt by never accepting to appear as coauthor with a student.

—Lars V. Ahlfors

Rae Michael Shortt (ed.), *Lars V. Ahlfors: Collected Papers, Vol I,* Boston: Birkhäuser, 1982, p. xii.

4   Elayne Arrington-Idowu spoke in the 1978 Atlanta panel of the disadvantages of growing up Black and female in the North. In her suburban Pittsburgh town she was not permitted to be a cheerleader or a drum majorette—and certainly not an angel in the Christmas play. It is with obvious joy that she tells about her two daughters who won national contests in baton twirling. When she was valedictorian of her high school class, she was not allowed to give the valedictory address; that was the only year the class president gave the graduation speech.

Her mother worked hard in a restaurant and there was little money for college. Thus they were overjoyed when she received a letter saying that on the basis of her high school grades and college board scores she had ranked first for a company scholarship, which would replace the tuition expenses, including funds for books. A few days later she was informed that the company refused to give its scholarship to a female; thus she would receive only the University tuition scholarship. She has written, "First of all I felt resentful—I resented the white male who received 'my scholarship,' as I thought of it. I had classes at the university with him and often heard him boast about the great scholarship that he had 'won.' Secondly, I felt compelled to prove that I could do anything that the male students could do (often collectively). They were not friendly and I didn't ask them any questions, lest they think that I was not capable of doing my own work. In effect, I was isolated, and it was me against all of them ... the worst effect of my undergraduate experiences was the lack of intellectual exchange with my peer group."

When she graduated from the University of Pittsburgh, her class standing was not listed because women were not included; she had to compare her average with the men on the list to discover where she stood. After college she was an aerospace engineer at Wright-Patterson Air Force Base for seven years, and then she enrolled in graduate school at the University of Cincinnati. There she was told by

her prospective advisor that she should spend an extra year preparing for the preliminary exams because although the general failure rate was 50 percent, the rate among "housewives like you" was 98 percent. She was startled to think of herself as a "housewife," but was persuaded to spend the extra year. —Patricia Kenschaft
"Black Women in Mathematics in United States," *Amer. Math. Monthly* 88 (October 1981) 600.

5 It was of the highest importance to Artin to help his students to develop their own mathematical personalities, to assist them to stand on their own feet, to kindle in them a deep love of mathematics. By putting all his strength to this effort and by using all his ingenuity, he created, not mathematical theories, but mathematicians.
—Richard Brauer
"Emil Artin," *Bull. of the Amer. Math. Soc.* 73 (January 1967) 39.

6 Artin, with his wide interests in all fields of human endeavor, became the stimulating center of a circle of friends. His strange nickname "Ma" which he always preferred to his given name Emil goes back to those days. It is short for "Mathematics"; he simply appeared to these young men as the embodiment of mathematics. —Richard Brauer
"Emil Artin," *Bull. of the Amer. Math. Soc.* 73 (January 1967) 27.

7 I always enjoyed mathematics, beginning with arithmetic in a one-room country school in Iowa. In high school and college an interest in mathematics was considered unusual for a girl but certainly was not discouraged. I entered college with a firm intention of majoring in Latin. Along with Latin I took mathematics because I liked it too, and taking calculus changed my mind about majoring in Latin. (In those days calculus was a college sophomore subject.) In the mathematics department my interest was encouraged, but more generally the attitude was that pursuing a Ph.D. in mathematics was something for a man to do, not a woman. —Mabel S. Barnes
"Centennial Reflections on Women in American Mathematics," *Assoc. for Women in Math. Newsletter* 18 (November–December 1988) 6.

8 Even in remote Nebraska I heard about a place called the Institute for Advanced Study opening in far away Princeton. I applied for admission and was accepted. ... Soon after I arrived the Director of the

School of Mathematics took me aside and warned me that Princeton was not accustomed to women in its halls of learning and I should make myself as inconspicuous as possible. However, otherwise I found a very friendly atmosphere and spent a valuable and enjoyable year there.

—Mabel S. Barnes
"Centennial Reflections on Women in American Mathematics," *Assoc. for Women in Math. Newsletter* 18 (November–December 1988) 7.

9   One day a Mr. Pullinger, to whom my father had been apprenticed, was visiting us. As a result of some questions he had put to me he recommended me to study mathematics. I was quite impressed but my memory played me a trick when a lady asked me a few days later what I was going to study. My reply was that I was going to study acrobatics. She then asked me where I was going to perform and I was at a loss for an answer. Since I have learned recently that Dr. Thomas Young was an expert tight rope walker and harlequin my mistake does not seem so bad after all.   —Harry Bateman

F. D. Murnaghan, "Harry Bateman 1882–1946," *Bull. of the Amer. Math. Soc.* 54 (January 1948) 88.

10   I remember well a feeling of amazement, mingled with discouragement, which came over me when I discovered the thoroughness of the man [Harry Bateman]. He already possessed a large, carefully indexed card-catalogue on each card of which was written in his minute, but beautifully clear, handwriting an abstract of a paper which he had read. I am told that in later years this card-catalogue crowded him out of his office and almost out of his home. No wonder, then, that his books and papers bristle with references which are a veritable mine of useful source material. His memory was phenomenal. No matter what stubborn integral or intractable differential equation you showed him, a moment's thought and a reference to the card-catalogue never failed to produce something useful.   —F. D. Murnaghan

"Harry Bateman 1882–1946," *Bull. of the Amer. Math. Soc.* 54 (January 1948) 90.

11   [E. T.] Bell, born in Scotland, was rather imposing in appearance and manner. Handsome, quick and forceful in speech, with a nose that gave a patrician quality to this profile, he threw off sparks in conversation. He was fond of making bold assertions, usually buttressed by a basis of factual truth, but sometimes more extreme than was warranted.

His writings on the history of mathematics are interesting, often vividly so, but not always entirely accurate, according to some professional historians of science and mathematics.

I had a number of interesting conversations with Bell about abstractions in mathematics. I remember one in October of 1935 while I was still a graduate student. He expressed the firm opinion that generalization by abstractions in analysis "does nothing really new and finds no new results." (I wrote these words in my diary at the time.) I disagreed, although I felt too inexperienced and respectful to get into an argument with him, . . . Bell's assertion was extreme, but behind it there was a valid note of caution. He was not alone among well-established mathematicians in being skeptical about abstractions in analysis. I recall very well, a few years later, hearing Professor Einar Hille say, at a meeting of the American Mathematical Society at Stanford, that there was a danger that young mathematicians might be tempted to succumb to the lure of generalization by abstraction in ways that would be easy, sterile, and lacking in substantial content, with too few points of contact with the ongoing body of significant work in mathematics.

—Angus E. Taylor
"A Life in Mathematics Remembered," *Amer. Math. Monthly* 91 (December 1984) 610.

12 At the beginning this course [in differential equations] was overflowing with students both from mathematics and from engineering and physics. After one look at the crowded classroom, [Richard] Bellman talked about prerequisites and assigned a long, highly theoretical problem set involving existence theorems and the Arzela selection theorem. By the second meeting of the class all of the engineering and physics students had dropped the course, but there were still a good many students left. Bellman promptly assigned another lengthy problem set. . . . By the third meeting most of the mathematics students were gone, and Bellman proceeded to lecture for the rest of the term to a few hardy souls, mostly auditors. No mention was ever again made of the assigned problem sets, for which no due dates had been specified, and no more problems were assigned.

—Halsey Royden
"A History of Mathematics at Stanford," in Peter Duren (ed.), *A Century of Mathematics in America, Part II,* Providence, RI: American Mathematical Society, 1989, p. 256.

13   Birkhoff was uncompromising in his appraisal of mathematics—by the test of originality and relevance. For him the systematic organization or exposition of a mathematical theory was always secondary in importance to its discovery. ... His choice of topics of investigation could be called objective rather than subjective. His problems were not necessarily chosen from among those which he could solve; indeed many of his papers from 1920 on were on problems which he left unsolved. Some of the current mathematical theories were regarded by Birkhoff as no more than relatively obvious elaborations of current examples.   —Marston Morse

> "George David Birkhoff and His Mathematical Work," *Bull. of the Amer. Math. Soc.* 52 (May 1946) 359.

14   When Birkhoff talked to me about his work in mathematics he generally betrayed a certain confidence that he would be able to develop said work farther and obtain results which would give him much personal satisfaction; however, there were a few exceptions. I recall that at one Annual Meeting of the American Mathematical Society in New York he was very much discouraged with the progress he was making in a particular line of investigation, so much so that I was unable to console him. However, a year later when I saw him again in New York, his discouragement was gone; he had, a few months before, discovered his Ergodic Theorem!   —H. S. Vandiver

> "Some of My Recollections of George David Birkhoff," *J. of Math. Anal. and Appl.* 7 (October 1963) 282.

15   [Harald Bohr] was a very kind person. Oh, well, we all can be kind you see. You talk to a boring student. Then you are kind because you feel it is your duty to be kind to a student. Or you talk to a nasty colleague and you are kind because you don't wish to collide with him, so you are kind out of duty or self-interest. But Harald Bohr was naturally kind. To be kind was an inborn instinct.

—George Pólya

> G. L. Alexanderson (ed.), *A Pólya Picture Album*, Boston: Birkhäuser, 1987, p. 67.

16   He [Borel] was by temperament a man of action as well as a man of thought ... he entered public life after the first world war, sat for 12 years in Parliament, held Cabinet office as Minister of the Navy

in the two Painlevé governments in 1925 and was vice-President of the influential Finance Committee of the Chamber from 1933 until his retirement from active politics in 1936. Only while he was actually Minister were his academic duties as a professor suspended; at all other times during these 12 parliamentary years the life of the politician had to be lived alongside that of the great international mathematician, the university professor and administrator, the director of research, the scientific publicist.   —E. F. Collingwood
"Émile Borel," *J. of the London Math. Soc.* 34 (October 1959) 489.

17 Most mathematicians today are still convinced that Nicolas Bourbaki does not exist. Instead, they consider Bourbaki simply to be the pseudonym for a group of French mathematicians. Mr. Boas, executive editor of the *Mathematical Reviews,* went so far as to print this opinion in an article for the *Encyclopædia Britannica.* The publishers of the *Encyclopædia Britannica* soon found themselves in an acutely embarrassing position, for they received a scalding letter signed by Nicolas Bourbaki in which he declared that he was not about to allow anyone to question his right to exist. And to avenge himself on Boas, Bourbaki began to circulate the rumour that the mathematician Boas did not exist, rather that the initials B.O.A.S. were simply used as a pseudonym for a group of the *Mathematical Reviews'* editors.   —Henri Cartan
"Nicolas Bourbaki and Contemporary Mathematics," *Math. Intell.* 2 (No. 4, 1980) 175.

18 His name is Greek, his nationality is French and his history is curious. He is one of the most influential mathematicians of the 20th century. The legends about him are many, and they are growing every day. Almost every mathematician knows a few stories about him and is likely to have made up a couple more. His works are read and extensively quoted all over the world. There are young men in Rio de Janeiro almost all of whose mathematical education was obtained from his works, and there are famous mathematicians in Berkeley and in Göttingen who think that his influence is pernicious. He has emotional partisans and vociferous detractors wherever groups of mathematicians congregate. The strangest fact about him, however, is that he does not exist.

This nonexistent Frenchman with the Greek name is Nicolas Bourbaki. ... The fact is that Nicolas Bourbaki is a collective pseudonym

used by an informal corporation of mathematicians. ... The pseudony-
mous group is writing a comprehensive treatise on mathematics starting
with the most general basic principles and to conclude, presumably,
with the most specialized applications. The project got under way in
1939, and 20 volumes (almost 3,000 pages) of the monumental work
have appeared.   —Paul Halmos
              "Nicolas Bourbaki," *Sci. Amer.* 196 (May 1957) 88.

19   Jean Dieudonné ... has been Bourbaki's chief scribe almost from
the beginning. Since Dieudonné is a prolific writer on mathematics
under his own name, there is a certain difficulty about distinguishing
his private work from his efforts for Bourbaki. According to one story,
he manages to keep the record straight in a truly remarkable manner.
The story is that Dieudonné once published, under Bourbaki's name,
a note which later was found to contain a mistake. The mistake was
corrected in a paper entitled "On an Error of M. Bourbaki" and signed
Jean Dieudonné.   —Paul Halmos
              "Nicolas Bourbaki," *Sci. Amer.* 196 (May 1957) 94.

20   Many of his [Brauer's] most important results have been given
alternative or better proofs, usually by others, sometimes by himself.
This is at least partly due to the fact that he was always primarily
interested in results and did not spend a great deal of time looking for
the "best" proof. However, his papers are very readable. He had a style
which enabled him to present complicated and computational proofs in
an understandable form. He frequently wrote a paper and put it away
for six months or a year before looking at it again. Then he either liked
it or rewrote it. As any mathematician knows, things that are obvious in
one's mind become a little less obvious a year later, so that his method
is an excellent way to test readability.   —Walter Feit
              "Richard D. Brauer," *Bull. of the Amer. Math. Soc.*
              (New series) 1 (January 1979) 15.

21   To Professor Cayley we owe a debt not only as an explorer, but as
one who followed out of set purpose the tracks often so faintly indicated
by those that first passed that way. Where he found a mere mountain-
path he left a broad road, steep it may be, but plainly marked out, and
with no hidden pitfalls or lurking dangers. While it is his creative power
that excites our admiration, it is this determination that others shall be
enabled to follow that endears him to us. This he has done consistently

for his own work as well as for that of others, and it is partly due to this that so large a proportion of the results and processes of his earlier papers have become the commonplaces of text-books. . . . Cayley was emphatically in touch with the mathematics of the day; his omnivorous reading, his rapid assimilation of new thoughts, his readiness to believe in others, his frank and genial response to any appeal for help, all combined to make him the ideal head of the mathematical world.

—Charlotte Angus Scott
"Arthur Cayley," *Bull. of the Amer. Math. Soc.* 1 (March 1895) 139.

22   Any sketch of Professor Cayley is self-condemned if it leaves out of the account the childlike purity and simplicity of his nature, the entire freedom from the professional touchiness on the score of priority to which mathematicians are as liable as other men. He was ever ready to say what he was working at, to indicate the lines of thought, to state what difficulties he was encountering. It is not every mathematician that will lecture to a class of specialists on the incomplete investigation of the night before, and end up with the remark, obviously genuine, "Perhaps some of you may find this out before I do." To this engaging sweetness of his nature must be ascribed also the urbanity of manner which, as one of its many manifestations, would not allow him to leave unacknowledged the slightest mathematical paper sent to him. His little note of thanks would frequently contain a few words of comment, just enough to show that he had made time to glance over the paper. Anecdotes illustrating his absorption in his work, his disregard for appearances, are well known to all that knew him, and will doubtless be forthcoming in the reminiscences of his contemporaries; but his greatness and his simplicity cannot be enshrined in anecdotes.

—Charlotte Angus Scott
"Arthur Cayley," *Bull. of the Amer. Math. Soc.* 1 (March 1895) 139.

23   [Alonzo Church] looked like a cross between a panda and a large owl. He spoke slowly in complete paragraphs which seemed to have been read out of a book, evenly and slowly enunciated, as by a talking machine. . . .

His one year course in mathematical logic was one of Princeton University's greatest offerings. It attracted as many as four students in 1961. . . . Every lecture began with a ten-minute ceremony of erasing the blackboard until it was absolutely spotless. We tried to save him the effort by erasing the board before his arrival, but to no avail. The ritual could not be disposed of; often it required water, soap, and brush, and was followed by another ten minutes of total silence while the blackboard was drying. Perhaps he was preparing the lecture while erasing; I don't think so. His lectures hardly needed any preparation. They were a literal repetition of the typewritten text he had written over a period of twenty years, a copy of which was to be found upstairs in the Fine Hall library. .... Occasionally, one of the sentences spoken in class would be at variance with the text upstairs, and he would warn us in advance of the discrepancy between oral and written presentation. ...

It may be asked why anyone would bother to sit in a lecture which was a literal repetition of an available text. Such a question would betray an oversimplified view of what goes on in a classroom. What one really learns in class is what one does not know at the time one is learning. The person lecturing to us was logic incarnate. ... We learned to think in unison with him as he spoke, as if following the demonstration of a calisthenics instructor. Church's course permanently improved the rigor of our reasoning.   —Gian-Carlo Rota
"Fine Hall in Its Golden Age: Remembrances of Princeton," in Peter Duren (ed.), *A Century of Mathematics in America, Part II,* Providence, RI: American Mathematical Society, 1989, p. 225.

24   I remember when [William] Claytor was on a post-doctoral at Michigan and they had a vacancy for which he was qualified. They would not offer him the position, and the student newspaper took up the issue but to no avail. I believe that incident in discrimination was one of the main chilling, if not killing, points in the research career of a brilliant mathematician. There are references in the literature to his work, but he lost his spirit.   —Walter Talbot
Virginia Newell et al (eds.), *Black Mathematicians and Their Works,* Ardmore, PA: Dorrance, 1980, p. 321.

25   [Richard Courant], a mathematician who hates logic, who abhors abstractions, who is suspicious of 'truth,' if it is just bare truth!
—K. O. Friedrichs
Constance Reid, *Courant in Göttingen and New York,* New York: Springer-Verlag, 1976, p. 1.

26   My father [Tobias Dantzig] taught me by giving me problems to
solve. He gave me thousands of geometry problems while I was still in
high school . . . I would say over ten thousand. After he gave me one and
I came back with a solution, he would say, "Well, I'll give you another
one."

It seemed as if he had an infinite storehouse of them. . . . It was I who
asked for the problems. I believe he gave them to me just to get rid of
me. It was almost as if he were saying, "Here's another problem. Now
go away and don't bother me." He was always busy with whatever he
was busy with—taking care of his students, writing, doing research, and
so on. Eventually, of course, he did run out of problems and had to go
to the Library of Congress to dig up additional ones.

—George B. Dantzig
Donald J. Albers and Constance Reid, "An Interview
with George B. Dantzig: The Father of Linear Programming," *Coll. Math. J.* 17 (September 1986) 297.

27   Max Dehn . . . possessed a radiance which makes one naturally
bow down before [his] memory; a quality, both intellectual and moral,
that is perhaps best conveyed by the word "wisdom" . . . for such a man,
truth is all one, and mathematics is but one of the mirrors in which it is
reflected—perhaps more purely than it is elsewhere.   —André Weil

Apprenticeship of a Mathematician, Boston: Birkhäuser Verlag, 1992, p. 52.

28   The fact that I neglected mathematics to a certain extent had its
cause not merely in my stronger interest in the natural sciences than
in mathematics but also in the following strange experience. I saw
that mathematics was split up into numerous specialties, each of which
could easily absorb the short lifetime granted to us. Consequently I saw
myself in the position of Buridan's ass which was unable to decide upon
any specific bundle of hay. This was obviously due to the fact that my
intuition was not strong enough in the field of mathematics in order to
differentiate clearly the fundamentally important, that which is really
basic, from the rest of the more or less dispensable erudition.

—Albert Einstein
"Autobiographical Notes," in Paul A. Schilpp (ed.),
Albert Einstein: Philosopher-Scientist, New York:
Tudor Publishing, 1951, p. 15.

29   [Einstein] thought that scientific greatness was primarily a question of character, the determination not to compromise or to accept incomplete answers. Let me mention the only occasion on which he said: 'This would make a good anecdote about me.' We had finished the preparation of a paper and we were looking for a paper clip. After opening a lot of drawers we finally found one which turned out to be too badly bent for use. So we were looking for a tool to straighten it. Opening a lot more drawers we came on a whole box of unused paper clips, Einstein immediately starting to shape one of them into a tool to straighten the bent one. When I asked him what he was doing, he said, 'Once I am set on a goal, it becomes difficult to deflect me.'

—Ernst G. Straus
"Memoir," in A. P. French (ed.), *Einstein: A Centenary Volume,* Cambridge, MA: Harvard University Press, 1979, p. 31.

30   One never knew where [Paul] Erdős was, not even the country. However, one could be sure that during the year that Erdős was everywhere. He was the nearest thing to an ergodic particle that a human being could be.   —Richard Bellman
Eye of the Hurricane, Singapore: World Scientific, 1984, p. 128.

31   Paul Erdős has the theory that God has a book containing all the theorems of mathematics with their absolutely most beautiful proofs, and when he wants to express particular appreciation of a proof he exclaims, "This is one from the book!"   —Ross Honsberger
Mathematical Morsels, Washington, DC: Mathematical Association of America, 1978, p. vii.

32   Paul [Erdős], then still a young student but already with a few victories in his bag, was always full of problems and his sayings were already a legend. . . . Our discussions centred around mathematics, personal gossip, and politics. It was the beginning of a desperate era in Europe. Most of us in the circle belonged to that singular ethnic group of European society which drew its cultural heritage from Heinrich Heine and Gustav Mahler, Karl Marx and Cantor, Einstein and Freud, later to become the principal target of Hitler's fury. . . . Many of us had leftist tendencies, following the simple reasoning that our problems can only be solved on a global, international scale and socialism was the only political philosophy that offered such a solution. Being a leftist had its dangers and Paul was quick to spread the news when one of our number got into trouble: "A. L. is studying the theorem of Jordan." It meant that following a police action A. L. had just verified that the interior of a prison cell is not in the same component as the exterior. I have a dim recollection that this is how I first heard about the Jordan curve theorem.

—Gy Szekeres
"A Combinatorial Problem in Geometry, Reminiscences," in Joel Spencer (ed.), *Paul Erdős: The Art of Counting, Selected Writings,* Cambridge, MA: MIT Press, 1973, p. xix.

33 His [Lipót Fejér's] papers are particularly well written, they are very easy to read. This is due to his style of work: When he found an idea, he tended it with loving care; he tried to perfect it, simplify it, free it from unessentials; he worked on it carefully and minutely until the idea became transparently clear. He eventually produced a work of art, not of too large dimensions, but highly finished.

He had artistic talents besides mathematics. He loved music and played the piano. He had a special gift for telling stories, he was a "raconteur." In telling his stories, he acted the part of the persons he was telling about, and underlined the points with little gestures.

—George Pólya
"Some Mathematicians I Have Known," *Amer. Math. Monthly* 76 (August-September 1969) 749.

34 Why did Hungary produce so many mathematicians? Hungary was a small country (it is even smaller today) not much industrialized, and it produced a disproportionately large number of mathematicians, several of whom were active in this country. Why was that so? ... a good part of the answer can be found in [Lipót] Fejér's personality: He attracted many people to mathematics by the success of his own work and by his personal charm. He sat in a coffee house with young people who could not help loving him and trying to imitate him as he wrote formulas on the menus and alternately spoke about mathematics and told stories about mathematicians. In fact, almost all Hungarian mathematicians who were his contemporaries or somewhat younger were personally influenced by him, and several started their mathematical career by working on his problems.

—George Pólya
"Some Mathematicians I Have Known," *Amer. Math. Monthly* 76 (August-September 1969) 749.

35 [William Feller's] lectures were loud and entertaining. He wrote very large on the blackboard, in a beautiful Italianate handwriting with lots of whirls. Sometimes only one huge formula appeared on the blackboard during the entire period; the rest was handwaving. His proofs—insofar as one can speak of proofs—were often deficient. Nonetheless, they were convincing, and the results became unforgettably clear after he had explained them. The main idea was never wrong.

He took umbrage when someone interrupted his lecturing by pointing out some glaring mistake. He became red in the face and raised his voice, often to full shouting range. It was reported that on occasion he had asked the objector to leave the classroom. The expression "proof by intimidation" was coined after Feller's lectures (by Mark Kac). During a Feller lecture, the hearer was made to feel privy to some wondrous secret, one that often vanished by magic as he walked out of the classroom at the end of the period. Like many great teachers, Feller was a bit of a con man.   —Gian-Carlo Rota

"Fine Hall in Its Golden Age: Remembrances of Princeton," in Peter Duren (ed.), *A Century of Mathematics in America, Part II,* Providence, RI: American Mathematical Society, 1989, p. 227.

36 In March 1884 he [Henry Fine] and [W. F.] Magie sailed together for Germany. According to his own account, he knew very little German and almost no mathematics. Nevertheless he developed so rapidly that he obtained the Ph.D. in Leipzig in May 1885. He used to tell how Klein advised him, in spite of his ignorance, to come into the advanced lectures, and assured him that he would be learning mathematics even if he did not seem to understand everything as it went along. Fine did so and after a few months was surprised, on looking back at his early notes, to find that the whole story was clear to him. —Oswald Veblen

"Henry Burchard Fine—In Memoriam," *Bull. of the Amer. Math. Soc.* 35 (September-October 1929) 727.

37 The savage pressure at which the Cambridge coaches of the nineteenth century drove their pupils became legendary: not a day, not an hour, was wasted; the perfect candidate should be able to write the bookwork automatically while his thoughts were busy with the rider, and the fingers could be trained even when the brain was weary; above all, curiosity about unscheduled mathematics was depravity. [A. R.] Forsyth did all that was required of him, but he had a phenomenal capacity for

work ... and he was able to indulge in reading far outside the common undergraduate range.   —E. H. Neville
"Andrew Russell Forsyth," *J. of the London Math. Soc.*, 17 (October 1942) 239.

38 [Gottlob Frege's] mathematical work was almost wholly confined to the field of mathematical logic and the foundations of mathematics. The investigations of these areas led him into work of a philosophical rather than a mathematical character, but here again, his work was restricted in scope ... His life was one of disillusionment and frustration. It was spent almost entirely, until his retirement, at the University of Jena, and his energies were absorbed completely by his academic work ... He believed his work to have found no response, and felt as isolated and unlistened to as much at Jena as in the general philosophical and mathematical communities. Yet, despite the apparently narrow scope of his work, and his own belief that it met with almost total misunderstanding or neglect, he would now be generally acknowledged, by philosophers and mathematicians at least, as one of the great figures of the past hundred years.   —Michael Dummett
Frege: Philosophy of Language, New York: Harper and Row, 1973, p. xiii.

39 [Lazarus] Fuchs was not a brilliant lecturer. He spoke in a quiet, undemonstrative manner, but what he said was full of substance. To the student there was the inspiration of seeing a mathematical mind of the highest order full at work. For Fuchs worked when he lectured. He was rarely well prepared, but produced on the spot what he wished to say. Occasionally he would get lost in a complicated computation. Then he would look around at the audience over his glasses with a most winning and child-like smile. He was always certain of the essential points of his argument, but numerical examples gave him a great deal of trouble. He was fully conscious of this failing, and I remember well one occasion when, after a lengthy discussion, he laid considerable emphasis upon the fact that "*in this case,* two times two is four".   —E. J. Wilczynski
"Lazarus Fuchs," *Bull. of the Amer. Math. Soc.* 9 (October 1902) 46.

40 The same year [1972] I met Kurt Gödel at the Institute of Advanced Study. No one in modern times has thought more logically than Gödel, no one has proved theorems of greater mathematical complexity. Yet the man I met was a joyful, twinkling sage—not some obsessed

fossil. What struck me about Gödel was his intellectual freedom—his ability to move back and forth between frankly mystical insights and utterly precise logical derivations.   —Rudy Rucker
Infinity and the Mind, Boston: Birkhäuser, 1982, p. 1.

4I   Until the end of his very long life, he [Hadamard] retained an extraordinary freshness of mind and character; in many respects, his reactions remained those of a fourteen-year-old boy. His kindness knew no bounds. The warmth with which Hadamard received me in 1921 [when I was 15] eliminated all distance between us. He seemed to me more like a peer, infinitely more knowledgeable but hardly any older; he needed no effort at all to make himself accessible to me.
—André Weil
Apprenticeship of a Mathematician, Boston: Birkhäuser Verlag, 1992, p. 29.

42   [William] Hamilton had great confidence in himself. He never seems to have debated as to whether what he was doing was important. He wrote down everything and kept the notes. Most of his notes were coherently and legibly written, and those selected for publication required little editing. He wrote a small clear hand, generally using large notebooks with dated entries. He seldom made an error. He liked long arithmetical calculations which he carried out with precision. Hamilton's two hundred-odd notebooks in the Library of Trinity College, Dublin, refute the idea that great originality and penetration in a mathematician imply a contempt for detail and arithmetical calculation. He liked to refer to himself in the words Ptolemy used of Hipparchus: a lover of labor and a lover of truth.   —J. L. Synge
"The Life and Early Work of Sir William Rowan Hamilton," *A Collection of Papers in Memory of Sir William Rowan Hamilton,* New York: Scripta Mathematica, 1945, p. 23.

43   How much of the emotional response which led him [G. H. Hardy] to become a conscientious objector in the first World War is due to the abhorrence of the social destructiveness of war itself and how much to his feeling to the perversion of a beautiful thing like mathematics to unworthy ends one cannot say. Perhaps the two motives are not fully distinct. It is, however, certain that Hardy carried his hostility to applied mathematics to the extent of a real doubt that much work,

which attached itself to his own but claimed an engineering motivation, really was genuinely associated with engineering.   —Norbert Wiener
"Godfrey Harold Hardy," *Bull. of the Amer. Math. Soc.* 55 (January 1949) 75.

44   Hardy always referred to God as his personal enemy. This was, of course, a joke, but there was something real behind it. He took his disbelief in the doctrines of religion more seriously than most people seem to do. He would not enter a religious building, even for such a purpose as the election of a Warden of New College. The clause in the New College by-laws, enabling a fellow with a conscientious objection to being present in Chapel to send his vote to the scrutineers, was put in on his behalf.   —E. C. Titchmarsh
"Godfrey Harold Hardy 1877–1947," *Collected Papers of G. H. Hardy,* Oxford: Clarendon Press, 1966, p. 5.

45   But several things happened to change my life during that spring of 1963. Betty Friedan's *The Feminine Mystique* was published. When I read it, I questioned for the first time the rationale of giving first priority to being a wife and mother, and sacrificing a career for myself for the sake of my husband's. The second thing that happened was that Hannah Neumann gave a Colloquium at Mount Holyoke to which I was invited, and I happened to sit next to her at the Colloquium dinner. I must have mentioned my new baby, and she proceeded to tell me some of her history: how she had interrupted her studies to have two children, but then having been evacuated during the war (as an "enemy alien") from the coast of England to Cambridge while her husband joined the British Army, she returned to school, using other students as sitters while she saw her adviser, and finished her Ph.D. By 1963, she had raised five children and become a renowned algebraist. The message that came across to me was that if she could finish a Ph.D. with two children, surely I could do so with one.   —Louise Hay
"How I Became a Mathematician (or how it was in the bad old days)," *Assoc. for Women in Math. Newsletter,* 19 (September-October 1989) 9.

46   She [Louise Hay] always seemed to say things you wouldn't hear others say. I can't imagine anyone but Louise paraphrasing Virginia Woolf, ". . . women will not achieve equality until they have earned the right to be hacks . . . not everyone is a genius." In Louise's eyes, there was room for a broad spectrum of mathematical achievement.

Perhaps that is why many of us who were at Circle then have remained in mathematics long after good people from better places have gone on to other things. —Rhonda Hughes

"Fond Remembrances of Louise Hay," *Assoc. for Women in Math. Newsletter* 20 (January-February 1990) 6.

47   In 1963 Hay returned to Cornell to complete a Ph.D. degree in mathematics. A remarkably energetic and dedicated person, she stayed at Cornell for only fifteen months, during which time she took the required graduate courses and Ph.D. examinations, started and completed her dissertation (1965), and had twins in November, 1964.

—Robert I. Soare

"Louise Hay: 1935–1989," *Assoc. for Women in Math. Newsletter* 20 (January-February 1990) 3.

48   There were a group of about six very bright undergraduates in that class [Topics in Algebra at Cornell], all of whom later went on to get Ph.D.'s in mathematics. I remember distinctly the excitement Yitz [Herstein] transmitted to us about the beauty of mathematics. Wielandt's elegant proof of the first Sylow theorem had just come out and was presented to the class in a way making clear just how lovely Yitz felt it was. When John Thompson's thesis was announced, Yitz got the students to go to Thompson's talks on it at Cornell. The previous year the problem had been slipped into our class as an unrequired exercise ... Yitz was one of the most significant shapers of my mathematical career. —Barbara Osofsky

Martha Smith, "I. N. Herstein: In Memoriam," *Assoc. for Women in Math. Newsletter* 18 (July-August 1988) 3.

49   Yitz [Herstein] loved life. He had an amazing capacity to be both an adventurer and a nurturer. The adventurer surfaced in his research, his travels, and his non-mathematical pursuits. In his research, Yitz was not so much a builder of theories as a tackler of problems. He reveled in, and excelled at, the kind of problem that requires a tour de force, a tortuous (and sometimes torturous to almost anyone else) path pursued by means of cleverly conceived and delicately arranged calculations. Irving Kaplansky aptly described a series of Yitz's papers as a "display of virtuosity." His propensity to toss out conjectures showed this same adventurous streak. (His ability to generate conjectures awed me as a graduate student. I soon realized part of his secret: he covered all bases. Half of his conjectures were apt to be inconsistent with the other half.) His non-mathematical interests ranged from pool playing, to the stockmarket, to painting (both as appreciator and artist), to punning. He was great fun just to sit around and talk with.

—Martha Smith
"I. N. Herstein: In Memoriam," *Assoc. for Women in Math. Newsletter* 18 (July-August 1988) 3.

50   Many people wanted to get their doctor's degree with him [Hilbert] ... Somebody would hand in a doctoral thesis on a subject proposed by Hilbert. If it wasn't written well, and it was easier to do things by himself rather than study what the person had written, then Hilbert handed it to some assistant. Very quickly every assistant noticed that Hilbert didn't read the thesis so they also did not read it. By this method very many theses were accepted by Hilbert, and he produced a very large number of Ph.D's, some of them with impossibly wrong and silly theses.

—Richard Courant
"Reminiscences from Hilbert and Göttingen," *Math. Intell.* 3 (No. 4, 1981) 163.

51   David Hilbert was one of the truly great mathematicians of his time. His work and his inspiring scientific personality have profoundly influenced the development of the mathematical sciences up to the present time. His vision, his productive power and independent originality as a mathematical thinker, his versatility and breadth of interest made him a pioneer in many different mathematical fields. He was a unique personality, profoundly immersed in his work and totally dedicated to his science, a teacher and leader of the very highest order, inspiring and most generous, tireless and persistent in all of his efforts.

—Richard Courant
Constance Reid, *Hilbert*, New York: Springer-Verlag, 1970, p. v.

52   [Hilbert's literary style] is one of great lucidity. It is as if you were on a swift walk through a sunny open landscape; you look freely around, demarcation lines and connecting roads are pointed out to you, before you must brace yourself to climb the hill; then the path goes straight up, no ambling around, no detours. His style has not the terseness of many of our modern authors in mathematics, which is based on the assumption that printer's labor and paper are costly but the reader's effort and time are not. In carrying out a complete induction Hilbert finds time to develop the first two steps before formulating the general conclusion from n to $n + 1$. How many examples illustrate the fundamental theorems of his algebraic papers—examples not constructed ad hoc, but genuine ones worth being studied for their own sake!

    —Hermann Weyl
"David Hilbert and His Mathematical Work," *Bull. of the Amer. Math. Soc.* 50 (September 1944) 616.

53   Witold [Hurewicz] was a gentle, elfin man, incredibly insightful and inventive, and he wrote mathematics like poetry.   —J. L. Kelley
"Once Over Lightly," in Peter Duren (ed.), *A Century of Mathematics in America, Part III*, Providence, RI: American Mathematical Society, 1989, p. 479.

54   Felix Klein, in his *History of Mathematics in the Nineteenth Century*, calls [Adolf] Hurwitz an "aphoristician." An aphorism is a concise weighty saying. The aphorism is short, but its author may have worked a long time to make it so short. Also Hurzwitz tended his ideas with loving care, until he arrived at the simplest attainable expression, devoid of superfluous ornament or ballast and transparently clear ... he spotted well circumscribed weighty problems capable of a surprisingly simple solution and presented the solution in perfect form. If you wish to have an easily accessible sample, read two pages in his collected works: the proof for the transcendence of the number e.   —George Pólya
"Some Mathematicians I Have Known," *Amer. Math. Monthly* 76 (August-September 1969) 750.

55   On all these topics he [J. H. Jeans] wrote with amazing fluency, in a highly readable mathematical style. He was a master of his mathematical techniques, which he never allowed to overwhelm his physical objectives, and it is fair to say that he scarcely wrote a dull page. Indeed it is difficult to describe the undercurrent of thrilling expectation which Jeans' technical papers and treatises conveyed to the interested reader. The present writer vividly remembers being almost swept off his feet when he first read the passages in Jeans' *Dynamical theory of gases* dealing with the systems of N molecules described in $6N$-dimensional phase-space (this was in 1919, before he knew Jeans personally); it was an emotional experience seldom equalled in the writer's mathematical experience. Power and generality—those were the features of Jeans' mathematical style at its best. He always led the mathematics, never

allowing it to dominate. For sheer beauty of technical exposition Jeans
must rarely have been surpassed.   —E. A. Milne
"James Hopwood Jeans," *J. of the London Math. Soc.*
21 (July 1946) 312.

56   Eleanor Green Dawley Jones was the second of six children of
a letter carrier in Norfolk, Virginia. She was educated in completely
segregated schools and the only whites she knew as a child were the
priests and nuns of her parish. When she graduated from high school at
the age of 15, she won a scholarship to Howard University. There she
studied under Elbert Cox, the first Black American to receive a Ph.D. in
mathematics, as well as several other Black men with doctorates. She
received her B.S. in 1949 and her M.S. in 1950, both in mathematics.
For a while after her graduation she taught in high school; in 1955 she
became an instructor at Hampton Institute. The Black men she had
known with doctorates served as role models, and it occurred to her
that she should work for a Ph.D. degree.

In 1962 she left Hampton Institute to work for a doctoral degree
in mathematics at Syracuse University. At that time no Black people
were allowed to pursue doctoral studies in any academic discipline in
Virginia, but the state would pay tuition and travel costs of Black citizens
who went out of the state for graduate study. Jones by then had two
small sons, whom she took with her to Syracuse. There she earned her
own living and that of her children while obtaining her doctorate, which
she did in 1966.   —Patricia Kenschaft
"Black Women in Mathematics in United States,"
Amer. Math. Monthly 88 (October 1981) 598.

57   Original as he [Felix Klein] undoubtedly was to a very high
degree, and anxious that his view should prevail if possible, his actuating
impulse, in his later years, was not so much a desire for discovery as a
desire to share his thoughts with others. Intensely sympathetic, capable
of great enthusiasm about the results of others (for instance, Hilbert's
early works on the completeness of the Binary Form system), he seems
to have done his thinking by conferences and lectures, and . . . to have
accepted it as a matter of course that many of his results would have
been obtained by others before him. He could not be like Sylvester's
oyster who, in darkness and obscurity, elaborates the pearl to deck a
princess. Thus he must be judged by the influence he exerted rather
than by the new results he found. This influence was enormous, and,

among those who are wise enough to study his papers, will remain for many years to come.   —H. F. Baker

"Felix Klein," *J. of the London Math. Soc.* 1 (January 1926) 29.

58   [Letter written to Grace C. Young on the death of Felix Klein by his wife]

Dear Gracy,

Many thanks for your sympathetic letter. As I read it, the time when you were here came vividly before my mind, and I saw my husband working with you in full strength as his first female doctorate student. He returned home delighted after the examination and said: "Now she has succeeded with Mark 1!" You are right when you strive to remember him only in those good years. I bear in my heart with the greatest grief the last sad two years, when my husband could not leave his room any more. It was infinitely sad to see him fade away more and more, at the end he was entirely helpless and could no longer get out of bed. But he never complained and was great even in suffering. . . .

My husband was completely clear to the last and always went on working, or at least read proofs until it was no longer possible. . . . From all over the world I received such lovely letters full of affection and gratitude, so many tell me that he showed them the way on which their life was built. I had him for fifty years, this wonderful man; how privileged I am above most women.   —Anna Klein

I. Grattan-Guinness, "A Mathematical Union, William Henry and Grace Chisholm Young," *Annals of Science* 29 (August 1972) 170.

59   [Kronecker] was a foe not only of artificial concepts but of all artificial methods and of all artificial or purely formal tendencies in mathematics. He would have rid mathematics of the artificial numbers and of its "symbolic" methods, and the devising of new functions seemed to him a foolish waste of energy. "God created numbers and geometry," I once heard him say, "but man the functions."

—Henry Fine

"Kronecker and His Arithmetical Theory of the Algebraic Equation," *Bull. of the New York Math. Soc.* 1 (1892) 183.

60   [Edmund] Landau was a man of commanding presence with a real sense of humor, an enthusiastic lecturer, meticulously dressed in a somewhat formal fashion. He was particularly annoyed by chalk dust. In those days the blackboards of our department classrooms were of black slate, and we had rather soft chalk ... Landau would write in unusually large script, quickly filling the front blackboards. He would sometimes dart about the room and write on the sidewall blackboard— once he even climbed over a couple of chairs to get to the board on the back wall. But then, the boards must needs be erased so that the writing could go on. Landau abhorred the usual felt erasers—too much dust. So, on the first day of his 8:00 and 9:00 classes, his assistant brought in a granite-ware kettle in which were a sponge and some water. Since she adamantly refused to use the sponge on the blackboard, Landau himself ... would grasp the sponge, wring the water out on the floor, make some passes at the board, and then call on one or two students or visitors to his lecture to come up and dry off the slate with paper towels. A very ineffective method of drying! The lecture would continue. But the slate was still slightly wet, so half the chalk marks didn't show. Eventually the board dried, however, and normal conditions returned ... on the last day of classes, Landau make a graceful and humorous farewell speech in his heavily accented English. His last 'goodbye' ended with the request. 'Please preserve the sponge to remember me by!'   —Harold Bacon

> Halsey Royden, "A History of Mathematics at Stanford," in Peter Duren (ed.), *A Century of Mathematics in America, Part II,* Providence, RI: American Mathematical Society, 1989, p. 246.

61   His [Landau's] working day often began at 7 a.m. and continued, with short intervals, until midnight. He loved lecturing, more perhaps even than he realized himself; and a lecture from Landau was a very serious thing, since he expected his students to work in the spirit in which he worked himself, and would never tolerate the tiniest rough end or the slightest compromise with the truth. ...

This was all part of his passion for order in the world of mathematics. He could not stand untidiness in his chosen territory, blunders, obscurity, or vagueness, unproved assertions or half substantiated claims ... the man who did his job incompetently, who spoilt Landau's world, received no mercy: that was the unpardonable sin in Landau's eyes, to make a mathematical mess where there had been order before.

> —G. H. Hardy and H. Heilbronn
> "Edmund Landau," *J. of the London Math. Soc.* 13 (1938) 309.

62   Few of Landau's papers fail to contain some sentence of the type: 'X proved such and such a theorem in the year n, Subsequently, I established a stronger result by a shorter route'. The British reader may sometimes be taken aback by this tone, but in the present instance the tendency to squirm is not appropriate. Landau did not, to be sure, take a despairing view of his ability but neither did he overvalue his own achievements; and his appreciation of other mathematicians' work was genuine and generous. Essentially, his passion was simply for facts; and if he *had* improved on X's argument, that fact ought to be recorded: to him that was all there was to it.   —L. Mirsky

"In Memory of Edmund Landau," *Math. Sci.* 2 (January 1977) 14.

63   [E. P.] Lane was a very fine man. I had come to Chicago in 1926 to run the high hurdles in the National Intercollegiate Track and Field Meet at Soldiers Field. I played in the finals and some members of the U.S. Olympic Committee urged me to keep working for the 1928 Olympics. So I worked on the Stagg Field track until an accident set off a series of leg infections. I was very sick in Billings Hospital in the days before antibiotics and it was Lane who came to the hospital to see me and make sure that I got the best available care. The only way I was ever able to express my thanks to him was to do a similar service to some of my own students in later years. I guess that is the only way we ever thank our teachers.   —W. L. Duren, Jr.

"Graduate Student at Chicago in the Twenties," *Amer. Math. Monthly* 83 (April 1976) 245.

64   Lebesgue excelled in looking at old things with new eyes. He knew the virtue of attentive examination of an example, of an anomaly, of an exception. He was suspicious of too general theories whose formalism and verbalism repelled him. He had a geometric vision of mathematical facts and preferred synthetic insights which satisfy and nourish the mind to analytic proofs which reassure it.   —P. Montel

"Notice Nécrologique sur M. Henri Lebesgue," *Comptes Rendus* 215 (4 August 1941) 199.

65   [Solomon Lefschetz] asserted (with much truth) that "he made up his mind in a flash, and then found his reasons". Naturally he made mistakes this way, but once he was really convinced that he was wrong he could be extremely generous. This can be illustrated from the occasion when I first met him. His paper on correspondences between curves

contained inter alia a very simple proof of the Riemann inequalities for
the integrals of the first kind on a curve. About the time it was written
Severi and other Italian geometers were concerned with the question
whether a double integral of the first kind could have all its periods zero,
and I noticed that Lefschetz's method of dealing with the Riemann inequalities could answer this question at once; and I wrote a short paper
on it. When this appeared Lefschetz "made up his mind in a flash"—I
was wrong and I must withdraw the paper. A correspondence lasting
for several months took place, and during this period Lefschetz was
travelling round Europe visiting mathematicians in various countries
to whom he voiced his criticisms of my paper. Eventually we reached
a state of armed neutrality, and he extended an invitation to me to
visit Princeton. When I arrived there I was immediately instructed to
conduct a seminar on my paper ... at the end of which he stood up
and publicly retracted all his criticisms, and then ... wrote to all his
European correspondents admitting that I was right and he was wrong.

> —William Hodge
> "Solomon Lefschetz," *Bull. of the London Math. Soc.*
> 6 (March 1974) 201.

66   This method of organizing seminars on topics in which he
[Lefschetz] was interested and then continually heckling the speaker
was typical of the way in which he got things done. It was somewhat
harassing for a young man not accustomed to it, but it was kindly
meant, and often helpful. Eventually it became so famous that it earned
Lefschetz a verse in the song sung by Princeton students about members
of the Faculty:

> Here's to Lefschetz (Solomon L.)
> Who's as argumentative as hell,
> When he's at last beneath the sod,
> Then he'll start to heckle God.

> —William Hodge
> "Solomon Lefschetz," *Bull. of the London Math. Soc.*
> 6 (March 1974) 201.

67   The Franco-Prussian war broke out in 1871 and the German
[Felix] Klein had to leave France in a hurry. .... Left without his friend,
[Sophus] Lie—who was an experienced hiker—decided to take advantage of the forced interruption in their studies to make a trek through
all of France, the Alps, and Italy. But in the wartime atmosphere the

plan proved to be rather unfortunate. Because of his poor French, conspicuous height and handsome but purely Nordic appearance, Lie was immediately arrested as a German spy and imprisoned. Apparently, French patriots found Lie's manner of looking around in an abstracted way (he was then thinking through some mathematical problem) and then feverishly scribbling in a little notebook (he was making mathematical jottings—in Norwegian) extremely suspicious. He spent about a month in the prison of Fontainebleau. ... As soon as he learned of Lie's arrest, Darboux used all his contacts in order to have Lie freed. But conditions in prison were not particularly bad, and Lie spent the time pondering over some aspects of Plücker's line geometry, to which his attention had been drawn by Klein.   —I. M. Yaglom

Felix Klein and Sophus Lie, Boston: Birkhäuser, 1988, p. 24.

68   Littlewood remained active in mathematics even at an advanced age: his last paper was published in 1972, when he was 87. One of his most intricate papers, concerning Van der Pol's equations and its generalizations, was written when he was over seventy: 110 pages of hard analysis, based on his joint work with Mary Cartwright. He called the paper "The Monster" and he himself said of it: "It is very heavy going and I should never have read it had I not written it myself." His last hard paper, breaking new ground, was published in the first issue of the Advances in Applied Probability, when he was 84. In this paper he gave very precise bounds for the probability in the tail of the binomial distribution. The bounds he gave are still the best; in fact, they are so fine that their precise form is rarely needed; Littlewood himself became interested in these estimates because he conducted long "card guessing" experiments with Ann [his daughter].   —Béla Bollobás

Littlewood's Miscellany, Cambridge: Cambridge University Press, 1986, p. 15.

69   In 1972 Littlewood had two bad falls and he fell again in January 1973. He was taken to the Evelyn Nursing Home in Cambridge, but he had very little interest in life. In my desperation I suggested the problem of determining the best constant in Burkholder's weak L_1 inequality (an extension of an inequality Littlewood had worked on). To my immense relief (and amazement), Littlewood became interested in the problem. He had never heard of martingales but he was keen to learn about them so he was happy to listen to my brief explanations and was willing to read some introductory chapters! All this at the age of 89 and in bad health! It seemed that mathematics did help to revive his spirits and he could leave the nursing home a few weeks later. From then on, Littlewood kept up his interest in the weak inequality and worked hard to find suitable constructions to complement an improved upper bound. Unfortunately, we did not have much success so eventually I published the improvement only after Littlewood's death.   —Béla Bollobás

> *Littlewood's Miscellany,* Cambridge: Cambridge University Press, 1986, p. 17.

70   Littlewood, on Hardy's own estimate, is the finest mathematician he had ever known. He was the man most likely to storm and smash a really deep and formidable problem; there was no one else who could command such a combination of insight, technique and power.

> —Henry Dale
> Béla Bollobás (ed.), *Littlewood's Miscellany,* Cambridge: Cambridge University Press, 1986, p. 22.

71   Probably the most important lesson I learned from Dr. [Lee] Lorch and his late wife Grace, is that my career and success as a mathematician should be cherished and are important—but that decency is more important than success.   —Charles Costley

> Vivienne Mayes, "Lee Lorch at Fisk: a Tribute," *Amer. Math. Monthly* 83 (November 1976) 710.

72   Dr. Lorch encouraged me in the pursuit of a mathematical career at a time when it was unpopular for both Blacks and women. He was well before his time in promoting the rights of all people. He refused to see a color line or sex line that limited ability, and for this reason he has profoundly affected the development of many persons who would otherwise have carried out the low expectations of the time.

> —Etta Zuber Falconer
> Vivienne Mayes, "Lee Lorch at Fisk: a Tribute," *Amer. Math. Monthly* 83 (November 1976) 709.

73   I have never expressed to Lady Lovelace my opinion of her as a student of these matters. I always feared that it might promote an application to them which might be injurious to a person whose bodily health is not strong. I have therefore contented myself with very good, quite right, and so on. But I feel bound to tell you that the power of thinking on these matters which Lady L. has always shown from the beginning of my correspondence with her, has been something so utterly out of the common way for any beginner, man or woman, but this power must be duly considered by her friends, with reference to the question whether they should urge or check her obvious determination to try not only to reach, but to go beyond, the present bounds of knowledge. . . .

All women who have published mathematics hitherto have shown knowledge, and power of getting it, but no one, except perhaps (I speak doubtfully) Maria Agnesi, has wrestled with difficulties and shown a man's strength in getting over them. The reason is obvious: the very great tension of mind which they require is beyond the strength of a woman's physical power of application. Lady L. has unquestionably as much power as would require all the strength of a man's constitution to bear the fatigue of thought to which it will unquestionably lead her. It is very well now, when the subject has not entirely engrossed her attention; by-and-bye when, as always happens, the whole of the thoughts are continually and entirely concentrated upon them, the struggle between the mind and body will begin.   —Augustus De Morgan

Ethel Colburn Mayne, *The Life and Letters of Anne Isabella Lady Noel Byron,* New York: Charles Scribner's Sons, 1929, p. 477.

CHAPTER 14

About Mathematicians, M–Z

1   Saunders Mac Lane came close to taking a high school teaching position [in the 1930s]. The circumstances were these: with his baccalaureate degree from Yale and a Master's from Chicago, Mac Lane completed his Ph.D. work at Göttingen in 1933, one of the last Americans to go to Germany for graduate work in mathematics before World War II. Next there was a one year post at Yale, and then Mac Lane was looking for a position in the spring of 1934. Jobs were very scarce, so he interviewed for a position at Exeter, a well-known private high school of the first rank. However, an opportunity opened up for a Benjamin Peirce Instructorship at Harvard, enabling him to stay in the university system. It is interesting to contemplate what course his career might have taken if this leading American mathematician had gone to Exeter instead of to Harvard.   —Ivan Niven
"The Threadbare Thirties," in Peter Duren (ed.), *A Century of Mathematics in America, Part I,* Providence, RI: American Mathematical Society, 1988, p. 219.

2   Vivienne Malone Mayes grew up in Waco, Texas, where she described the public schools as "strictly separate and strictly unequal." Although she was "victimized educationally" by the segregation, she has also written, "In every Black school I've attended there's always been at least one Black woman teacher or professor with whom I could identify ... No difference was made between boys and girls ... Every girl expected to work. Her hope was that through education she could escape the extremely low-paying jobs designated for Black women ... Girls held the majority in my upper-level math classes at Fisk ... After Fisk, I taught at two Black colleges. In both instances, girls outnumbered boys in every class." Her experiences at graduate school were in stark contrast. In her first class, "I was the only Black and the only woman. For nine weeks thirty or forty white men ignored me completely ... It seemed to me that conversations before class on mathematics between classmates quickly terminated if it appeared that I was listening ... My mathematical isolation was complete."

Mayes could not become a teaching assistant at the University of Texas in Austin because she was Black. There was even one professor who would not let Blacks attend his classes. She could not join her advisor, Don E. Edmondson, and other classmates to discuss mathematics over coffee at Hilsberg's Cafe because she was Black ... Only after the law changed to require Hilsberg's Cafe to serve Blacks did she notice that women were rarely included in these conversations no matter what their color. After several courses friendships did begin to develop, but throughout her graduate years there was only one other woman in most of her classes.   —Patricia Kenschaft

"Black Women in Mathematics in United States," *Amer. Math. Monthly* 88 (October 1981) 596.

3   Leon [Mirsky], ever disposed to keeping of written records, also adopted this habit [of keeping a mathematical diary]. For the first three years entries were sparse, with only 21 pages covered. However, from January 1946 onwards (as a result of a New Year resolution?) there is a torrent of material. During that year Leon filled three volumes totalling nearly 600 pages. Though the pace later slackened, he left altogether 35 volumes with 6652 pages. These diaries contain isolated results he had met and which he had found pleasing or striking and also a great deal of original work much of which was later used in published papers.

—H. Burkill, C. Hooley, W. Ledermann, H. Perfect

"Obituary," *Bull. of the London Math. Soc.* 18 (1986) 196.

4   During the 1940s and early 50s Leon [Mirsky] seemed to be immutably attached to the theory of numbers. However, when A. G. Walker ... asked him to give a lecture course in linear algebra ... he immediately became fascinated by this novel subject. The result was

his textbook on linear algebra, followed by some 35 papers spread over roughly ten years. Then, in the mid 1960s, Leon's research smoothly slid into the area of combinatorics ... But his earlier loves never lost their charm for him and the breadth of his interests was one reason why he was such a stimulating colleague. Even more important, though, was his whole attitude to research. He was always asking questions, posing problems and anxious only to know the answers, unconcerned as to who supplied them. No-one adhered more steadfastly than he to his maxim that research should be a cooperative rather than a competitive activity.
—H. Burkill, C. Hooley, W. Ledermann, H. Perfect
"Obituary," *Bull. of the London Math. Soc.* 18 (1986) 197.

5   He [Gösta Mittag-Leffler] was a Swede by birth who had studied with Weierstrass and had occupied a chair in mathematics at the University of Helsingfors ... This he gave up to accept a new appointment and to start the work in mathematics in Stockholm. To this he devoted his energy and ingenuity, his wife's fortune, and his many connections at home and abroad ... There was no library at the university and no room to build one, so, when he built his home in the fashionable suburb Djursholm, he made it into a library which in its days was probably the best mathematical research library in the world.   —Einar Hille
"In Retrospect," in Robert Kallman (ed.), *Einar Hille: Classical Analysis and Functional Analysis,* Cambridge, MA: MIT Press, 1975, p. xiv.

6   I reached Djursholm in March 1927 and was hospitably received by Mittag-Leffler and his staff. I was given a small but comfortable room on an upper floor; meals were taken *en famille* with Mittag-Leffler's secretaries and assistant. ... The old man presided. For my benefit the conversation, at first at any rate, was mostly in French, which he spoke excellently, or else in German, in which he was equally fluent; but soon I acquired a tolerable working knowledge of Swedish. Mittag-Leffler was a perfect host, and he knew it. I found the atmosphere, on the whole, quite pleasant, but a domineering strain in his make-up was unmistakable. When he was back in his study and wished for the presence of his secretary, his call "Fröken där!" was heard all over the house. Perhaps by that time he found it an imposition to have to remember her name ...   —André Weil
"Mittag-Leffler as I Remember Him," *Acta Mathematica* 148 (1982) 10.

7   Möbius was the epitome of the absentminded professor. He was shy and unsociable, timid with unfamiliar people, and so absorbed in his thoughts that he was forced to work out a whole system of mnemonic rules (which did not always work) so as not to forget his keys or his inseparable umbrella and handkerchief when he set out from home for a walk or for the university. His entire life passed in one city and in one building. His study in Göttingen and two or three short excursions through Germany in his youth were his principal "adventures." A complete picture of his life can be gained from the scientific diary Möbius wrote every night and by which we can trace the evolution of his views, interests, and ideas, the only things which changed in that fully regulated life. It is paradoxical that modesty and even shyness in everyday life combined in that impressive figure with boldness, fantasy and inventiveness in science, profound thoughts, and outstanding teaching abilities ... All of Möbius's works ... are distinguished not only by innovative thinking and deep insights but also by crispness of style, clarity of narrative and excellence of structure. The mathematical talent of most mathematicians diminishes with age ... But time did not diminish Möbius's gifts. What was perhaps his most impressive discovery—that of one-sided surfaces such as the famous "Möbius strip"—was made when he was almost seventy, and all the works found among his papers after his death show the same excellence of form and profundity of thought.   —I. M. Yaglom

Felix Klein and Sophus Lie, Boston: Birkhäuser, 1988, p. 39.

8   When [the history of mathematics in the United States] is attempted, particularly for the past forty years, the historian will doubtless be impressed by the tremendous influence of one man, E. H. Moore. In the late 1890's and early 1900's, the history of mathematics in this country is largely an echo of Moore's successive enthusiasms at the University of Chicago. Directly through his own work, and indirectly through that of the men he trained, Moore put new life into the theory of groups, the foundations of geometry and of mathematics in general, finite algebra, and certain branches of analysis as they were cultivated in America. Moore's interests frequently changed, and with each change, mathematics in this country advanced. His policy (as he related shortly before his death) in those early years of his great career, was to start some thoroughly competent man well off in a particular field, and then,

himself, get out of it. All his work, however, had one constant direction: he strove unceasingly toward the utmost abstractness and generality obtainable. It is to Moore's influence that much of the abstract development of the first two decades of this century in American algebra can be traced. Not the least of Moore's contributions to algebra was the encouragement he gave the University of Chicago's second Ph.D. in mathematics, L. E. Dickson, who took his degree at the age of 22 in 1896. After that, it was no longer necessary for young Americans to go abroad for their training in algebra, and very few have.   —E. T. Bell
"Fifty Years of Algebra in America, 1888–1938," *Semicentennial Addresses of the American Mathematical Society, Vol. II,* New York: American Mathematical Society, 1938, p. 3.

9   In the lecture room, Professor [E. H.] Moore's methods defied most established rules of pedagogy. Such rules, indeed, meant nothing to him in the conduct of his advanced courses. He was absorbed in the mathematics under discussion to the exclusion of everything else, and neither clock times nor meal times brought the discussion to a close. His discourse ended when some instinct told him that his topic for the day was exhausted. Frequently he came to his class with ideas imperfectly developed, and he and his students studied through successfully or failed together in the study of some question in which he was at the moment interested . . . It is easy to understand under these circumstances, however, that poor students often shunned his courses, and that good students whose principal interests were in other fields sometimes could not afford the time to take them. But it was a proud moment when one who was ambitious and interested found himself in the relatively small group of those who could stand the pace. It is no wonder that among the ablest mathematicians of our country at the present time those who drew their chief inspiration from Professor Moore are numerous.
—G. A. Bliss
"Eliakim Hastings Moore," *Bull. of the Amer. Math. Soc.* 39 (November 1933) 833.

10   I worked for the doctorate in mathematics under Professor R. L. Moore of the University of Texas. In three and a half years of graduate work, under his direction, I believe that I heard him lecture (in a style that a conventional professor would recognize as lecturing) for about two hours at most, and it may well have been less. All of his graduate courses worked in the same way: he would present postulates, definitions, and propositions; and the student's job was to find out which of the propositions were true, and present proofs or counter-examples. The theorems were not mere exercises; they were the substance of the sort of set-theoretic topology that Moore was teaching. Six months might elapse, between the time a problem was proposed and the time it was solved. At first, a very large number of the students' proofs were wrong. When a student had gone astray, Moore did not correct him; he would merely say that he didn't understand; and it took us quite a while to realize that anything that he "didn't understand" was surely wrong.

Under Moore's regime, all use of the literature is forbidden. Most of the time, therefore, a student of Moore doesn't even know whether the problems that he is working on are research problems. Eventually, they turn out to be, and the result is a thesis. Thus, at the time when I wrote my first research paper, I had never read one.   —Edwin E. Moise
"Activity and Motivation in Mathematics," *Amer. Math. Monthly* 72 (April 1965) 408.

II   So on the appropriate morning I went to the gymnasium to register ... There was a mass of people, but there were very few people at the mathematics table so I was sent over there. The man who was sitting at the table was an old white-haired gentleman. He and I discussed all kinds of things for a long time. I now know the kinds of things that he must have asked me. There would have been lots of sentences with *if* and *then*. I used *if* and *then* correctly. I also used *and* and *or* correctly from a mathematician's standpoint.

At the end of our conversation he signed me up for the courses that I had written on my slip of paper. When I went to my math class the next day, I found that the professor was R. L. Moore—the same man who had talked to me at the registration table.   —Mary Ellen Rudin
Donald J. Albers and Constance Reid, "An Interview with Mary Ellen Rudin," *Coll. Math. J.* 19 (March 1988) 120.

I2   Eyewitnesses say that when he [R. L. Moore] was about sixty-seven or sixty-eight years old there was a student who seemed to be taking up too much time bragging about his physical feats. Professor Moore offered to show this young man what he could do; he did some impressive one arm push-ups. He did them with his feet up in a chair so that his head was angled down toward the floor; he did seven of them and jumped back up onto his feet without losing wind. The student got the message. Professor Moore liked to box. The story persists that the first person he looked up when he went to Princeton as the first native American mathematician to tour on the American Mathematical Society Visiting Lectureship was the boxing coach, who was his sparring partner during the early days of his teaching career as an instructor at Princeton. Indeed it has been said that one of the secrets of his success as a teacher is that he is not afraid of a fight, either a physical one or a scholarly one. More to the point perhaps, he seems to inspire others with a feeling of their own mental strength, something quite different from being led to think that the professor is wonderful.

—Lucille S. Whyburn
"Student Oriented Teaching—The Moore Method,"
Amer. Math. Monthly 77 (April 1970) 355.

13 When her children were young, people often asked her [Cathleen Morawetz] whether she didn't worry about them when she was at work. Her reply was, "No, I'm much more likely to worry about a theorem when I'm with my children."

—G. B. Kolata
"Cathleen Morawetz: The Mathematics of Waves,"
Science 206 (12 October 1979) 207.

14 As a boy and a young man [Frank] Morley had shown exceptional promise as a chessplayer; throughout his life he could grasp the possibilities of a position at chess or of a hand at cards with astonishing ease and certainty. He had something of the same power in discussing a geometrical configuration, for he proved, not once but many times, that he could penetrate more deeply into its inner significance than the rest of us.

—Herbert W. Richmond
"Prof. Frank Morley," *Nature* 140 (20 November 1937) 880.

15 I suppose that a young prospective knight approaching King Arthur's table for the first time must have felt as I did when I first walked into Fuld Hall [at the Institute for Advanced Study] and took possession of my small office on the third floor. The professors of Mathematics at that time were Oswald Veblen, Hermann Weyl, John von Neumann, Carl Ludwig Seigel, Marston Morse and James W. Alexander. On the ground floor you passed Einstein's office and you were welcomed upon arrival by J. Robert Oppenheimer. The permanent members were Kurt Gödel, Deane Montgomery, and Atle Selberg. The officer in charge of the temporary members that year was Marston Morse and it was in that capacity that I first met him. His office was also on the third floor and I had seen him bounding up the stairs several times before my official "reporting to work", so to speak, occurred. . . .

I approached this interview with some nervousness, because in the few weeks which I had spent at Princeton before it took place, the whole mysterious world of pure mathematics had burst upon me and all I wanted to do was explore it. In no way did I want to write the book [on network theory, which I thought was part of the general plan of my appointment].

Well, after five minutes with Marston all my uneasiness had vanished. First of all I found that I really did not have to say very much! I think it is a fair statement that in all conversations with Marston, one only had to do twenty percent of the talking. His energy was such that it just naturally took over. He immediately dismissed my fears of having to write a book. It was a matter of course to him that at the Institute a young man should only do what he wanted to do; that this was the place where a young man should find himself, and the last place in the world for performing a chore. And once this technical part of our interview was over he immediately, again characteristically I think, started to speak about the subject that absorbed his interest at the time. . . . I remember leaving this interview with a light heart, newly liberated and buoyed by the energy and optimism I had just encountered. I was also elated by the directness of Marston's manner. There was not the slightest condescension in it. Although he dominated—I expect—all encounters, he treated everyone as an equal, with complete honesty, and in personal matters he showed great kindness and generosity.

—Raoul Bott
"Marston Morse and His Mathematical Works," *Bull. of the Amer. Math. Soc. (New series)* 3 (November 1980) 908.

16   Marston loved music and played the piano beautifully and effortlessly. He was devoted to Bach and very knowledgeable about all aspects of music, and so music was our first and quite natural bond. But beyond that and quite apart from certain affinities of taste, I think I immediately sensed and revered his spiritual nature. Marston was a deeply religious man, yet I never heard him "preach." One was conscious of this aspect of his life only indirectly and quite marvelously.

His daughter-in-law, Terry Morse, put it better than I ever could. "His personality had a light and a force which was very spiritual and mysterious. I think it was because he welcomed the ultimate mystery of life, embraced it, and took great joy in it, that we always came away from being with him feeling a heightened sense of awareness of the beauty and the possibilities in life," she wrote to Louise Morse after his death.

—Raoul Bott
"Marston Morse and His Mathematical Works," *Bull. of the Amer. Math. Soc.* (*New series*) 3 (November 1980) 909.

17   The major problem during this time [WW II] was accommodation. . . . It was not easy to find accommodation with two young children and was made no easier by having to compete with refugees from the bombing of London. . . . Hanna [Neumann] found a brilliant solution. She rented a caravan and got permission from a market gardener to park it on his farm. She also, as was necessary, had it declared "approved rooms" by the Oxford Delegacy of Lodgings.

It was then that the thesis was largely written; in a caravan by candlelight. The typing was done on a card-table by a haystack when the weather permitted. The thesis was submitted in mid-1943.

—M. F. Newman and G. E. Wall
"Hanna Neumann," *J. of the Australian Math. Soc.* 17 (February 1974) 8.

18   [The rise of the Nazi terror had] a direct effect on her [Hanna Neumann's] studies. Hanna had by now set her sights directly on a doctorate. However in her fourth year she was warned that in the oral examination [a] mathematician would personally examine her on "political knowledge" which was by now compulsory. She was advised to switch quickly to the Staatsexamen for which, though it had a similar requirement, the oral might be arranged with a different examiner. She could then go on and do a doctorate at another university.

. . . the Staatsexamen had requirements which placed more emphasis on breadth than those for the doctorate. Hanna chose to be examined in Mathematics, Physics and Philosophy. This involved an oral examination in all three subjects and extended essays in Mathematics and Philosophy. The switch also involved some last minute changes in her course for the eighth semester to meet the requirements in Philosophy. Fortunately she was able to find a Philosophy lecturer who

was sympathetic to her difficulties. He suggested the essay topic: The epistemological basis of number in Plato's later dialogues. . . . In order to be able to compare the translations of critical passages she acquired a rudimentary knowledge of Greek in a couple of months of private study. The mathematical essay was: The construction of relative cyclic fields. The summer semester of 1936 was spent on leave from courses preparing for the orals in August. Preparation was seriously disrupted by an attack of scarlet fever. Nevertheless she obtained distinctions in both Mathematics and Physics and good in Philosophy for an over-all award with distinction.   —M.F. Newman and G.E. Wall
"Hanna Neumann," *J. of the Australian Math. Soc.* 17 (February 1974) 5.

19   When she [Mary Frances Winston Newson] was honored at the Women's Centennial Congress in New York City in 1940, she was not present. It fell on the first day of classes for a new term at Eureka, and she felt she had to teach her classes. So she replied to the invitation, "Thank you, but I can't make it," and she didn't even mention it to her friends or colleagues. However, the whole community was made aware of the celebrity among them when the local newspaper announced with a bold headline, GETS NATIONAL HONOR AND TELLS NOBODY. [Her daughter Caroline Newson] Beshers recounted, "Mama said, 'Well, you know, I didn't have very many intimate friends there, and there wasn't anybody I really thought cared.' And that was absolutely typical of Mama. Anybody else would have mentioned it, I'm sure. We realize now how lonely she was most of the time."
                                           —Betsey S. Whitman
"Mary Frances Winston Newson: The First American Woman to Receive a Ph. D. in Mathematics from a European University," *Math. Teacher* 76 (November 1983) 577.

20   Within the past few days a distinguished mathematician, Professor Emmy Noether, formerly connected with the University of Göttingen and for the past two years at Bryn Mawr College, died in her fifty-third year. In the judgment of the most competent living mathematicians, Fraulein Noether was the most significant creative mathematical genius thus far produced since the higher education of women began. In the realm of algebra, in which the most gifted mathematicians have been busy for centuries, she discovered methods which have proved of

enormous importance in the development of the present-day younger
generation of mathematicians.   —Albert Einstein
"Letter to the Editor," *New York Times,* May 5, 1935.

21   Emmy Noether belonged to the small group of pioneering women
who were at that time rejecting the traditional decorous role, assigned
to their peers in the middle and upper classes, to knock at the doors
of academia.   When she attended the University of Erlangen there
were only three other women regularly enrolled: a Russian studying
philosophy, and two other German girls, one in medicine, and the other
in languages. What inspired Emmy Noether in 1900 to diverge from
the norm? Why did she decide that she did not want either to stay
home or to teach French and English to other well-brought-up young
ladies? Was it the cumulative effect of years of having been exposed to
mathematical talk by the Erlangen mathematicians who frequented the
Noether home? Was it the example of her younger brother Fritz, now
beginning his university studies, and undoubtedly full of enthusiasm for
mathematics which he probably discussed at home with his father? Was
it a sudden rebellion against the prescribed course, a desire to be herself,
to follow her own inclination? ... We shall probably never know and
can only speculate. What matters is that she did take the step, she did
persist, despite all the odds against women, and did go on to become
one of the most distinguished algebraists of her century.
                                              —E. P. and G. E. Noether
                         "Emmy Noether in Erlangen and Göttingen," in
                         Bhama Srinivasan and Judith Sally (eds.), *Emmy
                         Noether in Bryn Mawr,* New York: Springer-Verlag,
                         1983, p. 135.

22   She [Emmy Noether] had no didactical gifts, and the great
pains she took to explain her remarks by quickly spoken interjections
even before she had finished speaking were more likely to have the
opposite effect. And still how exceptionally great was the impact of
her talks, everything notwithstanding! The small, faithful audience,
mostly consisting of a few advanced students and often just as many
lecturers and foreign guests, had to exert themselves to the utmost to
keep up. When that was done, however, one had learned far more
than from the most excellent lecture. Completed theories were almost
never presented, but usually those that were still in the making. Each
of her lecture series was a paper. And nobody was happier than she

herself when such a paper was completed by her students. Completely unegotistical and free of vanity, she never claimed anything for herself, but promoted the works of her students above all. . . . She was a faithful friend to us and at the same time a strict and unprejudiced judge.

—B. L. van der Waerden
"Obituary of Emmy Noether" in James W. Brewer and Martha K. Smith (eds.), *Emmy Noether, A Tribute to Her Life and Work,* New York: Marcel Dekker, Inc., 1981, p. 98.

23   [Benjamin Pierce] inspired rather than taught. . . . I always had the feeling that his attitude toward his loved science was that of a devoted worshipper, rather than of a clear expounder. Although we could rarely follow him, we certainly sat up and took notice.

I can see him now at the blackboard, chalk in one hand and rubber in the other, writing rapidly and erasing recklessly, pausing every few minutes to face the class and comment earnestly, perhaps on the results of an elaborate calculation, perhaps on the greatness of the Creator, perhaps on the beauty and grandeur of Mathematics, always with a capital M. To him mathematics was not the handmaid of philosophy. It was not a humanly devised instrument of investigation, it was Philosophy itself, the divine revealer of TRUTH.   —W. E. Byerly
"Benjamin Peirce, Reminiscences," *Amer. Math. Monthly* 32 (January 1925) 5.

24   Professor [James] Pierpont was a large man with full beard and fairly long hair—both almost white—at a time when beards and long hair were rarely seen. He seldom wore a hat; always carried a book bag; and frequently wore a cape as an outergarment. He was fond of going to the movies in the afternoon—apparently regardless of what kind of picture was being shown—and was an eye-catching sight as he walked at a quick pace across the New Haven Green with hair flying and book bag over his shoulder. . . . Professor Pierpont was normally pleasant and good-natured but sometimes he became very agitated. I remember once when I inadvertently aroused his ire. He had asked a question for which I volunteered an answer.

Immediately he demanded the basis for my statement, and when I replied "Granville's Calculus," the storm broke. I had not been warned that W. A. Granville . . . had refused to take Professor Pierpont's advice when he wrote what became one of the most popular and best selling of the early calculus textbooks, but one that did not exhibit much rigor.

—Harold L. Dorwart
"Mathematics and Yale in the Nineteen Twenties," in Peter Duren (ed.), *A Century of Mathematics in America, Part II,* Providence, RI: American Mathematical Society, 1989, p. 91.

25 Pierpont was one of the most widely read men I have ever met. He could frequently be seen on the campus with his old-fashioned canvas book-bag over the shoulder, and during his close to forty years at Yale he carried a considerable part of the library in his bag. For many years he held the distinction of being the greatest borrower of books at the university library. His interest was in no way limited to mathematics. On the contrary his interests did not seem to have any limits at all. He devoured books on science, history, languages, geography, and travel with the same interest as novels and biographies.

Perhaps it might be worth while to recall a couple of his personal attitudes. He seemed to have equal mastery over both hands. He could write with them both and it always used to impress the undergraduates when he drew illustrations on the board using both arms simultaneously and independently.

He could read and write upside down with great facility and I still remember vividly my surprise at the first conference with him across the table where he used this method in explaining his formulas.

—Øystein Øre
"James Pierpont—In Memoriam," *Bull. of the Amer. Math. Soc.* 45 (June 1939) 482.

26 The record of [Poincaré's] life shows that he was not one of those who sit by the roadside waiting for inspiration. He was always at work, ever acquiring fresh knowledge by assimilating the work of others, and constantly giving verbal expression to the form in which the acquired knowledge presented itself to his mind and the relation in which it stood to the things that he had known before . . . All this knowledge and much besides he could bring to bear upon any matter to which it could be applied.

But there was another requisite—the indefinable thing that we call genius. His right is recognized now, and it is not likely that future

generations will revise the judgment, to rank among the greatest mathematicians of all time.   —A. E. H. Love
                    "Jules Henri Poincaré," *Proc. of the London Math. Soc.*
                    11 (1913) xlviii.

27   George Pólya is not only a distinguished gentleman but a most
kind and gentle man: His ebullient enthusiasm, the twinkle in his eye,
his tremendous curiosity, his generosity with his time, his spry energetic
walk, his warm genuine friendliness, his welcoming visitors into his
home and showing them his pictures of great mathematicians he has
known—these are all components of his happy personality.

As a mathematician, his depth, speed, brilliance, versatility, power,
and universality are all inspiring. Would that there were a way of
teaching and learning these traits!   —Frank Harary
                    "Homage to George Pólya," *J. of Graph Theory* 1
                    (Winter 1977) 289.

28   Pólya has become the Marx and Lenin of mathematical problem
solving; a few words of obeisance need to be offered in his name before
an author can get down to the topic at hand.   —Jeremy Kilpatrick
                    "George Pólya's Influence on Mathematics Educa-
                    tion," *Math. Mag.* 60 (December 1987) 299.

29   The driving force in his [George Pólya's] research was the search
for beauty and the joy of discovery.   —M. M. Schiffer
                    "George Pólya (1887–1985)," *Math. Mag.* 60 (Decem-
                    ber 1987) 268.

30   Dear Sir
I beg to introduce myself to you as a clerk in the Accounts Department of the Port Trust Office at Madras on a salary of only [20 pounds]
per annum. I am now about 23 years of age. I have had no university
education, but I have undergone the ordinary school course. After
leaving school I have been employing the spare time at my disposal
to work at Mathematics. I have not trodden through the conventional
regular course which is followed in a university course, but I am striking
out a new path for myself. I have made a special investigation of
divergent series in general and the results I get are termed by the local
mathematicians as 'startling'. . . .

Very recently I came across a tract published by you styled *Orders of
Infinity* in page 36 of which I find a statement that no definite expression
has been as yet found for the no of prime nos [sic] less than any given

number. I have found an expression which very nearly approximates to the real result, the error being negligible. I would request you to go through the enclosed papers. Being poor, if you are convinced that there is anything of value I would like to have my theorems published. I have not given the actual investigations nor the expressions that I get but I have indicated to the lines on which I proceed. Being inexperienced I would very highly value any advice you give me. Requesting to be excused for the trouble I give you. —Srinivasa Ramanujan

> G. H. Hardy, "Srinivasa Ramanujan," *Proc. of the London Math. Soc. (ser. 2)* 19 (1921) xlii.

31   The entire œuvre of Rényi is permeated with his love of mathematics. Throughout his life he was devoted to mathematics as a lover is to his beloved. But what truly characterizes Rényi and makes him unique among outstanding mathematicians is not this unconditional love of mathematics, which is common to all true mathematicians. What distinguishes Rényi as a mathematician was that he loved people with the same fervour with which he loved mathematics so that he wanted to make mathematics a gift to them, a source of pleasure and joy.

> —Pál Révész
> Alfréd Rényi, *A Diary on Information Theory,* New York: John Wiley, 1984, p. viii.

32   It was announced that Marcel Riesz would give a series of four lectures. . . . The day of the first lecture was warm, and the good-sized lecture room was full of faculty and students. Gábor Szegö introduced Riesz, who promptly took off his jacket and proceeded to lecture in his shirtsleeves and suspenders. A bowl of water and sponge had been provided. After filling up the blackboard, Riesz motioned imperiously to Szegö, who jumped up and washed off the blackboard while Riesz stood by and watched! Now Szegö was very distinguished and autocratic, wore elegant tailor-made suits, and was always regarded with awe by the students and most of the faculty. To see him in the role of a young European assistant to Riesz was startling! . . . Sitting directly behind me was George Pólya, who had brought Felix Bloch to hear a distinguished fellow Hungarian. Pólya was somewhat embarrassed by the performance and muttered apologies *sotto voce.*   —Halsey Royden

> "A History of Mathematics at Stanford," in Peter Duren (ed.), *A Century of Mathematics in America, Part II,* Providence, RI: American Mathematical Society, 1989, p. 256.

33   One of her [Julia Robinson's] first actions as president was to call me to express her concern over whether our respective organizations were doing all that they could to help mathematically talented young people from minority groups to achieve their potential. ...

No one working with Julia could fail to be impressed by the depth of her compassion, and by the extent of her dedication to the goal of removing barriers that limit the full development of the mathematical talents of young members of minority groups.   —Ivan Niven

"Julia Bowman Robinson," *Notices of the Amer. Math. Soc.* 32 (November 1985) 741.

34   I'm a mathematician because [R. L.] Moore caught me and demanded that I become a mathematician. He schooled me and pushed me at just the right rate. He always looked for people who had not been influenced by other mathematical experiences, and he caught me before I had been subjected to influence of any kind. I was pure, unadulterated. He almost never got anybody like that. ... I was always conscious of being maneuvered by him. I hated being maneuvered. But part of his technique of teaching was to build your ability to withstand pressure from outside—pressure to give up mathematical research, pressure to change mathematical fields, pressure to achieve non-mathematical goals. So he maneuvered you in order to build your ego. He built your confidence that you could do anything. No matter what mathematical problem you were faced with, you could do it. I have that total confidence to this day. ... I'm a problem solver, primarily a counterexample discoverer. Part of that is a Moore thing, too. That is, he didn't always give us correct theorems, at least half of his statements were false. So we had to think about them as a research mathematician might. I still have this feeling that if a problem can be stated in a simple form that I can really understand, then I should be able to solve it even if doing so involves building some complicated structure.   —Mary Ellen Rudin

Donald J. Albers and Constance Reid, "An Interview With Mary Ellen Rudin," *Coll. Math. J.* 19 (March 1988) 121.

35   The University of Rochester hadn't known I was coming with [my husband] Walter, but they immediately gave me a calculus class to teach. So I taught. I had a private office. I didn't really have a position, but—oh well, I was a temporary part-time something. And that's the kind of job I have had almost all my life until 1971, when I became a full professor.

I have had non-jobs wherever we happened to be. I loved my non-jobs. I always had all the goodies that go with being a mathematician. I had graduate students, I had seminars, I had colleagues who loved me. I never had committees. I never had a trigonometry class. I was always just asked, "Is there something you'd like to teach this semester?" And I would say, "I think I'll teach a graduate course in—" or maybe, "I think I'll take this semester off." I often had grant money. It didn't make that much difference in my life though, since Walter always had a good job. But I was a mathematician, and I always thought of myself as a mathematician.   —Mary Ellen Rudin

> Donald J. Albers and Constance Reid, "An Interview with Mary Ellen Rudin," *Coll. Math. J.* 19 (March 1988) 130.

36   In a manner that only a few mathematicians are capable of, you [Isaac Schur] practice the great art of Abel which consists in formulating the problems correctly, recasting them conveniently, separating them skillfully and then overcoming them individually.   —Max Planck

> W. Ledermann, "Isaac Schur and His School in Berlin," *Bull. of the London Math. Soc.* 15 (January 1983) 102.

37   Charlotte Scott received a scholarship to Girton in 1876 strictly on the basis of home tutoring. The college was growing; there were eleven students in her entering class. It was growing in more than size, and when she took the honors exam in 1880, she placed eighth in the entire university. And in mathematics! Because she was female, she could not be present at the conferring ceremony, nor could her name be officially mentioned. But when the name of the man who was credited with eighth was read, the students (all male) screamed "Scott of Girton" so loudly that his name could not be heard.   —Patricia Kenschaft

> "Why Did Charlotte Scott Succeed?" *Assoc. for Women in Math. Newsletter* 17 (March-April 1987) 9.

38   Behind Serge the geometer and the expositor, there remained always Serge the teacher and friend. An interesting figure he was in the lecture room. Of medium height and frail, half seated on the end of the table, gesticulating rapidly with his left hand, while his right whirled his watchchain about with astonishing angular velocity, his whole being was thrown into the task of driving home the essentials of what he had in mind. The subject matter of his course was new every year. There

was no limit to the amount of care and patience which he would bestow on one of his pupils. To one who apologized for taking so much of his valuable time with trivial difficulties, he wrote: "Surtout, il ne faut jamais hésiter à me consulter quand vous trouverez une difficulté. Il n'y a que les ignorantes et les paresseux qui n'ont jamais de difficultés." [Never hesitate to consult me when you are having difficulties. It is only the ignorant and the lazy who never have difficulties.] —J. L. Coolidge
> "Corrado Serge," *Bull. of the Amer. Math. Soc.* 33 (May-June 1927) 357.

39   [J.-P.] Serre is a prime example of what I call a "smart mathematician"—as opposed to a "dumb one." What he knows is so crystal clear in his mind that he can give us lesser mortals the feeling that it is indeed all child's play. He also had, and still has, the infuriating habit of never seeming to work. In public one sees him playing pingpong, chess, or reading the paper—never in the sort of mathematical fog so many of us inhabit most of the time ... Mrs. Serre comments that from her view "Serre works all the time." And indeed he claims that all his true work is done in his sleep!   —Raoul Bott
> "The Topological Constraints on Analysis," in Peter Duren (ed.), *A Century of Mathematics in America, Part II,* Providence, RI: American Mathematical Society, 1989, p. 532.

40   One of my fondest memories from the M.I.T. years is running into Allen [Shields] in the library at ungodly hours of the night. We shared reverential feelings for "classical" mathematics and had acquired the habit of browsing in sources like *Fundamenta Mathematica* and *Crelle's Journal* ... I'll never forget that atmosphere—we were the only living souls around; it seemed truly amazing that we had access to the departed, to Banach and Poincaré, to the Urysohn metrization theorem as seen through the eyes of *Urysohn,* and rather clearer than in our topology course.   —Harold S. Shapiro
> "Allen Lowell Shields—Some Reminiscences," *Math. Intell.* 12 (Spring 1990) 9.

41   On rare occasions [C.L. Siegel] made remarks of a general nature which expressed his attitude towards mathematics. The mathematical

universe, he said, is inhabited not only by important species but also by interesting individuals.
—Wilhelm Magnus
Gilbert Baumslag and Bruce Chandler (eds.), *Wilhelm Magnus Collected Papers,* New York: Springer-Verlag, 1984, p. 626.

42   Do you know what it is to be possessed by a problem, to have within yourself some urge that keeps you at it every waking moment, that makes you alert to every sign pointing the way to its solution; to be gripped by a piece of work so that you cannot let it alone, and to go on with deep joy to its accomplishment?

Dr. Smith has been so possessed these many years in his search for truth in the field of the history of mathematics and the history of the teaching of mathematics.

This search has led him to the ends of the earth whence he has returned with rich additions to knowledge in his chosen field.
—Lao G. Simons
"Dinner in Honor of Professor David Eugene Smith," *Math. Teacher* 19 (May 1926) 261.

43   I know I felt a certain amount of relief when, the summer after my first year in graduate school I met a woman mathematician for the first time. There was living evidence that what I wanted to do was not impossible.
—Martha K. Smith
John Ernest, "Mathematics and Sex," *Amer. Math. Monthly* 83 (October 1976) 605.

44   Hugo Dynoizy Steinhaus was born in 1887 in Jaslo, Poland, and trained in mathematics at Göttingen University, where he received his doctorate. At present he is professor emeritus at the University of Wroclaw (Breslau) and one of Poland's most distinguished mathematicians. He has published some 150 papers on pure and applied mathematics, edited mathematical journals, and received many mathematical awards. His interest in recreational mathematics is lifelong and unbounded. In the preface to the first edition of *Mathematical Snapshots,* he stated that the book's gimmicks and haphazard arrangements were designed to appeal "to the scientist in the child and the child in the scientist". "Perhaps", he concluded, "I have succeeded only in amusing myself."
—Martin Gardner
Hugo Steinhaus, *One Hundred Problems in Elementary Mathematics,* New York: Basic Books, 1964, p. 6.

45   Together with a splendid mathematical talent Szegö combines wide cultural interests and exceptional personal charm, which is difficult to forget after having seen him once even for a short time. A very important point . . . is his helpful attitude toward his fellow mathematicians. He is a rarely-encountered type of great talent who is not self-centered, but is much and effectively interested in the work of other mathematicians. Szegö is always ready to collaborate or to give valuable advice.   —J. D. Tamarkin

"Gábor Szegö: A Short Biography," in Richard Askey (ed.), *Gábor Szegö: Collected Papers, Vol I (1915–1927)*, Boston: Birkhäuser, 1982, p. 2.

46   The first time I met eminent proof theorist Gaisi Takeuti I asked him what set theory was really about. "We are trying to get exact description of thoughts of infinite mind," he said. And then he laughed, as if filled with happiness by this impossible task.   —Rudy Rucker

Infinity and the Mind, Boston: Birkhäuser, 1982, p. ix.

47   [Alfred Tarski] lectured frequently in Berkeley's Dwinelle Hall, many of whose rooms had small podiums; he always seemed to have an uncertain relationship with material objects and among them were these podiums which he'd constantly be backing into or almost backing off of, and one was always afraid of what would happen. But even though he'd teeter there, he never did fall off. And often, because of the forcefulness with which he wrote on the board, the chalk would explode in his hand. And then there was the business about the cigarettes. Since he was an inveterate chain smoker, he smoked while lecturing and there was always the cigarette and the chalk—and it looked like he was going to smoke the chalk and write with the cigarette! But somehow he always managed to put each one in the right place.   —Solomon Feferman

"Commemorative Meeting for Alfred Tarski," in Peter Duren (ed.), *A Century of Mathematics in America, Part III*, Providence, RI: American Mathematical Society, 1989, p. 400.

48   [Alfred] Tarski was a very inspiring teacher. He had a way of setting results into a framework so that they all fit nicely together, and he was always full of problems—he just bubbled over with problems. There are teachers whose lectures are so well organized that they convey the impression that mathematics is absolutely finished. Tarski's lectures were equally well organized; but because of the problems, you knew that there were still things that even you could do which would make for progress.   —Julia Robinson

Constance Reid, "The Autobiography of Julia Robinson," *Coll. Math. J.* 17 (January 1986) 15.

49   For me you were always, up to the end, youth personified. Not because you celebrated your fiftieth birthday by swimming across the Danube or things like that, but because your belief in mathematics never faltered no matter how hard life was for you. Although your love of mathematics went much deeper than loving one's own results, an important role in sustaining your interest was undoubtedly played by the many innovations which you presented to mathematics throughout your life.   —Gábor Halász

"Letter to Professor Paul Turán," in Paul Erdős (ed.), *Studies in Pure Mathematics, to the Memory of Paul Turán*, Boston: Birkhäuser Verlag, 1983, p. 13.

50   It is rare to meet an authentic genius. Those of us privileged to inhabit the world of scholarship are familiar with the intellectual stimulation furnished by talented colleagues. We can admire the ideas they share with us and are usually able to understand their source; we may even often believe that we ourselves could have created such concepts and originated such thoughts. However, the experience of sharing the intellectual life of a genius is entirely different; one realizes that one is in the presence of an intelligence, a sensitivity of such profundity and originality that one is filled with wonder and excitement.

Alan Turing was such a genius, and those, like myself, who had the astonishing and unexpected opportunity, created by the strange exigencies of the Second World War, to be able to count Turing as colleague and friend will never forget that experience, nor can we ever lose its immense benefit to us.   —Peter Hilton

"Reminiscences of Bletchley Park, 1942–1945," in Peter Duren (ed.), *A Century of Mathematics in America, Part I*, Providence, RI: American Mathematical Society, 1988, p. 295.

51   One day the amateur [Stan] Ulam went one up on the Warsaw mathematicians, who cultivated the equally new field of algebraic topology. While chatting at the Scottish Café with Borsuk, an outstanding Warsaw topologist, he saw in a flash the truth of what is now called the Borsuk–Ulam theorem. Borsuk had to commandeer all his technical resources to prove it. News of the result quickly swept across the ocean, and Ulam became an instant topologist. Stan took to café-mathematics like a fish to water . . .

In the casual ambiance of the Scottish Café, Stan blossomed into one of the most promising mathematicians of his generation. He also began to display the contradictory traits in behavior that after his operation were to become dominant: deep intuition and impatience with detail, playful inventiveness and dislike of prolonged work. He began to view mathematics as a game, one that a well-bred gentleman should not take too seriously. His insights have opened whole new areas of mathematics, all of them still actively cultivated today, but he himself could not bear to give his discoveries more than a passing interest and at times he would make merciless fun of those who did take them too seriously.

—Gian-Carlo Rota
"The Lost Cafe," in Necia Grant Cooper (ed.), *From Cardinals to Chaos,* Cambridge: Cambridge University Press, 1988, p. 24.

52   I have no doubt that when Van Vleck saw this promising field [linear homogeneous difference equations] in which he had begun to work taken up so quickly by others, there was no tinge of regret on his part, for he would know that there were many other beautiful fields to be explored, and would feel that it was relatively unimportant from the larger point of view what the formal assignment of credit might be, so long as the subject itself was developed. It was enough for him that all should work together earnestly and sincerely for the increase of mathematical knowledge.   —George Birkhoff
"Edward Burr Van Vleck—in Memoriam," *Bull. of the Amer. Math. Soc.* 50 (January 1944) 39.

53   When I first went to the Institute, he [John von Neumann] greeted me, and we were talking, and he invited me to come around and tell him about my thesis. Well, of course, I thought that was just his way of making a new young visitor feel at home, and I had no intention of telling him about my thesis. He was a big, busy, important man. But then a couple of months later, I saw him at tea and he said, "When are you coming around to tell me about your thesis? Go in and make an appointment with my secretary." So I did, and later I went in and started telling him about my thesis. He listened for about ten minutes and asked me a couple of questions, and then he stated telling *me* about *my* thesis. What you have really done is this, and probably this is true, and you could have done it in a somewhat simpler way, and so on. He was a really remarkable man. He listened to me talk about this rather obscure subject and in ten minutes he knew more about it then I did. He was extremely quick. I think he may have wasted a certain amount of time, by the way, because he was so willing to listen to second- or third-rate people and think about their problems.   —David Blackwell

Morris H. DeGroot, "A Conversation with David Blackwell," *Statistical Science* 1 (February 1986) 41.

54   John [von Neumann], with whom I had many conversations, could not separate mathematics from life; he saw mathematics wherever he looked. His feel for nature inspired him to be a better mathematician and his mathematics inspired him to better understand nature.

—C. V. Newsom
"The Image of the Mathematician," *Amer. Math. Monthly* 79 (October 1972) 879.

55   He [John von Neumann] is the only student of mine I was ever intimidated by. He was so quick. There was a seminar for advanced students in Zurich that I was teaching and von Neumann was in the class. I came to a certain theorem and I said it is not proved and it might be difficult. Von Neumann didn't say anything but after five minutes he raised his hand. When I called on him he went to the board and proceeded to write down the proof. After that, I was afraid of von Neumann.   —George Pólya

G. L. Alexanderson (ed.), *The Pólya Picture Album*, Boston: Birkhäuser, 1987, p. 154.

56   In his [von Neumann's] constant search for applicability and in his general mathematical instinct for all exact sciences, he brought to mind Euler, Poincaré, or in more recent times, perhaps Hermann Weyl. One should remember that the diversity and complexity of contemporary problems surpass enormously the situation confronting the first two named. In one of his last articles, Johnny deplored the fact that it does not seem possible nowadays for any one brain to have more than a passing knowledge of more than one-third of the field of pure mathematics.   —S. Ulam

"John von Neumann, 1903–1957," *Bull. of the Amer. Math. Soc.* 64 (May 1958, Part II) 8.

57   The accuracy of his [von Neumann's] logic was, perhaps, the most decisive character of his mind. One had the impression of a perfect instrument whose gears were machined to mesh accurately to a thousandth of an inch. "If one listens to von Neumann, one understands how the human mind should work," was the verdict of one of our perceptive colleagues.   —Eugene P. Wigner

Symmetries and Reflections, Cambridge, MA: MIT Press, 1970, p. 260.

58   To me, as a boy growing up in his presence and, later, as a humanistically inclined young chap, the strongest memories of my father [Hermann Weyl] are associated with his passionate interest in literature. . . . To watch Hermann read poetry . . . and to listen to him recite it aloud, one realized immediately how much it filled an inner need of his. Deep down in his psyche, I venture to say, mathematics and poetry were one; and it is because of this, methinks, that as a mathematician he really felt closer to intuitionism than to formalism.   —Michael Weyl

K. Chandrasekharan (ed.), *Hermann Weyl 1885–1985,* New York: Springer-Verlag, 1986, p. 95.

59   Dear Mrs. Wheeler,
. . . I remember the foot marks on the wall of the math seminar room. You had the habit of standing on one foot while leaning the sole of the other against the wall. I remember being hauled off a tennis court to be told that Modern Algebra was good for my soul. I remember your stopping the car at an intersection in the middle of nowhere while you tried to identify a bird call which only you had heard. I remember the very "practical" application of some theory in mathematical physics to a vibrating string with a finite number of discontinuities. But most of all I remember my father's words after he met you on Commencement Day in 1930. The thought of his daughter aspiring to be a female mathematician was a bit horrifying to him. However, after he met you, he said, "Such a woman I would like you to be." That, of course, was impossible. However, I hope I will be able to pass on to my students a bit of the feeling for mathematics which you have given yours.

—Annita Tuller Levine
Nancy J. Owens, "Anna Johnson Pell Wheeler," *Assoc. for Women in Math. Newsletter* 12 (July-August 1982) 5.

60   The course on point set topology contained beautiful mathematics and it was done in a fascinating way. [G. T.] Whyburn stated theorems, drew pictures, gave examples, and we were left to find proofs. Each day he listened with enormous patience to our clumsy presentations of proofs of previously announced results. If no one of us had a proof of a result and we all gave up on it, he presented a proof himself. Otherwise he just listed more results, all chopped up into lemmas and propositions that we might be able to prove. It was often brutally difficult and it was always enormous fun. It gave us great self-confidence and a really deep understanding of a body of material.   —J. L. Kelley
"Once Over Lightly," in Peter Duren (ed.), *A Century of Mathematics in America, Part III,* Providence, RI: American Mathematical Society, 1989, p. 477.

6I   I became acquainted with [Norbert] Wiener in September 1933, while still a student of electrical engineering, when I enrolled in his graduate course. It was at that time really a seminar course. At that level he was a most stimulating teacher. He would actually carry on his research at the blackboard. As soon as I displayed a slight comprehension of what he was doing, he handed me the manuscript of Paley–Wiener for revision. I found a gap in a proof and proved a lemma to set it right. Wiener thereupon sat down at his typewriter, typed my lemma, affixed my name and sent it off to a journal. A prominent professor does not often act as secretary for a young student. He convinced me to change my course from electrical engineering to mathematics. He then went to visit my parents, unschooled immigrant working people living in a run-down ghetto community, to assure them about my future in mathematics. He came to see them a number of times during the next five years to reassure them until he finally found a permanent position for me. (In those depression years positions were very scarce.) If this picture of extreme kindness and generosity seems at odds with Wiener's behavior on other occasions, it is because Wiener was capable of childlike egocentric immaturity on the one hand and extreme idealism and generosity on the other. Similarly his mood could shift quickly from a state of euphoria to the depths of dark despair.   —Norman Levinson
"Wiener's Life," *Bull. of the Amer. Math. Soc.* 72 (January 1966, Part II) 24.

62   [Raymond L.] Wilder wanted a better acquaintance with pure mathematics, and asked to enroll in one of Professor R. L. Moore's classes in topology. Moore at first refused him admission, since Wilder's interest in topology was only secondary. Moore remarked that he doubted that Wilder would like the rigors of proving theorems, and perhaps would not be much good at it even if he did. However, Wilder persisted that he was really interested in pure mathematics and answered some of Moore's questions (such as, "What is an axiom?") well enough that Moore relented and let him enroll. For a while he was ignored by Moore, but as Wilder was able to prove some difficult theorems, Moore's enthusiasm began to grow. Wilder continued his actuarial studies, but when Moore learned that Wilder had solved a problem that had baffled J. R. Kline and others, he suggested that Wilder write it up for a thesis promptly. The deadline for taking language and qualifying exams had already passed, but Moore cut through red tape and arranged for Wilder to take his exams after the deadline. Wilder took his Ph.D. in topology that very same year and gave up his actuarial studies.   —R. H. Bing

"Award for Distinguished Service to Professor Raymond L. Wilder," *Amer. Math. Monthly* 80 (February 1973) 117.

63   [Before our first meeting], Schlick admonished us urgently ... to let [Ludwig] Wittgenstein talk and then ask only very cautiously for the necessary elucidations.

When I met Wittgenstein, I saw that Schlick's warnings were fully justified.

But his behavior was not caused by any arrogance. In general, he was of a sympathetic temperament and very kind; but he was hypersensitive and easily irritated. Whatever he said was always interesting and stimulating, and the way in which he expressed it was often fascinating. His point of view and his attitude toward people and problems, even theoretical problems, were much more similar to those of a creative artist than to those of a scientist; one might almost say, similar to those of a religious prophet or a seer.   —Rudolf Carnap

Paul Arthur Schilpp, *The Philosophy of Rudolf Carnap*, LaSalle, IL: Open Court, 1963, p. 25.

64 Her [Grace C. Young's] energy and enthusiasm must have been quite extraordinary. She was a good tennis player in her younger days, and her interests, recorded in *Who's Who,* include music, domestic occupations, vine-culture, literature and languages, history (especially the sixteenth century), philosophy, chess, and formerly tennis, croquet and billiards. The domestic occupations involved in bringing up six children (two of whom, L.C. Young and R.C. Young, are mathematicians) would have been sufficient for most women, not to mention her collaboration with her husband in so much of his work, and her independent work on derivates in *Nature,* and poems; and her paper "On the solution of a pair of simultaneous Diophantine equations connected with the nuptial number of Plato" shows more than superficial knowledge of the history of Greek mathematics.   —Mary L. Cartwright
"Grace Chisholm Young," *J. of the London Math. Soc.* 19 (July 1944) 188.

65 On his fiftieth birthday, Klein was honored in Turin where Grace [Chisholm Young] was then studying. At dinner he was seated next to Grace, said to be his favorite pupil, and he whispered to her: "Ah, I envy you. You are in the happy age of productivity. When everyone begins to speak well of you, you are on the downward road."
—Sylvia Wiegand
"Grace Chisholm Young," *Assoc. for Women in Math. Newsletter* 7 (May-June 1977) 6.

66 Prof. Klein's seminary is quite different; it takes place every Wednesday at 11 o'clock, and lasts about two hours, and the members make 'Vortrag's [presentations] on their special subjects on different Wednesdays. The students who have been here some time, and some of the new students who have come from other Universities, have already got their special subjects; for the others, Prof. Klein has always suggestions as to special lines of work which they might take up, generally in connection with the lectures. Miss Winston made her Vortrag on the last Wednesday before the Christmas holiday. It would be nervous work in any case to make a Vortrag before an audience of about a dozen men, half of whom are Doctors, and one Prof. Klein; but the strain is considerably increased by having to speak German. There are about a dozen of us in our lectures; we are a motley crew: five are Americans,

one a Swiss-French, one a Hungarian, and one an Italian. This leaves a
very small residuum of German blood.   —Grace Chisholm Young
                    Mary L. Cartwright, "Grace Chisholm Young," *J. of
                    the London Math. Soc.* 19 (July 1944) 187.

67   [William H.] Young was the most original of the younger Cambridge mathematicians; twenty years later he was the most prolific. Yet
no one suggested to him that he might have it in him to be a great
mathematician; that the years between twenty-five and forty should be
the best of a mathematician's life; that he should set to work and see
what he could do. . . .

I still find it difficult to visualize Young's own attitude during these
early years of unproductivity. The productivity, when it did come, was
so astonishing; it seems at first as if it must have been the sequel to
years of preparation, by a man who had succeeded at last in finding his
subject and himself. One would have supposed that anyone so original,
however he might be occupied, must surely have found something significant to say, but actually the idea of research seems hardly to have
occurred to Young. Mr. Cowell says that Young once told him that
he "deliberately accepted ten years of drudgery," that he "fancied his
knowledge of the Stock Exchange," and that he thought that he could
"win his leisure" by thirty-five; but "leisure" meant freedom, comfort,
reading, and travel; not a life of mathematical research. The truth
seems to be that Young had really no time to think of anything but
his teaching; that the atmosphere of Cambridge was mathematically
stifling; that no one was particularly anxious to look out for or encourage
originality; and that he was too much absorbed in his routine, in his
pupils and their performance, to dream of higher ambitions.

However that may be, the dreams were to come and the "drudgery"
to end, and the end came quickly after Young's marriage. In 1896 he
married Grace Chisholm, the second of his wrangler pupils. . . .

The great break in Young's life came, quite suddenly, in 1897; and
here perhaps I had better quote Mrs. Young's own words. "At the end
of our first year together he proposed, and I eagerly agreed, to throw up
lucre, go abroad, and devote ourselves to research": it seems to imply a
revolution in Young's whole attitude to mathematics. But Mrs. Young
had studied in Göttingen before her marriage, and knew what the air of
a centre of research was like, so that possibly the revolution was a little
less abrupt than it appears. At any rate, the Youngs left Cambridge for

Göttingen in September. "Of course all our relations were horrified, but we succeeded in living without help, and indeed got the reputation of being well off": Young's "banker's instincts" had served him well.

—G. H. Hardy
"William Henry Young," *J. of the London Math. Soc.*
17 (October 1942) 220.

68   He [William H. Young] made mathematics exciting. He would have agreed completely with Hardy's dictum: "It is one of the first duties of a professor to exaggerate a little both the importance of his subject, and his own importance in the subject." Often one could not follow his leaping mind during the lectures, but afterwards, when one had read about the matter, the line of reasoning became clear. He spoke to us more as a learned society than as a collection of students, and he brushed away the tradition that the best student was one who reproduced faithfully what had been fed in. He made us well read; even at times when understanding was a little insecure, at least we began to have a feeling for mathematics as distinct from the acquisition of a technique. It was one of the more memorable experiences of my life to sit at the feet of one who knows so much mathematics.

—Graham Sutton
"The Centenary of the Birth of W. H. Young," *Math. Gaz.* 49 (February 1965) 20.

69   I hope you [wife Grace C. Young] enjoy this working for me. On the whole I think it is, at present at any rate, quite as it should be, seeing that we are responsible only to ourselves as to division of laurels. The work is not of a character to cause conflicting claims. I am very happy that you are getting on with the ideas. I feel partly as if I were teaching you, and setting you problems which I could not quite do myself but could enable you to. Then again, I think of myself as like Klein, furnishing the steam required—the initiative, the guidance. But I feel confident too that we are rising *together* to new heights. You do need a good deal of criticism when you are at your best, and in your best working vein.

The fact is that our papers ought to be published under our joint names, but if this were done neither of us get the benefit of it. No. Mine the laurels now and the knowledge. Yours the knowledge only. Everything under my name now, and later when the loaves and fishes are no more procurable in that way, everything or much under your name.

This is my programme. At present you can't undertake a public career. You have your children. I can and do. Every post which brings an answer from you to my last request or suggestion gives me a pleasurable excitement. Life here is more interesting with such stimulants. I am kept working and thinking, too, myself. Everything seems to say we are on the right tack just now.   —William H. Young

I. Grattan-Guinness, "A Mathematical Union, William Henry and Grace Chisholm Young," *Annals of Science* 29 (August 1972) 141.

CHAPTER 15

Anecdotes and Miscellaneous Humor

1   At parties, I often respond to the question as to what I do by saying that I am a tennis coach. I get tired of the automatic response to the statement that I am a mathematician.   —Richard Bellman
Eye of the Hurricane, Singapore: World Scientific, 1984, p. 33.

2   [Stefan] Bergman was a prolific writer. Of course he worked in the days before the advent of word processors. His method of writing was this: First, he would write a manuscript in longhand and give it to the secretary. When she had it typed up he would begin revising, stapling strips of paper over the portions that he wished to change. Strips would be stapled over strips, and then again and again, until parts of the manuscript would become so thick that the stapler could no longer penetrate. Then the manuscript would be returned to the secretary for a retype and the whole cycle would begin again. Sometimes it would repeat ad infinitum. Bergman once told a student that "a mathematician's most important tool is the stapler."
—Steven G. Krantz
"Mathematical Anecdotes," *Math. Intell.*   12 (Fall 1990) 34.

3   There is considerable evidence that [Stefan] Bergman thought about mathematics constantly. Once he phoned a student, at the stu-

dent's home number, at 2:00 a.m. and said "Are you in the library? I want you to look something up for me!"

On another occasion, when Bergman was at Brown, one of Bergman's graduate students got married. The student planned to attend a conference on the West Coast, so he and his new bride decided to take a bus to California as a sort of makeshift honeymoon. There was a method in their madness: the student knew that Bergman would attend the conference, but that he liked to get where he was going in a hurry. The bus seemed the least likely mode of transportation for Bergman. But when Bergman heard about the impending bus trip, he thought it a charming idea and purchased a bus ticket for himself. The student protested that this trip was to be part of his honeymoon, and that he could not talk mathematics on the bus. Bergman promised to behave. When the bus took off, Bergman was at the back of the bus and, just to be safe, Bergman's student took a window seat near the front with his wife in the adjacent aisle seat. But after about ten minutes Bergman got a great idea, wandered up the aisle, leaned across the scowling bride, and began to discuss mathematics. It wasn't long before the wife was in the back of the bus and Bergman next to his student—and so it remained for the rest of the bus trip!   —Steven G. Krantz
"Mathematical Anecdotes," *Math. Intell.* 12 (Fall 1990) 34.

4   So I came to Brown in 1935 and here became aware for the first time that some people made a distinction between men and women in mathematics. For example, I was assigned to teach a course in remedial algebra at Pembroke College, then a separate college for women at Brown, and Hugh Hamilton was assigned to teach the same course to the Brown boys. When we discovered that I had 3 girls in my class and he had 45 boys, it seemed natural to both of us, he from California and I from Wisconsin, to make two classes of 24 students each. But the chairman, C. R. Adams, would not hear of the idea, saying that the Brown boys would not stand being taught by a woman instructor. I pointed out that I had taught boys in Madison the previous year, but nothing was done, and we continued for a full semester—I with 3 girls and Hamilton with 45 boys.   —Dorothy Bernstein
"Women Mathematicians before 1950," *Assoc. for Women in Math. Newsletter* 9 (July-August 1979) 10.

5   In 1950, on his fifty-ninth birthday, Besicovitch was elected to
the Rouse Ball Chair of Mathematics, succeeding the first holder J.
E. Littlewood. Twenty-three years earlier, on his thirty-sixth birthday,
thinking that the years of greatest intensity of life were passing, he had
said "I have had four-fifths of my life." When J. C. Burkill reminded
him of this in 1950, he received a postcard which read "Numerator was
correct".   —S. J. Taylor
"Abram Samoilovitch Besicovitch," *Bull. of the Lon-
don Math. Soc.* 7 (July 1975) 194.

6   [Salomon] Bochner had a number of standard responses to any
problem you asked him about. They ranged from "I think this is not
very interesting" to "I think this cannot be." Once I got "I think this
is difficult" and then solved the problem. When I took the result to
Bochner, he said, "I think this is trivial." As [D. V.] Widder used to say,
"Everything is trivial when you know the proof."   —Ralph P. Boas
"Ralph P. Boas, Jr.," in D. Albers, G. Alexanderson,
C. Reid (eds.), *More Mathematical People,* New York:
Harcourt Brace Jovanovich, 1990, p. 29.

7   During my first year at Berkeley I arrived late one day at one of
[Jerzy] Neyman's classes. On the blackboard there were two problems
that I assumed had been assigned for homework. I copied them down.
A few days later I apologized to Neyman for taking so long to do the
homework—the problems seemed to be a little harder to do than usual.
I asked him if he still wanted it. He told me to throw it on his desk.
I did so reluctantly because his desk was covered with such a heap of
papers that I feared my homework would be lost there forever. About
six weeks later, one Sunday morning about eight o'clock, Anne and I
were awakened by someone banging on our front door. It was Neyman.
He rushed in with papers in hand, all excited: "I've just written an
introduction to one of your papers. Read it so I can send it out right
away for publication." For a minute I had no idea what he was talking
about. To make a long story short, the problems on the blackboard
that I had solved thinking they were homework were in fact two famous
unsolved problems in statistics. That was the first inkling I had that
there was anything special about them.   —George B. Dantzig
Donald J. Albers, "An Interview with George B.
Dantzig: the Father of Linear Programming," *Coll.
Math. J.* 17 (September 1986) 301.

8 Morgenstern had many stories to tell about Gödel. One concerned the occasion when in April 1948, Gödel became a U.S. citizen, with Einstein and Morgenstern as witnesses. Gödel was to take the routine citizenship examination, and he prepared for it very seriously, studying the United States Constitution assiduously. On the day before he was to appear, Gödel came to Morgenstern in a very excited state saying: "I have discovered a logical-legal possibility by which the U.S.A. could be transformed into a dictatorship." Morgenstern realized that, whatever the logical merits of Gödel's argument, the possibility was extremely hypothetical in character, and he urged Gödel to keep quiet about his discovery at the examination. The next morning, Morgenstern drove Gödel and Einstein from Princeton to Trenton, where the citizenship proceedings were to take place. Along the way Einstein kept telling one amusing anecdote after another in order to distract Gödel, apparently with great success. At the office in Trenton, the official was properly impressed by Einstein and Morgenstern, and invited them to attend the examination, normally held in private. He began by addressing Gödel: "Up to now you have held German citizenship." Gödel corrected him, explaining that he was Austrian. "Anyhow", continued the official, "it was under an evil dictatorship ... but fortunately, that's not possible in America." "On the contrary," Gödel cried out, "I know how that can happen!!" All three had great trouble restraining Gödel from elaborating his discovery, so that the proceedings could be brought to their expected conclusion. —Solomon Feferman

"Gödel's Life and Work," in Solomon Feferman (ed.), *Kurt Gödel Collected Work, Vol. I,* New York: Oxford University Press, 1986, p. 12.

9 [W.S.] Gosset, or Student, was an Oxford-trained chemist who had become a statistician as a result of circumstances ... [While employed at a brewery] Gosset became interested in the statistical treatment of brewing problems and, when he had been working as a brewer for five years, submitted a report on "The Application of the 'Law of errors' to the Work of the Brewery." Shortly afterwards he met Karl Pearson and then began to attend Pearson's lecture at University College. In his spare time he worked on the problem of small sample ... The result of this study was "Student's t-statistic" for testing a normal mean. One story has it that when the work was published Gosset signed himself

"Student" because the brewery did not want it known that one of its employees was writing scientific papers. According to another, Karl Pearson suggested using the pseudonym in preference to his having to designate the author of a paper in *Biometrika* as a brewer.

—Constance Reid
Neyman from Life, New York: Springer-Verlag, 1982, p. 54.

IO   At the Bologna Congress, ... the meetings started in Bologna and ended in Florence. That's about a three-hour train ride and for this there was a special train. I recall we were in a compartment that was very noisy, and [Jacques] Hadamard was tired and wanted to have some peace. So he told the people in the compartment about a difficult problem, a puzzle. As soon as he told it, everyone started working on it, and it suddenly became quiet so Hadamard could sleep.

—George Pólya
G. L. Alexanderson (ed.), *A Pólya Picture Album,* Boston: Birkhäuser, 1987, p. 87.

II   I must tell you one [of G. H. Hardy's jokes] about myself. In working with Hardy, I once had an idea of which he approved. But afterwards I did not work sufficiently hard to carry out that idea, and Hardy disapproved. He did not tell me so, of course, yet it came out when he visited a zoological garden in Sweden with Marcel Riesz. In a cage there was a bear. The cage had a gate, and on the gate there was a lock. The bear sniffed at the lock, hit it with his paw, then he growled a little, turned around and walked away. "He is like Pólya," said Hardy. "He has excellent ideas, but does not carry them out." —George Pólya
"Some Mathematicians I Have Known," *Amer. Math. Monthly* 76 (August-September 1969) 752.

I2   You must know that Hardy had a running feud with God. In Hardy's view God had nothing more important to do than frustrate Hardy. This led to a sort of insurance policy for Hardy one time when he was trying to get back to Cambridge after a visit to [Harald] Bohr in Denmark. The weather was bad and there was only a small boat available. Hardy thought there was a real possibility the boat would sink. So he sent a postcard to Bohr saying: "I proved the Riemann

Hypothesis. G. H. Hardy." That way if the boat sank, everyone would think that Hardy had proved the Riemann Hypothesis. God could not allow so much glory for Hardy so he could not allow the boat to sink.

—George Pólya

G. L. Alexanderson (ed.), *A Pólya Picture Album*, Boston: Birkhäuser, 1987, p. 89.

13 There is a German legend about Barbarossa, the emperor Frederick I. The common people of Germany liked him and as he died in a crusade and was buried in a far away grave, the legend sprang up that he was still alive, asleep in a cavern and would wake and come out, even after hundreds of years, when Germany needed him.

Somebody allegedly asked the famous German mathematician, David Hilbert, 'If you were to revive, like Barbarossa, after five hundred years, what would you do?' 'I would ask,' said Hilbert, 'Has somebody proved the Riemann hypothesis?' —Béla Bollobás

Littlewood's Miscellany, Cambridge: Cambridge University Press, 1986, p. 16.

14 Many such stories are told about Hilbert['s absentmindedness]. Are they true? I doubt it, but some are quite good. Here is one of the very well known ones: There is a party in Hilbert's house and Frau (I mean Mrs.) Hilbert suddenly notices that her husband forgot to put on a fresh shirt. "David," she says sternly, "go upstairs and put on another shirt." David, as it befits a long married man, meekly obeys and goes upstairs. Yet he does not come back. Five minutes pass, ten minutes pass, yet David fails to appear and so Frau Hilbert goes up to the bedroom and there is Hilbert in his bed. You see, it was the natural sequence of things: He took off his coat, then his tie, then his shirt, and so on, and went to sleep. —George Pólya

"Some Mathematicians I Have Known," *Amer. Math. Monthly* 76 (August-September 1969) 747.

15 In discharging conscientiously his duties as a professor, he [Adolf Hurwitz] took care of many Ph.D. candidates, treating them with much consideration and patience. Among so many there were some who needed a lot of help, and even the patient Hurwitz was once led to

say: "A Ph.D. dissertation is a paper of the professor written under aggravating circumstances.   —George Pólya
"Some Mathematicians I Have Known," *Amer. Math. Monthly* 76 (August-September 1969) 751.

16 It may come as no surprise that my ability to communicate in English was severely limited when I came to Baltimore. The hardest problem was ordering meals, since I invariably got something that didn't even vaguely resemble what I thought I ought to be getting. I finally solved the problem of lunches, which I ate in a drugstore a block from where I lived. I learned to say reliably, "Cream cheese sandwich and coffee." Unfortunately, the young man who served me would always respond: "On toast?" and all I could do was to smile inanely. The result was satisfactory, since I liked what I got, and my smiles were taken as signs of acquiescence. I looked up "toast" in the somewhat inadequate Polish-English, English-Polish pocket dictionary I carried and it gave just one meaning: "Gentlemen, the King!" Having been logically conditioned, I assumed that "on toast" must be some kind of salutation and I proceeded on this assumption. For a period of about two weeks the following ritual took place at lunch:

I: "Cream cheese sandwich and coffee."
Waiter: "On toast?"
I (bowing slightly and smiling): "On toast!"

Somehow it dawned on me that something was not quite right and I finally asked van Kampen. He laughed a little longer than I thought was kind, and finally said: "Why didn't you at least once answer in the negative? You would have soon known what 'on toast' meant." "I didn't want to risk being impolite," I replied and he laughed again.

—Mark Kac
Enigmas of Chance, New York: Harper and Row, 1985, p. 82.

17 Mark Kac once estimated this number [of persons who read a mathematical paper] to be three, which I gather are the author, the referee, and one other who may be the reviewer. Some editors have facetiously estimated it to be two, the referee and the reviewer.

—M. S. Klamkin
"On the Ideal Role of an Industrial Mathematician and Its Educational Implications," *Amer. Math. Monthly* 78 (January 1971) 58.

18   The twentieth century saw an upsurge of interest in the Fermat problem by amateurs because of a prize of 100,000 marks offered by a wealthy German mathematician, P. Wolfskel, in 1909 for a published solution of the problem. The prize money was never awarded and it disappeared in inflation.

Thousands of erroneous self-published proofs were submitted but the whole lot failed to advance the problem one inch. ... The great German number theorist E. Landau is said to have had post cards printed with the following message: "Dear Sir or Madam: Your proof of Fermat's Last Theorem has been received. The first mistake is on page ... line ..." He would give these cards to graduate students to be filled in and posted.   —D. H. Lehmer

                                        E. T. Bell, *The Last Problem*, New York: Simon and
                                        Schuster, 1961, p. 305.

19   [Alfred] Errera was a Belgian and was a student of Landau's. He was a multimillionaire—Landau was a multimillionaire too, by the way ... To be invited to his house for dinner was quite something. The dinner was very elaborate, with many courses, different wines and so on. There were various footmen and such. Anyway, one time Errera gave a dinner in honor of Paul Lévy, who was notoriously absent-minded. The next day, Lévy and Errera met somewhere and Errera, who was very polite, said: "I had great pleasure last evening." Lévy said: "Ah, and where were you last evening?"   —George Pólya

                                        G. L. Alexanderson (ed.), *A Pólya Picture Album*,
                                        Boston: Birkhäuser, 1987, p. 96.

20   The prevalent lifestyle in America fifty years ago was based on an unwritten but commonly understood contract between husband and wife that it was his responsibility to work outside the home to support the family financially, and her responsibility to manage the household. ... "Responsibility to manage the household" meant doing everything possible to free the husband for his work, in a very full sense. For example, in 1939 Hans Rademacher had an auto even though neither he nor his wife could drive; a friend drove them around occasionally. I offered to teach Rademacher, who was in his forties at the time, how to drive. After thinking it over he astonished me by proposing that rather than teaching him how to drive he would prefer that I teach his wife. So I taught his wife to drive in that spring of 1939. Hans Rademacher never did take up driving, to my knowledge. He spoke frequently about the need for large blocks of uninterrupted time to think about mathematics.   —Ivan Niven

> "The Threadbare Thirties," in Peter Duren (ed.), *A Century of Mathematics in America, Part I*, Providence, RI: American Mathematical Society, 1988, p. 217.

21   Ed Burgess ... remembers the following incident, which I don't remember at all. We were discussing locking doors. I said that I would never lock the door to my house unless my husband insisted. Ed says that [R. L.] Moore literally pounced on that saying, "Husband! But, Miss Estill, I thought that you were going to be a mathematician."

—Mary Ellen Rudin

> Donald J. Albers and Constance Reid, "An Interview with Mary Ellen Rudin," *Coll. Math. J.* 19 (March 1988) 123.

22   Jimmie [Savage] was terribly conscientious ...

John Williams, Jimmie, and I were writing a report that we couldn't finish on time. We finally decided it would have to be delivered by hand. All three of us piled on a train to Washington from New York at about 8 P.M., continuing to write and polish as we went. About halfway to Washington, we had a reasonably good report all finished, when it occurred to Jimmie that we hadn't looked at the problem as well as we could and we should start over ... he insisted that we buckle down and rewrite the paper from scratch. It was hard to take, but we did it and had it typed in time for delivery the next morning.

—Frederick Mosteller

> *The Writings of Leonard Jimmie Savage, a Memorial Selection*, Washington, DC: American Statistical Association, 1981, p. 27.

23   Allen [Shields] liked to play with words. His letters were spiced with all sorts of intentional and outrageous distortions. A Banach space was sometimes call a Bone Ache space. He referred to Chubby Chef's inequality. A proposed course in measure theory with modest prerequisites became a course on the LaVague integral ... One page [of a manuscript he was sending me in sections] contained a sentence

that read, "Without loss of genitalia, we may assume. ..." Later he told
me he was just checking to see if I was reading my mail. —Peter Duren
"In Remembrance of Allen Shields," *Math. Intell.* 12
(Spring 1990) 12.

24 When, about fifteen years ago, after failing to attend an important meeting of the committee of the Polish Academy of Sciences,
he [Hugo Steinhaus] received a letter chiding him (along with several
others) for not having "justified his absence," he wired the President
of the Academy that "as long as there are members who have not yet
justified their presence, I do not have to justify my absence."
—Mark Kac
"Hugo Steinhaus—A Reminiscence and a Tribute,"
Amer. Math. Monthly 81 (June-July 1974) 578.

25 Steinhaus liked to use statistical arguments even in jest. I
remember especially one such occasion. Each week I read *Nature* in
the hope that a position would be advertised which did not require the
applicant to be a British subject. Sure enough, one week the Imperial
College of Science and Technology in London announced an opening
for an assistant lecturer in mathematics at the salary of one hundred
and fifty pounds sterling per annum, and being a British subject was not
a requirement. The yearly salary, roughly equivalent to seven hundred
and fifty dollars, seemed so measly that I could not imagine any self-
respecting British subject coveting the job. I went to Steinhaus and
asked him whether I should apply. At the time I didn't know a word of
English but I was willing to perjure myself by claiming that my English
was adequate. "Let me see," said Steinhaus. "I would estimate your
chances of getting the job as being about one in a thousand, and if you
multiply this by one hundred and fifty pounds, you get three shillings;
this is much more that the cost of mailing the letter, so you should
apply." I did, and the job went to a British subject who after all did
covet it.   —Mark Kac
Enigmas of Chance, New York: Harper and Row,
1985, p. 53.

26 The course (Steinhaus' seminar) had a small attendance and one
day only one other student and I were present. Steinhaus went through
the lecture without so much as a glance at the depleted audience and at
the end I asked him what was the minimal number of listeners to whom

he would feel compelled to lecture. *"Tres facit collegium"* ("Three make a college" is a loose translation), he replied. The very next time I was the sole survivor. As the professor started to speak I interrupted him by saying, "What about the *'tres facit collegium'*?" "God," he said, "is always present" and continued to lecture. Steinhaus was an avowed atheist, by the way. —Mark Kac

Enigmas of Chance, New York: Harper and Row, 1985, p. 38.

27 Many years later, when I became chairman of the Mathematics Department of the University of Colorado, I noticed that the difficulties of administering N people is not really proportional to N but to N^2. This became my first "administrative" theorem. —S. M. Ulam

Adventures of a Mathematician, New York: Charles Scribner's Sons, 1976, p. 91.

28 I heard the following from Theodore von Kármán himself. Still, I would not swear that it actually happened; he liked good stories too much, and the best stories do not happen, they are invented. At that time he had a double position: He was professor at Aachen in Germany and also lectured at Cal Tech in Pasadena. As an important aeronautical engineer, he was consultant to several airlines, and so he got free transportation whenever he found an unoccupied seat on a plane of one of these lines. So he commuted more or less regularly between Aachen and Pasadena. He gave similar lectures at both places. Once he was somewhat tired when he arrived in Pasadena, but started lecturing. That was not so difficult: He had notes which he also used in Aachen. He talked, but as he looked around he had the impression that the faces in the audience looked even more blank than usual.

And then he caught himself: He was speaking in German! He became quite upset. "You should have told me—why did you not tell me?" The students were silent, but finally one spoke up: "Don't get upset, Professor. You may speak German, you may speak English, we will understand just as much." —George Pólya

"Some Mathematicians I Have Known," *Amer. Math. Monthly* 76 (August-September 1969) 748.

29 One famous story [about John von Neumann] concerns a complicated expression that a young scientist at the Aberdeen Proving

Ground needed to evaluate. He spent ten minutes on the first special case; the second computation took an hour of paper and pencil work; for the third he had to resort to a desk calculator, and even so took half a day. When Johnny came to town, the young man showed him the formula and asked him what to do. Johnny was glad to tackle it. "Let's see what happens for the first few cases. If we put $n = 1$, we get ..."—and he looked into space and mumbled for a minute. Knowing the answer, the young questioner put in "2.31?" Johnny gave him a funny look and said "Now if $n = 2, \ldots,$" and once again voiced some of his thoughts as he worked. The young man, prepared, could of course follow what Johnny was doing, and, a few seconds before Johnny finished, he interrupted again, in a hesitant tone of voice: "7.49?" This time Johnny frowned, and hurried on: "If $n = 3$, then ... ." The same thing happened as before—Johnny muttered for several minutes, the young man eavesdropped, and, just before Johnny finished, the young men exclaimed: "11.06!" That was too much for Johnny. It couldn't be! No unknown beginner could outdo him! He was upset and he sulked till the practical joker confessed.   —Paul Halmos

"The Legend of John von Neumann," *Amer. Math. Monthly* 80 (April 1973) 386.

30   He [von Neumann] could, it is said, memorize the names, address, and telephone numbers in a column of the telephone book on sight ... he said once that he knew all the numbers in it—the only other thing he needed, to be able to dispense with the book altogether, was to know the names that the numbers belonged to.   —Paul Halmos

"The Legend of John von Neumann," *Amer. Math. Monthly* 80 (April 1973) 383.

31   There is the famous fly puzzle. Two bicyclists start twenty miles apart and head toward each other, each going at a steady rate of 10 m.p.h. At the same time a fly that travels at a steady 15 m.p.h. starts from the front wheel of the southbound bicycle and flies to the front wheel of the northbound one, then turns around and flies to the front wheel of the southbound one again, and continues in this manner till he is crushed between the front wheels. Question: what total distance did the fly cover? The slow way to find the answer is to calculate what distance the fly covers on the first, northbound, leg of the trip, then on the second, southbound, leg, then on the third, etc., etc., and, finally, to sum the infinite series so obtained. The quick way is to observe that the bicycles meet exactly one hour after their start, so that the fly had just an hour for his travels; the answer must therefore be 15 miles. When the question was put to von Neumann, he solved it in an instant, and thereby disappointed the questioner: "Oh, you must have heard the trick before!" "What trick?" asked von Neumann; "all I did was sum the infinite series." —Paul Halmos

"The Legend of John von Neumann," *Amer. Math. Monthly* 80 (April 1973) 386.

32 I became a civilian computer in the range firing section of Aberdeen Proving Grounds. Oswald Veblen was in charge. I was bunked in barracks with Norbert Wiener and Philip Franklin. I learned a lot from these enthusiasts, but at times they inhibited sleep when they talked mathematics far into the night. On one occasion I hid the light bulb, hoping to induce earlier quiet. —D. V. Widder

"Some Mathematical Reminiscences," in Peter Duren (ed.), *A Century of Mathematics in America, Part I,* Providence, RI: American Mathematical Society, 1988, p. 80.

33 Probably the most famous Wiener story concerns a day when the Wiener family was moving to a new home. Wiener's wife knew Norbert only too well. So on the night before, as well as the morning of, the moving day she reminded him over and over that they were moving. She wrote the new address for him on a slip of paper (the new house was just a few blocks away), gave him the new keys, and took away his old keys. Wiener dutifully put the new address and keys into his pocket and left for work. During the course of the day, Wiener's thoughts were elsewhere. At one point somebody asked him a mathematical question, and Wiener gave him the answer on the back of the slip of paper his wife had given him. So much for the new address! At the end of the day Wiener, as was his habit, walked home—to his old house. He was puzzled to find nobody home. Looking through the window, he could see no furnishings. Panic took over when he discovered that his key would not fit the lock. Wild-eyed, he began alternately to bang on the door and to run around in the yard. Then he spotted a child coming down the street. He ran up to her and cried "Little girl, I'm very upset.

My family has disappeared and my key won't fit in the lock." She replied,
"Yes, daddy. Mommy sent me for you."   —Steven G. Krantz
"Mathematical Anecdotes," *Math. Intell.* 12 (Fall
1990) 38.

34   I once asked Edwin B. Wilson, a famed universalist among
mathematicians, how he came to switch from analysis to statistics at
Yale. With a humorous twinkle he said: "An immutable law of academia
is that the course must go on, no matter if all the substance and spirit has
gone out of it with the passing of the original teacher. So when [Josiah
Willard] Gibbs retired, his courses had to go on. And the department
said: 'Wilson, you are it.'"   —W. L. Duren, Jr.
"Graduate Student at Chicago in the Twenties," *Amer.*
Math. Monthly 83 (April 1976) 246.

35   When I was sixteen or seventeen, Aneurin Bevan [the great
politician who founded the British health service in the Attlee govern-
ment] asked my father what I was going to be when I grew up. My father
[Prime Minister Harold Wilson] said, "Well it looks as though he's going
to be a mathematician." Bevan replied, "Just like his father, all bloody
facts, no bloody vision!"   —Robin Wilson
D. L. Albers and G. L. Alexanderson, "A Conversation
with Robin Wilson," *Coll. Math. J.* 21 (May 1990) 183.

36   [Ernst] Zermelo was apparently a rather frustrated man who had
some justified grievances (the details of which I never found out about).
He did not wish to meet [Kurt] Gödel when these two scholars attended
the same congress.
    Some people had planned a lunch in an inn on top of a small mountain
and I was invited. Some friends of Zermelo were in the group and
they thought he ought to meet Gödel. But Zermelo had mistaken
somebody else for Gödel and replied he could not speak to somebody
with such a stupid face. Well, the misunderstanding was explained
to Zermelo. But then he said there would not be enough food if we
also invited Gödel. Finally he said climbing the mountain would be
too much for him. Finally, Gödel, who knew nothing of all this, was
somehow introduced to Zermelo. And then a miracle happened almost
instantaneously. Only seconds later the two scholars were engaged in

deep contemplations and Zermelo walked up the mountain without
even knowing that he did it!   —Olga Taussky-Todd

> "An Autobiographical Essay," in Donald J. Albers
> and G. L. Alexanderson (eds.), *Mathematical People,*
> Boston: Birkhäuser, 1985, p. 318.

37   Once when walking past a lounge in the University of Chicago
that was filled with a loud crowd watching TV, [Antoni Zygmund] asked
one of his students what was going on. The student told him that the
crowd was watching the World Series and explained to him some of the
features of this baseball phenomenon. Zygmund thought about it all for
a few minutes and commented, "I think it should be called the World
Sequence."   —Ronald Coifman and Robert S. Strichartz

> "The School of Antoni Zygmund," in Peter Duren
> (ed.), *A Century of Mathematics in America, Part
> III,* Providence, RI: American Mathematical Society,
> 1989, p. 348.

38   In an Engineering College, mathematics are thrown at you in
chunks, as you might throw a man a wrench.

Theirs not to reason why
Theirs not to make reply
Theirs but to use it or die.

> quoted in W. W. Sawyer, "Pressures on American
> Mathematics Teachers," *SIAM Review* 1 (January
> 1959) 36.

39   A Note on Piffles
                    By A. B. Smith

A. C. Jones in his paper "A Note on the Theory of Boffles", Proceedings of the National Society, 13, first defined a Biffle to be a non-definite
Boffle and asked if every Biffle was reducible.

C. D. Brown in "On a paper by A. C. Jones", Biffle, 24, answered in
part this question by defining a Wuffle to be a reducible Biffle and he
was then able to show that all Wuffles were reducible.

H. Green, P. Smith and D. Jones in their review of Brown's paper,
Wuffle Review, 48, suggested the name Woffle for any Wuffle other than
the non-trivial Wuffle and conjectured that the total number of Woffles

would be at least as great as the number so far known to exist. They asked if this conjecture was the strongest possible.

T. Brown, "A collection of 250 papers on Woffle Theory dedicated to R. S. Green on his 23rd Birthday" defined a Piffle to be an infinite multi-variable sub-polynormal Woffle which does not satisfy the lower regular Q-property. He stated, but was unable to prove, that there were at least a finite number of Piffles.

T. Smith, L. Jones, R. Brown and A. Green in their collected works "A short introduction to the classical theory of the Piffle", Piffle Press, 6 gns., showed that all bi-universal Piffles were strictly descending and conjectured that to prove a stronger result would be harder. It is this conjecture which motivated the present paper.   —A. K. Austin

"Modern Research in Mathematics," *Math. Gaz.* 51
(May 1967) 150.

40   There is an amusing legend about Flavius Josephus, a famous historian who lived in the first century A.D.

The story goes as follows: In the Jewish revolt against Rome, Josephus and 39 of his comrades were holding out against the Romans in a cave. With defeat imminent, they resolved that, like the rebels at Masada, they would rather die than be slaves to the Romans. They decided to arrange themselves in a circle. One man was designated as number one, and they proceeded clockwise around the circle of 40 men, killing every 7th man (the numbers 40 and 7 are different in other versions of the tale). Now it is obvious whose turn it was to be killed on the first time around: numbers 7, 14, 21, 28, and 35. From this point on, the outcome is not as clear. The next number would be 42; however, this has to be reduced modulo 40 to 2, and man number 2 is indeed the next to go. But the next after that is not man number 9. We are counting men, not seats in the circle. Seat number 7 is unoccupied. So the next man to be slaughtered is number 10.

Let us interrupt at this point, in order to finish telling the story. Josephus (according to the story) was among other things an accomplished mathematician; so he instantly figured out where he ought to sit in order to be the last to go ... But when the time came, instead of killing himself he joined the Roman side. And so he lived to write his famous histories: *The Antiquities* and *The Jewish Wars.* —I. N. Herstein and I. Kaplansky

Matters Mathematical, New York: Harper and Row,
1974, p. 121.

41   THERE'S A DELTA FOR EVERY EPSILON (Calypso)

There's a delta for every epsilon,
It's a fact that you can always count upon.
There's a delta for every epsilon
  And now and again,
  There's also an N.

But one condition I must give:
The epsilon must be positive.
A lonely life all the others live,
  In no theorem
  A delta for them.

How sad, how cruel, how tragic,
How pitiful, and other adjec-

Tives that I might mention.
The matter merits our attention.
If an epsilon is a hero,
Just because it is greater than zero,
It must be mighty discouragin'
To lie to the left of the origin.

This rank discrimination is not for us,
We must fight for an enlightened calculus,
Where epsilons all, both minus and plus,
  Have deltas
  To call their own.
          —Tom Lehrer
     Amer. Math. Monthly 81 (June-July 1974) 612.

42   The Publication System: A Jaundiced View

This is the paper X wrote.

This is the editor, all distraught,
Who tore his hair at the horrible thought
Of printing the paper X wrote.

This is the friend whose help was sought
by E, the editor, all distraught,

Who tore his hair and groaned at the thought
Of the horrible paper X wrote.

This is the proof, all shiny and new,
of 2.1 and 2.2
Conceived by F, whose help was sought
By E, the editor, all distraught,
Who tore his hair and groaned at the thought
Of the terrible paper X wrote.

This is the Referee's Report
Which says SUCH THINGS ARE BETTER SHORT
And gives the proof, all shiny and new,
Of 2.1 and 2.2
Proposed by F, whose help was sought
By E, the editor all distraught
Who tore his hair and groaned at the thought
Of the odious paper X wrote.

This Covering Note pretends to be
Detached about the referee.
("He doesn't tell you how to fix
The proof of Theorem 2.6.")

It quotes the Referee's Report
Which says Such Things are Better Short
And gives the proof, all shiny and new
Of 2.1 and 2.2
Proposed by F, whose help was sought
By E, the editor, all distraught,
Who tore his hair and groaned at the thought
Of the pitiful paper X wrote.

"But we are sure it can be mended;
If wholly changed it could be splendid."
Typing on a new machine,
F answers for his magazine. Signed $E_1 = F_2 = X_3$

Ian Stewart and John Jaworski (eds.), *Seven Years of Manifold, 1968–1980,* Nantwich: Shiva Publishing, 1981, p. 90.

43   Pereant

I've proved some theorems, once or twice,
And thought that they were rather nice.
My presentations were rejected
By referees who had detected
Those theorems that I thought my own
In journals I have never known,
And in a strange and knotty tongue.
Oh! For a world still fresh and young,
When fame was won by work alone.
Abstracting journals weren't known,
And (if report can be believed)
No information was retrieved,
Nor academic reputations
Achieved by counting up citations.

—Ralph P. Boas

"The Verses of Boas," *Two-Year Coll. Math. J.* 14
(September 1983) 342.

44   Formalism

The devil is very neat. It is his pride
To keep his house in order. Every bit
Of trivia has its place. He takes great pains
To see that nothing ever does not fit.

And yet his guests are queasy. All their food,
Served with a flair and pleasant to the eye,
Goes through like sawdust. Pity the perfect host!
The devil thinks and thinks and he cannot cry.

Constructivism

Computation is the heart
Of everything we prove.
Not for us the velvet wisdom
Of a softer love.

If Aphrodite spends the night,
Let Pallas spend the day.

When the sun dispels the stars
Put your dreams away.
—Errett Bishop
"Schizophrenia in Contemporary Mathematics," in R.O. Wells, Jr. (ed.), *Errett Bishop: Reflections on Him and His Research,* Providence, RI: American Mathematical Society, 1985, p. 14.

45 Young Irving Joshua Bush, who later took the name of Matrix . . . grew up a devout believer in the biblical prophecies of his parents' faith, and, owing to a natural bent in mathematics, was particularly intrigued by the numerical aspects of those prophecies. At the age of seven he surprised his father by pointing out that there was 1 God, 2 testaments, 3 persons in the Trinity, 4 Gospels, 5 books of Moses, 6 days of creation, and 7 gifts of the Holy Spirit.

"What about 8?" his father had asked.

"It is the holiest number of all," the boy replied, "The other numbers with holes are 0, 6, and 9, and sometimes 4, but 8 has two holes, therefore it is the holiest."
—Martin Gardner
The Magic Numbers of Dr. Matrix, New York: Prometheus, 1985, p. 4.

46 A too persistent research student drove his supervisor to say "Go away and work out the construction for a regular polygon of 65537 ($= 2^{16} + 1$) sides." The student returned 20 years later with a construction (deposited in the Archives at Göttingen).
—John E. Littlewood
Béla Bollobás (ed.), *Littlewood's Miscellany,* Cambridge: Cambridge University Press, 1986, p. 60.

47 Schoolmaster: 'Suppose x is the number of sheep in the problem.' Pupil: 'But, Sir, suppose x is not the number of sheep.' (I asked Prof. Wittgenstein was this not a profound philosophical joke, and he said it was.)
—John E. Littlewood
Béla Bollobás (ed.), *Littlewood's Miscellany,* Cambridge: Cambridge University Press, 1986, p. 59.

48 [In 1940] over lunch, Wiener and Aurel Wintner amused themselves (and me) by inventing titles for articles in a journal to be called *Trivia Mathematica.* Wiener was enormously amused by the results, and insisted on showing them to Tibor Radó, who was well known to have no sense of humor, and was not amused. [The list follows.]

Anouncement of the Revival
of a Distinguished Journal
TRIVIA MATHEMATICA
founded by Norbert Wiener and Aurel Wintner
in 1939

"Everything is trivial once you know the proof."   —D. V. Widder

The first issue of *Trivia Mathematica (Old Series)* was never published. *Trivia Mathematica (New Series)* will be issued continuously in unbounded parts. Contributions may be written in Basic English, English BASIC, Poldavian, Peanese and/or Ish, and should be directed to the Editors at the Department of Metamathematics, University of the Bad Lands. Contributions will be neither acknowledged, returned, nor published.

The first issue will be dedicated to N. Bourbaki, John Rainwater, Adam Riese, O. P. Lossers, A. C. Zitronenbaum, Anon, and to the memory of T. Radó, who was not amused. It is expected to include the following papers.

On the well-ordering of finite sets.

A Jordan curve passing through no point on any plane.

Fermat's last theorem. I: The case of even primes.

Fermat's last theorem. II: A proof assuming no responsibility.

On the topology im Kleinen of the null circle.

On prime round numbers.

The asymptotic behavior of the coefficients of a polynomial.

The product of large consecutive integers is never a prime.

Certain invariant characterizations of the empty set.

The random walk on one-sided streets.

The statistical independence of the zeros of the exponential function.

Fixed points in theorem space.

On the tritangent planes of the ternary antiseptic.

On the asymptotic distribution of gaps in the proofs of theorems in harmonic analysis.

Proof that every inequation has an unroot.

Sur un continu d'hypothèses qui équivalent à l'hypothèse du continu.

On unprintable propositions.

A momentous problem for monotonous functions.

On the kernels of mathematical nuts.

The impossibility of the proof of the impossibility of a proof.
A sweeping-out process for inexhaustible mathematicians.
On transformations without sense.
The normal distribution of abnormal mathematicians.
The method of steepest descents on weakly bounding bicycles.
Elephantine analysis and Giraffical representation.
The twice-Born approximation
Pseudoproblems for pseudodifferential operators.

  The Editors are pleased to announce that because of a timely subvention from the National Silence Foundation, the first issue will not appear.   —R. P. Boas

> "Memories of Bygone Meetings," in Peter Duren
> (ed.), *A Century of Mathematics in America, Part
> I*, Providence, RI: American Mathematical Society,
> 1989, p. 95.

49   Mathematicians, like cows in the dark, all look alike to me.
                                              —Abraham Flexner

> Armand Borel, "The School of Mathematics at the
> Institute for Advanced Study," in Peter Duren (ed.),
> *A Century of Mathematics in America, Part III*, Providence, RI: American Mathematical Society, 1989, p.
> 129.

CHAPTER 16

Mathematics Education

1 The aims in teaching geometry should be, according to my views:
1. That the pupil should acquire an accurate, thorough knowledge of geometrical truths.

2. That he should develop the power of original, logical, geometrical reasoning.

3. That he should acquire a habit of thought which will give him a practical sagacity; which will develop his judgment, increase his resourcefulness, and fit him to cope more successfully with the many and varied problems of his after life; which will teach him to take a many-sided view of things, so that if the avenue of attack is blocked, he should be able to promptly, cheerfully and successfully attack from another quarter.   —W. E. Bond
"The Aims in Teaching Geometry and How to Attain
Them," Math. Teacher 1 (September 1908) 30.

2 It would appear, on the face of it, that girls and boys in these days and this country enjoy equal opportunities. They may read the same books and play the same games; they pass through the same grade school and, in most towns, the same high school; finally, they receive, as a rule, the same preparation for college. But is even this all that is involved?

Whoever will watch groups of girls and boys in any grade school must realize that out of sight, in the homes, distinctions are introduced which

result ultimately in mental handicap for the girl. This discrimination manifests itself primarily in compelling her attention in matters of dress. Observe the hat constructed for the little girl's wearing and contrast it with the cap worn by a boy of her own age. Good brains go to waste under a hat like that because it must receive the attention that the boy may save to bestow on a hundred things worth while. The rest of the girl's apparel corresponds of course to her hat. What is the prevailing style, how shall her clothes be made and trimmed, and does she look pretty in them, are considerations that grow with the girl's growth. If she is destined to be a member or, let us say, an associate member of the leisure class she can not proceed far in her teens before her social environment compels acceptance of the notion that a girl must be, first of all, attractive and pleasing—if possible, a social ornament. A girl is free to elect science in the high school, but what does the freedom avail if science appears undesirable on the ground that it in no way contributes to her accomplishments. Further than this, a girl loses as a rule the informal preparation for science that a boy secures. The proprieties and dainty clothing cost her many a lesson that her brother learns; and who concern themselves to take a girl to the blacksmith shop, the power-house, and the stone-quarry, to the places where the steam-shovel and the pile-driver are at work. ... Opportunity is rendered ineffective and the world of natural phenomena inviting to observation and analysis is denied to girls because they are assigned to an artificial environment demanding an emotional response; and then we wonder at it when young women in their junior and senior years in college elect music and literature in preference to mechanics and philosophy; we wonder and we frame theories about feminine predilection.   —Ellen Hayes
"Women and Scientific Research," *Science* 32 (16 December 1910) 865.

3   It is a curious fact that the one striking example of rigorous mathematical reasoning with which everyone is familiar is taken from geometry rather than from algebra. Euclid's *Elements* has stood for 2000 years as the supreme illustration of the mathematical manner of reasoning. Axiom, theorem; hypothesis, conclusion; proposition, demonstration, corollary; the defense of every statement by reference to a previously established truth—all the apparatus and method of mathematical reasoning call up at once in our minds a text-book in geometry, never a text-book in algebra ...

Until recent years, elementary algebra has been largely a miscellaneous collection of rules for the manipulation of algebraic expressions, and is not at all the developed science that elementary geometry has long since become. In fact, if it were not for the study of plane geometry in our schools, it is doubtful whether our school children would ever derive, from their study of algebra alone, any clear notion of what is meant by a mathematical demonstration.

This fact is the more remarkable, because, on account of the simpler nature of the concepts with which it deals, algebra is better suited than geometry to serve as an illustration of what is essentially involved in mathematical reasoning. In geometry, the very concreteness and familiarity of the subject-matter is apt to obscure the logical structure of the science, while in algebra, the more abstract character of the content of the theorems makes it easier to fix the attention on their formal logical relations. —Edward V. Huntington
"The Fundamental Propositions of Algebra," in J. W. A. Young (ed.), *Monographs on the Topics of Modern Mathematics Relevant to the Elementary Field,* New York: Longmans, Green, 1911, p. 152.

4 We [my student and I] are both greatly amazed; and my share in the satisfaction is a double one, for he sees twice over who makes others see. —Jean Henri Fabre
The Life of the Fly, New York: Dodd, Mead and Co, 1915, p. 300.

5 No student ought to complete a course in mathematics without the feeling that there must be something in it, without catching a glimpse, however fleeting, of its possibilities, without at least a few moments of pleasure in achievement and insight. —Helen A. Merrill
"Why Students Fail in Mathematics," *Math. Teacher* 11 (December 1918) 51.

6 It is clearly impossible to arrange a scale of hardness in studies such as is used in mineralogical tests. But if the formation of such a scale were attempted, mathematics would probably head most of the lists. Once label a subject *very hard,* and let that label be flaunted before the young pupils' sight, and they are handicapped from the start. They magnify every difficulty, are discouraged too easily, accept failures as all but inevitable. This disadvantage works in many ways. Children are pitied for having to work hard examples, they are made to tremble at the very thought of algebra and geometry. If they express any pleasure in the subject they are called grinds or sharks, or are told "Just wait till you get to radicals." Students who have just finished a course in algebra and geometry delight in terrifying those in the class below them, exaggerating its difficulties, discouraging them from reasonable efforts to succeed by instilling a belief in the futility of such attempts, magnifying the slaughter wrought by examinations, or perhaps declaring that the only way they themselves got through was by committing all the proofs to memory, a tale which can rarely be true, but which is often swallowed with avidity. If it were possible to eliminate from the young minds, that cling so tenaciously to some forms of tradition, this conventional view of mathematics, I believe that we should find pleasure in learning and in teaching mathematics wonderfully increased, and failures in the subject correspondingly diminished. Is there any way in which we can achieve this? It is worth much thought and effort.　　　　—Helen A. Merrill

"Why Students Fail in Mathematics," *Math. Teacher* 11 (December 1918) 51.

7　We have come to believe that a pupil in school should feel that he is living his own life naturally, with a minimum of restraint and without tasks that are unduly irksome; that he should find his way through arithmetic largely by his own spirit of curiosity; and that he should be directed in arithmetic as he would be directed in any other game,—not harshly driven, hardly even led, but proceeding with the feeling that he is being accompanied and that he is doing his share in finding the way.

—D. E. Smith

The Progress of Arithmetic, New York: Ginn and Company, 1923, p. 12.

8　Our work is great in the classroom if we feel the nobility of that work, if we love the human souls we work with more than the division of fractions, if we love our subject so much that we make our pupils love it, and if we remember that our duty to the world is to help fix in the minds of our pupils the facts of number that they must have in after life.

—D. E. Smith

The Progress of Arithmetic, New York: Ginn and Company, 1923, p. 58.

9　In the development of the individual in his relations to the world, there is no initial separation of science into constituent parts, while there is ultimately a branching into the many distinct sciences. The troublesome problem of the closer relation of pure mathematics to its applications: can it not be solved by indirection, in that through the whole course of elementary mathematics, including the introduction to the calculus, there be recognized in the organization of the curriculum no distinction between the various branches of pure mathematics, and likewise no distinction between pure mathematics and its principal applications? Further, from the standpoint of pure mathematics: will not the twentieth century find it possible to give to young students during their impressionable years, in thoroughly concrete and captivating form, wonderful new notions of the seventeenth century?

By the way of suggestion these questions have been answered in affirmative, on condition that there be established a thoroughgoing laboratory system of instruction in primary schools, secondary schools, and junior colleges—a laboratory system involving a synthesis and development of the best pedagogic methods at present in use in mathematics and the physical sciences. —E. H. Moore

> "On the Foundations of Mathematics," in Charles Austin (ed.), *The First Yearbook: A General Survey of Progress in the Last Twenty-five Years,* New York, National Council of Teachers of Mathematics, 1926, p. 56.

IO *The primary purposes of the teaching of mathematics should be to develop those powers of understanding and of analyzing relations of quantity and of space which are necessary to an insight into and a control over our environment and to an appreciation of the progress of civilization in its various aspects, and to develop those habits of thought and of action which will make those powers effective in the life of the individual.*

All topics, processes, and drill in technique which do not directly contribute to the development of the powers mentioned should be eliminated from the curriculum.

> —National Committee on Mathematical Requirements
> J. W. Young (ed.), *The Reorganization of Mathematics in Secondary Education,* New York: Houghton Mifflin, 1927, p. 13.

II Before teachers can properly correlate mathematics with other fields, they ought to learn how to correlate the various parts of mathematics. They should first learn how and where arithmetic and informal geometry can be correlated, how and where algebra can be best correlated with arithmetic and informational geometry, and so on. Unless

we can do this, there is small chance that we can successfully correlate mathematics with science, music, the arts, and other applied fields.
—W. D. Reeve
"Mathematics and the Integrated Program in Secondary Schools," *Teachers College Record* 36 (March 1935) 503.

12   In colonial days scientific and mathematical knowledge had a certain definite standing, largely for its practical value but in part also for its own sake. George Washington was a scientifically-minded gentleman farmer for much of his life, and in his youth was a skilled surveyor, familiar with trigonometry; Benjamin Franklin discovered experimentally the electrical nature of the lightning discharge, theorized concerning electricity as a fluid, and had enough mathematical interest to devise ingenious magic squares; Thomas Jefferson regarded geometry and trigonometry as "most valuable to everyman," algebra and logarithms as "often of value," while he classed "conic sections, curves of the higher orders, perhaps even spherical trigonometry, algebraic operations beyond the $2d$ dimension, and fluxions" as a "delicious luxury"; in his later years Jefferson spent much of his time in mathematical reading, and was ever a true friend of mathematics. The interest in science and mathematics continued to be genteel and amateurish among American scholars and devotees until toward the middle of the last century, with few notable exceptions.   —George Birkhoff
"Fifty Years of American Mathematics," *Semicentennial Addresses of the American Mathematical Society, Vol. II,* New York: American Mathematical Society, 1938, p. 270.

13   Far seeing university and college presidents, desirous of improving the intellectual status of the institutions which they serve . . . strengthen their mathematical staffs. For, in doing so, no extraordinary laboratory or library expenses are incurred; furthermore, the subject of mathematics is in a state of continual creative growth, ever more important to engineer, scientist, and philosopher alike; and excellent mathematicians from here and abroad are within financial reach.   —George Birkhoff
"Fifty Years of American Mathematics," *Semicentennial Addresses of the American Mathematical Society, Vol. II,* New York: American Mathematical Society, 1938, p. 277.

14 Many teachers and textbook writers have never recognized the power of sheer intellectual curiosity as a motive for the highest type of work in mathematics, and as a consequence they have failed to organize and present the work in a manner designed to stimulate the student's interest through a challenge to his curiosity.

—Charles H. Butler and F. Lynwood Wren
The Teaching of Secondary Mathematics, New York: McGraw-Hill, 1941, p. 110.

15 When a student makes really silly blunders or is exasperatingly slow, the trouble is almost always the same; he has no desire at all to solve the problem, even no desire to understand it properly, and so he has not understood it. Therefore, a teacher wishing seriously to help the student should, first of all, stir up his curiosity, give him some desire to solve the problem. The teacher should also allow some time to the student to make up his mind to settle down to his task.

Teaching to solve problems is education of the will. Solving problems which are not too easy for him, the student learns to persevere through success, to appreciate small advance, to wait for the essential idea, to concentrate with all his might when it appears. If the student had no opportunity in school to familiarize himself with the varying emotions of the struggle for the solution his mathematical education failed in the most vital point.
—George Pólya
How to Solve It, Princeton: Princeton University Press, 1945, p. 88.

16 It has been said, often enough and certainly with good reason, that teaching mathematics affords a unique opportunity to teach demonstrative reasoning. I wish to add that teaching mathematics also affords an excellent opportunity to teach plausible reasoning ... A student of mathematics should learn, of course, demonstrative reasoning; it is his profession and the distinctive mark of his science. Yet he should also learn plausible reasoning; this is the kind of reasoning on which his creative work will mainly depend. The general student should get a taste of demonstrative reasoning; he may have little opportunity to use it directly, but he should acquire a standard with which he can compare alleged evidence of all sorts aimed at him in modern life. He needs, however, in all his endeavors plausible reasoning. At any rate, an

ambitious teacher of mathematics should teach both kinds of reasoning
to both kinds of students.   —George Pólya
"On Plausible Reasoning," *Proceedings of the International Congress of Mathematics—1950, Vol. I,* Providence, RI: American Mathematical Society, 1952, p.
746.

17   To those people who have never been able to stand mathematics,
I should like to remark that their dislike may have been formed early
in life by school experiences. Many aversions to history have been built
up by teachers who taught history by riding herd over a collection of
dates, and to geography by a method of presentation in which drill on
the capitals of the forty-eight states formed a significant part. And if
the above examples seem extreme, consider grammar-school arithmetic
with its twin tormentors—the addition and multiplication tables.

There is some chance, however, of history and geography's receiving
a better treatment in later schoolwork. But mathematics remains in a
comatose condition all through grammar school. All too often, in fact,
it barely comes to life in high-school or in freshman and sophomore
college work. Thus, even in college, the student frequently still does
not come into contact with living mathematics—the mathematics of
the contemporary mathematician. Instead, he largely studies formal
manipulation, useful in solving problems of physics and engineering but
not useful in fostering an understanding of modern mathematics which
is so highly unmanipulational.

For real mathematics is a constantly expanding subject in which ideas
and not manipulations play the dominant role.   —Roy Dubisch
The Nature of Number, New York: Ronald Press, 1952,
p. v.

18   I do not contend that the study of mathematics will automatically
produce intellectually honest people. Nevertheless, I do contend that
mathematics is the ideal subject in which to point out to the student the
virtues of intellectual honesty. In this age of the advertising man and
his more vicious cousin, the propaganda technician, is there any more
important function for education to perform?   —Moses Richardson
"Mathematics and Intellectual Honesty," *Amer. Math.
Monthly* 59 (February 1952) 76.

19   There are at least four fundamental purposes that the study of
mathematics should attain. First, it should serve as a functional tool in

solving our individual everyday problems. These questions How much? How many? What form or shape? and Can you prove it? arise every day in the lives of every citizen. . . .

In the second place, mathematics serves as a handmaiden for the explanation of the quantitative situations in other subjects, such as economics, physics, navigation, finance, biology, and even the arts. The mathematics used in these areas of practice is exactly the same mathematics and involves the same mathematical concepts and skills. It is only the things to which the mathematics is applied that are different, and this is immaterial if one really understands the mathematics. . . .

In the third place, mathematics, when properly conceived, becomes a model for thinking, for developing scientific structure, for drawing conclusions, and for solving problems. Its postulational nature, that is, accepted relations (axioms or postulates), undefined terms, definitions, theorems, and a logic, aids all other areas of knowledge to approach scientific perfection. This same structure aids us in problem solving methods in which we collect, organize, and analyze data, and deduce conclusions for future action. For example, one who understands the mathematical method can easily frame the problem. . . .

In the fourth place, mathematics is the best describer of the universe about us. In an age that has become statistical and scientific in much of its human endeavor, the need for people to understand these phenomena is not only a cultural necessity but to some extent a necessity for intelligent action.   —Howard F. Fehr
"Reorientation in Mathematics Education," *Teachers College Record* 54 (May 1953) 435.

20 University teaching in mathematics should: (a) answer the requirements of all those who need mathematics for practical purposes; (b) train specialists in the subject; (c) give to all students that intellectual and moral training which any University, worthy of the name, has the duty to impart.

These objects are not contradictory but complementary to each other. Thus, a training for practical purposes can be made to play the same part in mathematics as experiments play in physics and chemistry. Thus again, personal and independent thinking cannot be encouraged without at the same time fostering the spirit of research.   —André Weil
"Mathematical Teaching in Universities," *Amer. Math. Monthly* 61 (January 1954) 34.

21   The only instruction which a professor can give, in my opinion, is to think in front of his students.   —Henri Lebesgue

> A. Denjoy, L. Felix, and P. Montel. "Henri Lebesgue, le Savant, le Professeur, l'homme," *L'Enseignement Mathématique* 3, ser. 2 (January-March 1957) 8.

22   If you tell students that the marks which they make for numbers are numerals and not numbers, a natural reply is "What are numbers then?" The student writes 'Empire State Building' and can point to the Empire State Building, whereas he writes '5' but cannot point to 5. One of the immediate advantages of pointing out the distinction between numbers and numerals is that it raises the question: What are numbers? In a conventional course, students can be told that the number 5 exists independently of its name just as, for example, does the concept justice. The student never thinks that the word 'justice' is justice itself and in a similar way he can appreciate that the numeral '5' is not 5 itself. He has more or less vague ways of deciding whether a given act exemplifies justice (i.e., is just). He is likely to be much surer in deciding whether a given set exemplifies fiveness (i.e., has five members).

—UICSM Project Staff

> "Words, 'words', "words"," *Math. Teacher* 50 (March 1957) 195.

23   We believe that a student will come to understand mathematics when his textbook and teacher use unambiguous language and when he is enabled to discover generalizations by himself.   —Max Beberman

> *An Emerging Program of Secondary School Mathematics,* Cambridge, MA: Harvard University Press, 1958, p. 4.

24   A criticism of the discovery method runs something like this. It consumes too much time. Since the most important thing you can do for high school students is to help them acquire consummate skill in manipulation so that they can solve lots of problems, it is best to give, by rule and by example and with dispatch, all of the manipulative algorisms. Do this so that the student will have the maximum amount of time for practice. Occasionally, the teacher should ask a few questions as he derives a formula at the blackboard, but this type of questioning should not be pushed far because the student cannot be expected to know a derivation he has not seen carried out prior to that time. (Since only the brightest can ever reproduce derivations anyway, you can't include them on tests. Also, college entrance examination questions are multiple-choice, so there really is no good reason to waste effort on derivations.) —Max Beberman

An Emerging Program of Secondary School Mathematics, Cambridge, MA: Harvard University Press, 1958, p. 35.

25 The problem of providing a curriculum together with instructional material for all students, with their varied interests and abilities, is a tremendous task. Five points must be borne in mind in planning such a curriculum:

1. No one can predict exactly which mathematical skills will be important and useful in the future.

2. No one can predict exactly what career any particular student will choose when he leaves school.

3. Teaching which emphasizes understanding, insight, and imagination, without neglecting basic skills, is the best for all students, whatever their ability, and makes the best preparation for any vocation that uses mathematics.

4. An understanding of the role of mathematics in our society is essential for intelligent citizenship.

5. Any normal individual can appreciate some, at least, of the beauty and power of mathematics, and the appreciation is an important part of a civilized person's cultural background. —E. G. Begle

"The School Mathematics Study Group," *Math. Teacher* 51 (December 1958) 616.

26 The world of today demands more mathematical knowledge on the part of more people than the world of yesterday, and the world of tomorrow will demand even more. It is therefore important that mathematics be taught in a vital and imaginative way which will make students aware that it is a living, growing subject which plays an increasingly important part in the contemporary world. —E. G. Begle

"The School Mathematics Study Group," *Math. Teacher* 51 (December 1958) 616.

27 Educators today seem to have lost sight of the fact that mathematics is an essential element in the cultural heritage of the Western world. When they teach the painting, the sculpture, the literature, and the philosophy of the Renaissance, they ignore the reawakening of mathematical thought that took place concurrently. It was at this time,

for example, that mathematicians began pondering the nature of chance and developing the theory of probability that has enabled physicists, economists, statisticians, and social scientists to deal rationally with the basically uncertain world. When mathematics is taught, it is presented mainly as a collection of slightly related techniques and manipulations. The profound, yet simple, concepts get little attention. If art appreciation were taught in the same way, it would consist mostly of learning how to chip stone and mix paints.   —George A. W. Boehm
The New World of Mathematics, New York: Dial, 1958, p. 8.

28   Mathematical examination problems are usually considered unfair if insoluble or improperly described; whereas the mathematical problems of real life are almost invariably insoluble and badly stated, at least in the first balance. In real life, the mathematician's main task is to formulate problems by building an abstract mathematical model consisting of equations, which will be simple enough to solve without being so crude that they fail to mirror reality. Solving equations is a minor technical matter compared with this fascinating and sophisticated craft of model-building, which calls for both clear, keen common-sense and the highest qualities of artistic and creative imagination.
—John Hammersley
Mina Rees, "Mathematics in the Market Place," *Amer. Math. Monthly* 65 (May 1958) 335.

29   A creative mathematician is the intersection of several unlikely events. For the most part we are ignorant of the nature of these events and of their probabilities. Some of them are at present quite beyond our controls. An example is the probability of a genetic composition necessary for intensive and highly abstract thinking. Others are clearly subject to our influence. For example, the probability of an early acquaintance with living mathematics and with the joy of mathematical achievement is determined by educational practices.
—Kenneth O. May
"Undergraduate Research in Mathematics," *Amer. Math. Monthly* 65 (April 1958) 241.

30   [Informal advice to teachers]
1. There is one infallible teaching method: you will infallibly succeed in boring your audience with your subject if you are bored with it

yourself. Hence the first commandment for teachers: *Be interested in your subject.*

2. No amount of courses in teaching methods will enable you to explain understandably a point that you do not understand yourself. Hence the second commandment for teachers: *Know your subject.*

3. Our knowledge about any subject consists of "information" and of "know-how." In mathematics "know-how" is the ability to solve problems and it is much more important than mere possession of information. You have to show your students how to solve problems—can you show it if you don't know it? Hence a special commandment for mathematics teachers: *Acquire, and keep up, some aptitude for problem solving.*

—George Pólya
"On the Curriculum of Prospective High School Teachers," *Amer. Math. Monthly* 65 (February 1958) 104.

31 By what standard should we judge the success of a high school curriculum in mathematics? By essentially the same standard, I say, as we would judge the curriculum in French: by the facility that the students acquire in using the language—since mathematics is essentially a language. After graduation, your former student will go to college or into some profession. In the one place as in the other, he may face a problem capable of mathematical treatment. If he can reduce it to a neat computation, or set up an equation for it, or express it by a diagram, the result of your teaching is excellent. If, without being able to produce them, he can read graphs and formulas, and appreciate them, too, the result is still very good. If however, he cannot read graphs, cannot read formulas, and does not care for them a bit, the result is poor.

—George Pólya
"On the Curriculum of Prospective High School Teachers," *Amer. Math. Monthly* 65 (February 1958) 104.

32 That gifted young people must be given the fullest opportunity to taste its pleasures and be seduced by its charms is a first requirement of any program of mathematical education. —Mina Rees
"Mathematics in the Market Place," *Amer. Math. Monthly* 65 (May 1958) 332.

33   The present syllabus in our high schools corresponds almost exactly to what was known in the year 1640.   —W. W. Sawyer
"Pressures on American Mathematics Teachers,"
SIAM Review 1 (January 1959) 32.

34   We may well ask of any item of information that is taught or that we lead a child to discover for himself whether it is worth knowing. I can only think of two good criteria and one middling one for deciding such an issue: whether the knowledge gives a sense of delight and whether it bestows the gift of intellectual travel beyond the information given, in the sense of containing within it the basis of generalization. The middling criterion is whether the knowledge is useful. It turns out, on the whole, as Charles Sanders Peirce commented, that useful knowledge looks after itself. So I would urge that we as school men let it do so and concentrate on the first two criteria. Delight and travel, then.

It seems to me that the implications of this conclusion are that we opt for depth and continuity in our teaching rather than coverage, and that we re-examine afresh what it is that bestows a sense of intellectual delight upon a person who is learning.   —Jerome Bruner
"On Learning Mathematics," *Math. Teacher* 53 (December 1960) 617.

35   Euclid's system has outlasted centuries of development in mathematics. The aims of modern instruction in the schools transcend the limits of Euclid less than we might suppose. But Euclid is a prefabricated house, and its instruction is static. It is our aim to make instruction dynamic, and this cannot be done by giving our pupils a systematically ordered catalogue of tasks to accomplish, which is essentially what we do in teaching Euclid.   —O. Botsch
New Thinking in School Mathematics, Organization of the European Economic Cooperation, 1961, p. 77.

36   The first [principle] . . . is that a mathematical theory can only be developed axiomatically in a fruitful way when the student has already acquired some familiarity with the corresponding material—a familiarity gained by working long enough with it on a kind of experimental, or semiexperimental basis, i.e., *with constant appeal to intuition.*

The other principle . . . is that when logical inference is introduced in some mathematical question, it should always be presented with

absolute honesty—that is, without trying to hide gaps or flaws in the argument; any other way, in my opinion, is worse than giving no proof at all.   —Jean Dieudonné
New Thinking in School Mathematics, Organization of the European Economic Cooperation, 1961, p. 39

37   We shall continue to fight our battle with those students who come to us sure that they will not be able to "do" mathematics, since they have been told at home that no one in their family, on either side, ever could. When we present mathematics to them as something other than a series of manipulations, we may even arouse their interest and upset some time-honored family traditions.   —W. E. Slesnick
Robert W. Ritchie (ed.), *New Directions in Mathematics*, Englewood Cliffs, NJ: Prentice-Hall, 1963, p. 17.

38   [How] do we teach a child to cut his losses, but at the same time be persistent in trying out an idea; to risk forming an early hunch without at the same time formulating one so early and with so little evidence that he is stuck with it while he waits for appropriate evidence to materialize; to pose good testable guesses that are neither too brittle nor too sinuously incorrigible? . . . Practice in inquiry . . . is needed—but in what form? Of only one thing am I convinced: I have never seen anyone improve in the art and technique of inquiry by any means other than engaging in inquiry.   —Jerome Bruner
On Knowing—Essays for the Left Hand, Cambridge, MA: Harvard University Press, 1962, p. 94.

39   Creativity is the heart and soul of mathematics at all levels. The collection of special skills and techniques is only the raw material out of which the subject itself grows. To look at mathematics without the creative side of it, is to look at a black-and-white photograph of a Cezanne; outlines may be there, but everything that matters is missing.
—R. C. Buck
"Teaching Machines and Mathematics Programs," *Amer. Math. Monthly* 69 (June-July 1962) 562.

40   Mathematicians seem to have forgotten that for two thousand years Euclid's geometry was a model of rigor. Not even the greatest mathematicians observed its deficiencies. Similarly the foundation of the real number system was not created until the latter part of the nineteenth century. Neither Euler nor Gauss could have defined a real number, and it is unlikely that they would have enjoyed the gory details.

But both managed to understand mathematics and to make a "fair" number of contributions to the subject. Rigorous proof is not nearly so important as proving the worth of what we are teaching; and most teachers, instead of being concerned about their failure to be sufficiently rigorous, should really be concerned about their failure to provide a truly intuitive approach. . . . The general principle, then, is that the rigor should be suited to the mathematical age of the student and not to the age of mathematics.   —Morris Kline
Mathematics: A Cultural Approach, Reading, MA: Addison-Wesley, 1962, p. vii.

41   There is a distinction between what may be called a *problem* and what may be considered an *exercise*. The latter serves to drill a student in some technique or procedure, and requires little if any, original thought. Thus, after a student beginning algebra has encountered the quadratic formula, he should undoubtedly be given a set of exercises in the form of specific quadratic equations to be solved by the newly acquired tool. The working of these exercises will help clinch his grasp of the formula and will assure his ability to use the formula. An exercise, then, can always be done with reasonable dispatch and with a minimum of creative thinking. In contrast to an exercise, a problem, if it is a good one for its level, should require thought on the part of the student. The student must devise strategic attacks, some of which may fail, others of which may partially or completely carry him through. He may need to look up some procedure or some associated material in texts, so that he can push his plan through. Having successfully solved a problem the student should reconsider it to see if he can devise a different and perhaps better solution. He should look for further deductions, generalizations, and applications, and allied results. In short, he should live with the thing for a time, and examine it carefully in all lights. To be suitable, a problem must be such that the student cannot solve it immediately. One does not complain about a problem being too difficult, but rather too easy.

It is impossible to overstate the importance of problems in mathematics. It is by means of problems that mathematics develops and actually lifts itself by its own bookstraps. Every research article, every doctoral thesis, every new discovery in mathematics, results from an attempt to solve some problem.

The posing of appropriate problems, then, appears to be a very suitable way to introduce the promising student to mathematical research.

And, it is worth noting, the more problems one plays with, the more problems one may be able to propose on one's own. The ability to propose significant problems is one requirement to be a creative mathematician.

—Howard Eves
A Survey of Geometry, Vol. 1, Boston: Allyn and Bacon, 1963, p. ix.

42 Teaching is not a science, but an art. . . .

Teaching obviously has much in common with the theatrical art. For instance, you have to present to your class a proof which you know thoroughly having presented it already so many times in former years in the same course. You really can not be excited about this proof—but, please, do not show that to your class: if you appear bored, the whole class will be bored. Pretend to be excited about the proof when you start it, pretend to have bright ideas when you proceed, pretend to be surprised and elated when the proof ends. You should do a little acting for the sake of your students who may learn, occasionally, more from your attitudes than from the subject matter presented. . . .

Less obviously, teaching has something in common also with music. You know, of course, that the teacher should not say things just once or twice, but three or four or more times. Yet, repeating the same sentence several times without pause and change may be terribly boring and defeat its own purpose. Well, you can learn from the composers how to do it better. One of the principal art forms of music is "air with variations." Transposing this art form from music into teaching you begin by saying your sentence in its simplest form; then you repeat it with a little change; then you repeat it again with a little more color, and so on; you may wind up by returning to the original simple formulation. Another musical art form is the "rondo." Transposing the rondo from music into teaching, you repeat the same essential sentence several times with little or no change, but you insert between two repetitions some appropriately contrasting illustrative material. I hope that when you listen the next time to a theme with variations by Beethoven or to a rondo by Mozart you will give a little thought to improving your teaching.

Now and then, teaching may approach poetry, and now and then it may approach profanity. May I tell you a little story about the great Einstein? I listened once to Einstein as he talked to a group of physicists in a party. "Why have all the electrons the same charge?" said he. "Well, why are all the little balls in the goat dung of the same size?" Why did Einstein say such things? Just to make some snobs to raise their eyebrows? He was not disinclined to do so, I think. Yet, probably, it went deeper. I do not think that the overheard remark of Einstein was quite casual. At any rate, I learnt something from it: Abstractions are important; use all means to make them more tangible. Nothing is too good or too bad, too poetical or too trivial to clarify your abstractions. As Montaigne put it: The truth is such a great thing that we should not disdain any means that could lead to it. Therefore, if the spirit moves you to be a little poetical, or a little profane, in your class, do not have the wrong kind of inhibition.   —George Pólya

"On Learning, Teaching, and Learning Teaching," *Amer. Math. Monthly* 70 (June-July 1963) 606.

43 A considerable portion of my high school trigonometry course was devoted to the solution of oblique triangles. I pride myself on the fact that I was the best triangle solver my high school ever turned out. When I went to Princeton I found that I was up against very stiff competition. But whereas other freshmen might outdo me in many ways, I felt confident that I would shine when the time came to solve triangles. All through my undergraduate years I was waiting for that golden moment. Then I waited all through graduate school, through my work with Einstein, at Los Alamos, and while teaching and consulting for more than a dozen years. I have still not had an excuse for using my talents for solving oblique triangles.

If a professional mathematician never uses these dull techniques in a highly varied career, why must all high school students devote several weeks to the subject?   —John G. Kemeny

Random Essays on Mathematics, Education and Computers, Englewood Cliffs, NJ: Prentice-Hall, 1964, p. 13.

44 I think in all fields we owe it to our best students to encourage creative endeavor. The great advantage that we have in mathematics is that, again and again, examples have shown it possible to get students at a remarkably early age to do creative mathematics. There have been major contributions to mathematics by men in their late teens. Even if your students aren't going to do creative work, at least give them a first taste of developing something that may not be new to the mathematical world, but is new to them; something that has not been spoon-fed, but

that they have honestly discovered for themselves—preferably something that you, yourself have never heard of. I know that at first it is frightening to have your students know something you don't know, but it is the greatest achievement of a teacher to enable his students to surpass him.
— John G. Kemeny
Random Essays on Mathematics, Education and Computers, Englewood Cliffs, NJ: Prentice-Hall, 1964, p. 46.

45 The hundredth anniversary of the last covered wagon is approaching. Let us pay tribute to our ancestors who had the courage to set out west in a covered wagon, with some simple farm implements for equipment, and with the inevitable shotgun for protection. But if you want to follow in their footsteps I would suggest that in place of a covered wagon you acquire a well-rounded liberal education, in place of farm implements you equip yourself with an insatiable interest in human problems, and in place of the shotgun you would be well advised to arm yourself with the weapons of modern mathematics. —John G. Kemeny
Random Essays on Mathematics, Education and Computers, Englewood Cliffs, NJ: Prentice-Hall, 1964, p. 26.

46 Mathematics is capable of being learned as an *activity,* and that knowledge which is acquired in this way has a power which is out of all proportion to its quantity.

For this reason, it seems to me quite unrealistic to judge a curriculum by its general outline, or to judge a course by its syllabus. We can "cover" very impressive material, if we are willing to turn the student into a spectator. But if you cast the student in a passive role, then saying that he has "studied" your course may mean no more than saying of a cat that he has looked at a king. Mathematics is something that one *does.*
— Edwin E. Moise
"Activity and Motivation in Mathematics," *Amer. Math. Monthly* 72 (April 1965) 409.

47 One sometimes encounters quite curious conceptions as to what studying really means. If only everything is made quite palatable to the student, then, in the opinion of some, it ought to be an easy matter to advance to a mastery of the material, child's play to attain the loftiest heights of knowledge. It is thought to be an error if toil and effort are required on the way to the heights and that therefore, through the fault of the teacher, the goal is reached by only a few, and only slowly and gradually even by those. Of course everyone realizes that in, say, skiing and horseback riding, it is not sufficient to listen to instructions on the motions and carriage of the body, in order to handle oneself properly from the beginning on the skis or in the saddle; rather, many a drop of sweat and an occasional tumble must precede the assurance sought for.

Why should it not be similar in the intellectual field, in the acquisition of a body of knowledge: that genuine success is accorded only to serious, persistent effort along with occasional correction of false conceptions? And that even the best teacher can indeed guide the student and help him to avoid unnecessary obstacles on the way to acquiring skills and knowledge, but neither can nor should spare him persistent work; and that in addition, where talent is lacking, the hardest labor of love must be content with modest results. In this respect the serious study of mathematics is hardly an exception.   —Heinrich Tietze
Famous Problems of Mathematics, New York: Gray-lock Press, 1965, p. ix.

48   The arithmetic and the algebra that we learn in school have been known for centuries, and the geometry taught in the schools is for the most part some thousands of years old. This explains not only why there is scarcely any further change in the content of instruction, but also why the manner of presentation has assumed an established, almost rigid form which conceals the fact that this knowledge had once to be attained by laborious struggle. And this also explains why an outsider to mathematics, in view of the ancient and firm stock of knowledge transmitted to him in school, usually finds it hard to conceive that in mathematics also there are a host of problems. But we can only conceive of a science as living if, besides solved problems, it has also unsolved ones, and if the answers to earlier questions lead to new questions and stimulate new research.   —Heinrich Tietze
Famous Problems of Mathematics, New York: Gray-lock Press, 1965, p. xv.

49   Indeed, only a few are mathematically gifted in the sense that they are endowed with the talent to discover new mathematical facts. But by the same token, only a few are musically gifted in that they are able to compose music. Nevertheless there are many who can understand and perhaps reproduce music, or who at least enjoy it. We believe that the number of people who can understand simple mathematical ideas is not relatively smaller than the number of those who are commonly called musical, and that their interest will be stimulated if only we can eliminate the aversion toward mathematics that so many have acquired from childhood experiences.

—Hans Rademacher and Otto Toeplitz
The Enjoyment of Mathematics, Princeton: Princeton University Press, 1966, p. 5.

50 The only way to learn mathematics is to do mathematics. That tenet is the foundation of the do-it-yourself, Socratic, or Texas method, the method in which the teacher plays a role of an omniscient but largely uncommunicative referee between the learner and the facts.

—Paul Halmos
A Hilbert Space Problem Book, Princeton: Van Nostrand, 1967, p. vii.

51 People do acquire a little brief authority by equipping themselves with jargon: they can pontificate and air a superficial expertise. But what we should ask of the educated mathematician is not what he can speechify about, nor even what he knows about the existing corpus of mathematical knowledge, but rather what can he now do with his learning and whether he can actually solve mathematical problems arising in practice. In short, we look for deeds not words.   —J. M. Hammersley
"On the Enfeeblement of Mathematical Skills by 'Modern Mathematics' and by Similar Soft Intellectual Trash in Schools and Universities," *Inst. of Math. and Its Appl. Bull.* 4 (October 1968) 67.

52 What concerns me, then, is the emphasis on a good thing, efficient teaching of concepts, and the possible neglect of the essential thing, learning to learn.   —Harold C. Trimble
"The Heart of Teaching," *Math. Teacher* 61 (May 1968) 485.

53 The Ph.D. in mathematics is viewed today as a research degree. The training of the student proceeding toward this degree is totally oriented to the production of research scholars. Perhaps more significant, the total emphasis is that of the importance of doing research. How realistic is all this? Even more pertinent, how effective and constructive is it? ... Using the vaguest criteria, the general estimate is that between 20 and 25 percent of our Ph.D's go on to become researchers. What happens to the other 75%? For the most part they end up teaching in four-year colleges and lesser established universities.

In what state do the people making up this 75% arrive in the institutions where they will take up their life's work—teaching? Very often they arrive poorly educated. Since everything in their graduate training has been pointed towards the production of an original, publishable, research thesis, too often they have narrowed or have been narrowed in order to learn enough about some small slice of mathematics so as to be able to write something original. They have been given a view of mathematics through a tiny slit and have very little of a global view of mathematics or of their own particular sub-field. Now they are to teach across the whole undergraduate mathematics curriculum, which today involves much non-trivial subject matter, not as algebraists, topologists or analysts but as mathematicians. Are they prepared to do so? On many subjects that they will be required to teach they will know little more than their students and will have relatively little more appreciation of how these things fit into the large picture. How can they guide and imbue their students with a proper feeling for their subject? True, they are more mature, especially if it comes to the structure of hemi-demi groupoids with chain conditions say, the topic of their thesis. Unfortunately this sophistication on a very small corner of mathematics does not help them at all in carrying out their every-day function as good teachers and in speaking with some authority about their chosen discipline to their students.

Unfortunately, this sophistication about hemi-demi groupoids with chain conditions does not even help them very much as researchers, either. How much is there to say about such gadgets and, in fact, is it worth saying anything about them? The specialized knowledge about them is of no use when trying to switch to try one's hand at some other research. . . .

Worse than this, there is something else amiss in the picture. Many of this 75% have been inculcated throughout their whole graduate education with the feeling that being a mathematician is synonymous with being a research mathematician. Anything less is failure. So now one suffers from a sense of guilt, from a sense of not delivering the goods expected, from the feeling of being a failure in one's chosen profession. This frequently leads to a demoralization, an indifference to "lesser" duties—that is, teaching—and imagined failure now becomes actual failure. Why should people doing the honest job of being good teachers and responsible members of their departments have to feel ashamed of what they are doing?

Another factor now enters the scene. Their colleges and universities have been conditioned—by our own profession unfortunately—that they must have research mathematicians in their departments. So these administrations start applying pressure, often economic in nature, that their department members produce research. The net effect of this is to intensify the frustration and sense of failure in a great part of their mathematics staff.
—I. N. Herstein
"On the Ph.D in Mathematics," *Amer. Math. Monthly*
76 (August-September 1969) 819.

54   [R. L.] Moore used a great many techniques for teaching. I think he had a certain charm about his personality that attracted students to him. Probably none of Moore's students inspire the loyalty among students that Dr. Moore has engendered among his students . . . He not only taught in the classroom but he taught in the halls. He taught through influence of his wife . . . Also I remember walking to school on a number of occasions with other professors and they would say, "Moore has been telling me about the theorem that you have proved in class and he says that he is very impressed with you." This is one of the techniques he had of encouraging his students by talking about them to other people and letting the word come back to them.   —R. H. Bing
Lucille S. Whyburn, "Student Oriented Teaching—
The Moore Method," *Amer. Math. Monthly* 77 (April
1970) 352.

55   The essence of the [R.L.] Moore Method is to use an axiomatic treatment to create in the student a spirit of self-confidence and pleasure in personal creative endeavor.   —Lucille S. Whyburn
"Student Oriented Teaching—The Moore Method,"
Amer. Math. Monthly 77 (April 1970) 352.

56   Youth can be poisoned mentally. Worthless products of art and literature fabricated by the advertising and pleasure industry are a menace to youth, not because they poison the natural sources of morals and taste but because their consumption requires no activity. There is one defence against it—to excite the mind into activity—it does not matter perhaps in which field. A child that has discovered science, art or morals by its own activity is protected against mental infection just as it is against physical infection.   —Hans Freudenthal
Mathematics as an Educational Task, Dordrecht: D.
Reidel Publishing Co., 1973, p. 58.

57   A smooth lecture . . . may be pleasant; a good teacher challenges, asks, annoys, irritates, and maintains high standards—all that is generally not pleasant.   —Paul Halmos
"The Teaching of Problem Solving," *Amer. Math. Monthly* 82 (May 1975) 468.

58   I believe that the ultimate caricature of good mathematical teaching is linear error-free programming. Under this scheme, instead of taking care to ensure that every student is provided with the most stimulating challenges that he can react to successfully, people use their best efforts to create a situation in which nobody is faced with any challenge at all.   —Edwin E. Moise
"The Problem of Learning to Teach," *Amer. Math. Monthly* 82 (May 1975) 470.

59   It is probably true that the nature of mathematics and its role in our culture have never been well understood, even by the educated portion of society. . . . As mathematicians and teachers, with a concern for our subject and a sense of responsibility to our society, it behooves us to exert every effort to bring as many of our fellow-citizens as possible to appreciate mathematics—literally, to understand it, to enjoy it, and to esteem it.   —R. A. Rosenbaum
"The Vicious Versus," in Dalton Tarwater (ed.), *The Bicentennial Tribute to American Mathematics 1776–1976,* Washington, DC: Mathematical Association of America, 1977, p. 171.

60   The consequences of good teaching are to be observed not so much in the student's immediate reaction to the learning experience, but in his subsequent activities. If the student chooses voluntarily to take further mathematics courses at the university, I would say that is evidence of good teaching. If, in his subsequent life and career, he chooses to place himself in situations in which he is required to use mathematics and enjoys those activities, then he has been taught effectively and well. I do not accept that student's success in tests which take place during or immediately following the termination of a given course as evidence relevant to the question whether the teacher of that course was good.   —P. J. Hilton
"Teaching and Research: A False Dichotomy," *Math. Intell.* 1 (No. 1, 1978) 76.

61 How can we, the teachers of today, use the problem literature? Our assigned task is to pass on the torch of mathematical knowledge to the technicians, engineers, scientists, humanists, teachers, and not least, research mathematicians of tomorrow: do problems help?

Yes, they do. The major part of every meaningful life is the solution of problems; a considerable part of the professional life of technicians, engineers, scientists, etc., is the solution of mathematical problems. It is the duty of all teachers, and of teachers of mathematics in particular, to expose their students to problems much more than to facts. It is, perhaps, more satisfying to stride into a classroom and give a polished lecture on the Weierstrass M-test than to conduct a fumble-and-blunder session that ends in the question: "Is the boundedness assumption of that test necessary for its conclusion?" I maintain, however, that such a fumble session, intended to motivate the student to search for a counterexample, is infinitely more valuable. ... In a problem course, however, exposure means the acquiring of an intelligent questioning attitude and of some technique for plugging the leaks that proofs are likely to spring; in a lecture course, exposure sometimes means not much more than learning the name of a theorem, being intimidated by its complicated proof, and worrying about whether it would appear on the examination.
                                                           —Paul Halmos
"The Heart of Mathematics," *Amer. Math. Monthly* 87 (August-September 1980) 523.

62 Many teachers are concerned about the amount of material they must cover in a course. One cynic suggested a formula: since, he said, students on the average remember only about 40% of what you tell them, the thing to do is to cram into each course 250% of what you hope will stick.
                                                           —Paul Halmos
"The Heart of Mathematics," *Amer. Math. Monthly* 87 (August-September 1980) 523.

63 Why must we cover everything that we hope students will ultimately learn? Even if ... we think that the Weierstrass M-test is supremely important, and that every mathematics student must know that it exists and must understand how to apply it—even then a course on the pertinent branch of analysis might be better for omitting it. Suppose that there are 40 such important topics that a student *must* be exposed to in a term. Does it follow that we must give 40 complete lectures and hope that they will all sink in? Might it not be better to give

20 of the topics just a ten-minute mention (the name, the statement, and an indication of one of the directions in which it can be applied), and to treat the other 20 in depth, by student-solved problems, student-constructed counterexamples, and student-discovered applications? I firmly believe that the latter method teaches more and teaches better. Some of the material doesn't get *covered* but a lot of it gets *discovered* (a telling old pun that deserves to be kept alive), and the method thereby opens doors whose very existence might never have been suspected behind a solidly built structure of settled facts. As for the Weierstrass M-test, or whatever else was given short shrift in class—well, books and journals do exist, and students have been known to read them in a pinch.
                                                             —Paul Halmos
                      "The Heart of Mathematics," *Amer. Math. Monthly*
                      87 (August-September 1980) 523.

64   The best way to conduct a problem seminar is, of course, to present problems, but it is just as bad for an omniscient teacher to do all the asking in a problem seminar as it is for an omniscient teacher to do all the talking in a lecture course. . . . Just as you should not tell your students all the answers, you should also not ask them all the questions. One of the hardest parts of problem solving is to ask the right question and the only way to learn to do so is to practice. On the research level especially, if I pose a definite thesis problem to a candidate, I am not doing my job of teaching him to do research. How will he find his next problem, when I am no longer supervising him?   —Paul Halmos
                      "The Heart of Mathematics," *Amer. Math. Monthly*
                      87 (August-September 1980) 524.

65   My purpose in teaching this course [Foundations of Mathematics], as in the others I had taught over the years, was to learn the material myself.   —Philip Davis and Reuben Hersh
                      The Mathematical Experience, Boston: Birkhäuser,
                      1981, p. 2.

66   It is indeed surprising to what extent even research scientists in areas closely related to mathematics regard mathematics as an essentially completed subject. . . . Well, who is at fault here? Don't we use mathematical text books at the university level which contain over a thousand pages of neatly presented results but do not mention any single open problem? How can we expect the non-specialist to know that there are still open problems left in mathematics if we usually present mathematics as a closed subject? How then can we expect leading administrators to have any understanding of the necessity of mathematical research if virtually nobody knows that there are open problems at all on which research could be done? Isn't it correct to say that what we know is very little in comparison to what we do not know and that mathematics is not an exception but rather a good example of that rule? How do we manage to educate a "scientific society" which is not aware of the very basic situation of science, namely that by far most problems are open (and are growing faster in number than the solved ones), and why are we doing that? Are we afraid that people would loose their respect for us if they knew how relatively little we know?

—Wolfgang Haken
"Controversial Questions about Mathematics," *Math. Intell.* 3 (No. 3, 1981) 118.

67   A child should not be forced to do by hand anything that can be done better and more easily with a pocket calculator. ... It may be objected that the use of a pocket calculator teaches the child nothing about the concept of number, or about the meanings of the operations performed on numbers, or about the reasons why the little machine gives the right answers; but this objection is a nullity, because the algorithms are also worthless in all three of these respects.

—Edwin E. Moise
"Mathematics, Computation, and Psychic Intelligence," in Viggo P. Hansen (ed.), *Computers in Mathematics Education,* Reston, VA: National Council of Teachers of Mathematics, 1984, p. 37.

68   Psychic intelligence is an inclination to use whatever cognitive intelligence one has—for learning, for adaptive behavior, and for pleasure. ... Any time we convey to a student that knowledge is the ability to give the expected response, we are propagating psychic stupidity. The same thing happens if we assign to the student interminable chores that neither demand nor repay thought ... algorithmic drill stands alone in the elementary curriculum: it is the only subject whose study ordinarily damages the mentality of the child.   —Edwin E. Moise
"Mathematics, Computation, and Psychic Intelligence". in Viggo P. Hansen (ed.), *Computers in Mathematics Education,* Reston, VA: National Council of Teachers of Mathematics, 1984, p. 36.

69   I have observed in my research that great mathematician-teachers seem to fall into two classes—those like Klein (and at a later period in Göttingen, Hecke and Siegel), who presented the subject complete and finished, a perfect jewel; and those like Hilbert and Courant, who struggle with the subject in front of their students in the classroom. You remember Courant's remark that in Hilbert's lectures you could "feel his intellectual muscle." Some students are stimulated by one type; and some, by the other.   —Constance Reid

> G. L. Alexanderson, "An Interview with Constance Reid," *Two-Year Coll. Math. J.* 11 (September 1980) 234.

70   Mathematics was by far my favorite subject, but I hardly knew what the subject was. The only idea of real mathematics which I had came from *Men of Mathematics*. In it I got my first glimpse of a mathematician per se. I cannot overemphasize the importance of such books about mathematics in the intellectual life of a student like myself completely out of contact with research mathematicians.

> —Julia Robinson

> Constance Reid, "The Autobiography of Julia Robinson," *Coll. Math. J.* 17 (January 1986) 10.

71   So if you want to see where kids' views about mathematics are shaped, the first place to go is into mathematics classrooms. I packed up my videotape equipment, and off I went.

Borrowing a term from anthropologists, what I observed in mathematics classes was the practice of schooling—the day-to-day rituals and interactions that take place in mathematics classes, and (de facto) define what it is to do mathematics. One set of practices has to do with homework and testing. The name of the game in school mathematics is "mastery." Students are supposed to get their facts and procedures down cold. That means that most homework problems are trivial variants of things the students have already learned. For example, one "required" construction in plane geometry (which students memorize) is to construct a line through a given point, parallel to a given line. A homework assignment given a few days later contained the following problem: Given a point on a scale of a triangle, construct a line through that point parallel to the base of the triangle. This isn't a problem; it's an exercise. It was one of 27 "problems" given that night; the three previous assignments had contained 28, 45, and 18 problems respectively.

The test on locus and constructions contained 25 problems, and the students were expected to finish (and check!) the test in 54 minutes—an average of two minutes and ten seconds per problem. Is it any wonder that students come to believe that any problem can be solved in ten minutes or less?

I also note that the teacher was quite explicit about how the students should prepare for the test. His advice—well intentioned—to the students when they asked about the exam was as follows: "You'll have to know all your constructions cold so that you don't spend a lot of time thinking about them." In fact, he's right. Certain skills should be automatic, and you shouldn't have to think about them. But when this is the primary if not the only message that students get, they abstract it as a belief: mathematics is mostly, if not all, memorizing.

—Alan H. Schoenfeld
"Confessions of an Accidental Theorist," *For the Learning of Mathematics* 7 (February 1987) 37.

72 One reason that the black women who have achieved in mathematics have been able to overcome their relatively poor pre-college schooling is their family support. There was never any question as they were growing up as to whether they would have a job outside the home. They always expected to earn money; the only question was how. The black women in mathematics that I have known seem to have more family support for their careers than many, probably most, of the white women mathematicians I know, although this may merely indicate that without this support black women are doomed to early termination of their education. Every black woman with a doctorate in mathematics that I have interviewed had a family member, usually a parent, who earned money and sacrificed for her education.

All of these women also remember a secondary school teacher who said in effect, "You are gifted in mathematics. It would be worth the struggle for you to try to go far with it."   —Patricia Kenschaft
"Black Women in Mathematics," *Assoc. for Women in Math. Newsletter* 18 (September-October 1988) 7.

73 So frequently we hear it asserted that mathematics is a language, but what does this mean for our pupils? It seems to me that they meet mathematics, if at all, as a foreign language at an age when they are still struggling for mastery of their natural language. Furthermore, they meet this foreign language in a written form, i.e., in symbols, before they have had the opportunity to "speak" it, a practice which has never been found productive in the teaching of English or French. In order to encourage young children to embrace their own language, to use it creatively, to experiment with it, we speak it, we tell stories, we sing nursery rhymes, we do as many and varied things with the language as we can. Is that how children encounter mathematics? If not, why not? The language of pattern, of shape, of relationships can be spoken, played, observed in order to encourage an equal facility and interest.

—Leone Burton
"Femmes et Mathématiques: Y-a-t-il une Intersec-
tion?," *Assoc. for Women in Math. Newsletter* 18
(January-February 1989) 8. French version published
in Louise Lafortune (ed.), *Femmes et Mathématiques*,
Les Editions du remue-ménage, Montréal, 1986.

74   A good teacher helps a pupil by judicious questioning and encouragement so that she recognises and reclaims the required mathematical knowledge. The outcome of this dialogue is the formal mathematics of our school curricula, the content of which is thus validated by the style of teaching. This model of teaching can be supported by one or both of two images. One is the filling of the empty vessel—the transfer of knowledge from the teacher to the pupil. The other is the peeling of the onion—the uncovering process already described. . . .

Recently a different metaphor, that of construction and exploration, has been used to challenge the underlying assumptions of transfer and uncovering. In exploring and constructing emphasis shifts from product to process, from single solution to alternatives. Pupils are no longer seen as empty vessels but are recognized as lively and profound thinkers engaged upon trying to make sense of the new, in the context of what is already understood. Content can no longer be subscribed in the same way since it is created through a method of personal enquiry which results from questions in the mind of the learner. In the classroom, therefore, the pupil is expected to engage in a process of constructing understanding. The teacher's role becomes one of providing the resources which are necessary to support and stimulate pupils while they work through their cognitive conflicts towards a resolution which is personal. More time is spent by the teacher in observing and supporting groups or individual pupils than in informing the class. The results of the observation and interaction are used to make decisions about the next appropriate activity for those pupils. This style of classroom places a high value on the use of intuition, on the role of questions and the use of imagination to resolve those questions, on the creativity of the learners both in choosing their method and in communicating their results.   —Leone Burton

"Femmes et Mathématiques: Y-a-t-il une Intersection?," *Assoc. for Women in Math.* Newsletter 18 (November-December 1988) 18. French version published in Louise Lafortune (ed.), *Femmes et Mathématiques,* Les Editions du remue-ménage, Montréal, 1986.

75   Teach the student, not just the subject.   —Ralph Beatley

Garrett Birkhoff, "Mathematics at Harvard, 1836–1944," in Peter Duren (ed.), *A Century of Mathematics in America, Part II,* Providence, RI: American Mathematical Society, 1989, p. 49.

76   A modest competence in mental arithmetic and a five-dollar calculator would, I think, ensure arithmetic competence as measured by the usual standard tests, as well as saving an enormous amount of student and teacher time.   —J. L. Kelley

"Once Over Lightly," in Peter Duren (ed.), *A Century of Mathematics in America, Part III,* Providence, RI: American Mathematical Society, 1989, p. 473.

77   "Knowing" mathematics is "doing" mathematics. A person gathers, discovers, or creates knowledge in the course of some activity having a purpose. This active process is different from mastering concepts and procedures. We do not assert that informational knowledge has no value, only that its value lies in the extent to which it is useful in the course of some purposeful activity. It is clear that the fundamental concepts and procedures from some branches of mathematics should be known by all students; established concepts and procedures can be relied on as fixed variables in a setting in which other variables may be unknown. But instruction should persistently emphasize "doing" rather than "knowing that."

—NCTM Commission on Standards for School Mathematics
Curriculum and Evaluation Standards for School Mathematics, Reston, VA: National Council of Teachers of Mathematics, 1989, p. 7.

78   Each individual's knowledge of mathematics is uniquely personal. Mathematics becomes useful to a student only when it has been

developed through a personal intellectual engagement that creates new
understanding.   —National Research Council
    Everybody Counts, Washington, DC: National
Academy Press, 1989, p. 6.

79 Everyone depends on the success of mathematics education;
everyone is hurt when it fails. —National Research Council
    Everybody Counts, Washington, DC: National
Academy Press, 1989, p. 7.

80 Mathematics is the worst curricular villain in driving students to
failure in school. When mathematics acts as a filter, it not only filters
students out of careers, but frequently out of school itself.
        —National Research Council
    Everybody Counts, Washington, DC: National
Academy Press, 1989, p. 7.

81 To the Romans a *curriculum* was a rutted course that guided
the path of two-wheeled chariots. Today's mathematics curriculum—a
course of study—follows a deeply rutted path directed more by events
of the past than by the changing needs of the present. Vast numbers of
specific learning objectives, each with associated pedagogical strategies,
serve as mileposts along the trail mapped by texts from kindergarten
until twelfth grade. Problems are solved not by observing and responding to the natural landscape through which the mathematics curriculum passes, but by mastering time-tested routines conveniently placed
along the path near every anticipated problem. Students who progress
through this curriculum develop a kind of mathematical myopia in
which the goal is to solve artificial word problems rather than realistic
world problems. —Mathematical Sciences Education Board
    Reshaping School Mathematics, Washington, DC: Na-
tional Academy Press, 1990, p. 4.

82 The world is changing, with an increasing emphasis on science
and technology in every aspect of life: the service sector, the man-
ufacturing sector, and so forth. Consequently, quantitative skills are
prerequisites to enjoying a decent standard of living.

  This, of course, has special significance for women and minorities,
groups that have traditionally been shut out of many technical jobs and
careers because of weak mathematics preparation ... increasingly, the

nation will have to depend on the talents and the abilities of the traditionally underrepresented groups. Therefore, this is really an economic necessity for our nation. ...

We will move beyond using mathematics merely as a tool to control the wealth in this country and move toward using education in mathematics to protect the wealth of this country.

—Mathematical Sciences Education Board
Making Mathematics Work for Minorities, Mathematical Sciences Education Board, 1990, p. 2.

83   A good student is one who will teach you something.

—Irving Kaplansky
D. J. Albers, "Interview with Irving Kaplansky," *Coll. Math. J.* 22 (March 1991) 109.

AUTHOR INDEX

The numbers in this index do not indicate a page. The digit(s) before the hyphen refer to the chapter. The two digits after the hyphen refer to the number of the quotation within the chapter. For example, 2-21 indicates that the quotation is the 21st quotation in Chapter 2.

Adler, I.　2-21, 3-19, 3-20, 12-06
Ahlfors, L. V.　8-35, 13-03
Aleksandrov, A. D.　1-34, 2-26, 9-24
Aleksandrov, P. S.　7-09, 8-21
Allendoerfer, C.　6-12
Anderson, J.　1-44, 4-49, 4-50
Anon　15-38, 15-42
Appel, K.　12-17
Arkhangel'skii, A.V.　13-02
Atiyah, M.　2-35, 4-59, 6-19, 7-12
Austin, A.　15-39

Babbage, C.　7-07
Bacon, H.　13-60
Baker, H. F.　13-57
Barnes, M.　13-07, 13-08
Bateman, H.　13-09
Beatley, R.　16-75
Beberman, M.　16-23, 16-24
Begle, E. G.　16-25, 16-26
Bell, E. T.　9-06, 14-08
Bellman, R.　1-50, 4-32, 4-34, 4-60, 4-61, 8-10, 12-03, 12-04, 13-30, 15-01
Bernstein, D.　5-14, 15-04
Bers, L.　1-55, 2-38, 4-73, 4-74, 4-75, 8-31, 10-34
Bing, R. H.　14-62, 16-54
Birkhoff, G. D.　1-07, 1-08, 3-10, 9-04, 9-07, 11-05, 14-52, 16-12, 16-13
Bishop, E.　15-44
Black, M.　2-28, 2-29
Blackwell, D.　8-27, 14-53
Bliss, G. A.　14-09
Board of Education of NYC　11-10
Boas, R. P.　8-38, 15-06, 15-43, 15-48
Bôcher, M.　6-01
Bochner, S.　1-39, 1-40
Boehm, G.　16-27
Bollobás, B.　13-68, 13-69, 15-13

Bond, W. E.　16-01
Botsch, O.　16-35
Bott, R.　14-15, 14-16, 14-39
Bourbaki, N.　1-19
Boyer, C.　1-17, 1-18, 2-11
Brauer, R.　13-05, 13-06
Brock, P.　4-32, 12-03, 12-04
Brooks, E.　1-01
Bruner, J.　5-02, 6-11, 8-09, 16-34, 16-38
Buck, R. C.　3-15, 16-39
Burkill, H.　14-03, 14-04
Burton, L.　2-39, 4-76, 16-73, 16-74
Butler, C.　16-14
Byerly, W.　14-23

Cambridge Conference　3-17
Cantor, G.　11-15
Carathéodory, C.　8-16
Carmichael, R.D.　1-06, 10-05
Carnap, R.　14-63
Cartan, H.　13-17
Cartwright, M.　14-64
Chandrasekhar, S.　10-30
Coifman, R.　10-39, 15-37
Collingwood, E. F.　13-16
Cooley, H.　1-35
Coolidge, J. L.　3-06, 14-38
Costley, C.　13-71
Coughlin, M.　11-17
Courant, R.　1-11, 2-09, 4-52, 9-14, 9-27, 13-50, 13-51
Coxeter, H. S. M.　3-21

Dale, H.　13-70
Dantzig, G.　13-26, 15-07,
Dantzig, T.　2-06, 2-07, 4-08, 4-09
Davis, P.　1-44, 1-47, 4-49, 4-50, 4-53, 4-54, 7-10, 12-19, 16-65
DeBruijn, N. G.　4-30
DeMorgan, A.　9-01, 13-73

Dickson, L. E.   6-07, 8-06

Dieudonné, J.   3-23, 4-38, 16-36

Doob, J. L.   3-28

Dorwart, H.   14-24

Dresden, A.   1-05, 2-01

Dubisch, R.   16-17

Dukas, H.   11-13

Dummett, M.   13-38

Duren, P.   15-23

Duren, W. L.   13-63, 15-34

Dyson, F.   2-31, 3-18, 8-22

Eilenberg, S.   3-22

Eilenberger, G.   2-36, 11-19

Einstein, A.   4-17, 8-05, 10-07, 13-28, 14-20

Eves, H.   16-41

Fabre, J. H.   7-01, 8-01, 11-01, 11-02, 16-04

Falconer, E.   8-18, 13-72

Feferman, S.   14-47, 15-08

Fehr, H.   11-09, 16-19

Feit, W.   4-51, 13-20

Fine, H.   13-59

Flexner, A.   15-49

Forder, H.   3-07

Forsythe, G.   12-10, 12-11

Freudenthal, H.   16-56

Friedrichs, K.   4-57, 13-25

Fry, T.   4-22

Gardner, M.   6-17, 10-21, 14-44, 15-45

Gleason, A.   1-38, 4-39, 4-86

Goodstein, J.   9-34

Goodstein, R.   3-13

Graham, R.   1-56, 6-23, 7-17, 8-36, 9-39

Greenberg, J.   9-34

Griffin, F. L.   10-08

Guy, R.   4-55

Hadamard, J.   4-77, 4-78, 6-05, 9-12, 10-13

Hájos, G.   5-04

Haken, W.   12-17, 16-66

Halász, G.   14-49

Halmos, P.   1-41, 1-48, 4-42, 4-56, 4-79, 5-09, 5-10, 5-16, 6-14, 7-11, 7-18, 8-32, 9-31, 10-24, 12-20, 13-18, 13-19, 15-29, 15-30, 15-31, 16-50, 16-57, 16-61, 16-62, 16-63, 16-64

Hambidge, J.   11-03

Hammersley, J.   16-28, 16-51

Hamming, R. W.   9-38, 12-08, 12-09, 12-16

Harary, F.   14-27

Hardy, G. H.   9-10, 9-11, 10-10, 10-11, 13-61, 14-67

Harrop, R.   12-15

Hawkins, D.   6-24

Hay, L.   4-84, 13-45

Hayes, E.   16-02

Heilbronn, H.   5-13, 13-61

Helmholtz, H.   10-03

Hersh, R.   1-47, 4-54, 7-10, 12-19, 16-65

Herstein, I. N.   3-27, 5-07, 15-40, 16-53

Hilbert, D.   1-21, 4-19, 8-02

Hille, E.   14-05

Hilton, P.   14-50, 16-60

Hodge, W.   13-65, 13-66

Hodges, A.   9-35

Hoffmann, B.   11-13

Hofstadter, D.   3-24

Hogben, L.   9-05

Holgate, T.   3-02

Honsberger, R.   1-43, 10-27, 13-31

Hooley, C.   14-03, 14-04

Hughes, R.   13-46

Huntington, E.   16-03

Huntley, H. E.   4-43, 10-25, 10-26, 11-12

Jeans, J.   11-06

Johns, F.   4-64

Jones, S.   1-03

Jordan, C.   4-25

Kac, M.   4-65, 4-68, 6-20, 7-13, 7-14, 8-28, 8-29, 9-21, 10-28, 15-16, 15-24, 15-25, 15-26

Kaplansky, I.   5-19, 15-40, 16-83

Karpinski, L.   6-02

Karp, C.   6-13
Kasner, E.   1-09, 2-08, 3-01, 3-12, 10-12
Kelley, J. L.   8-37, 13-53, 14-60, 16-76
Kemeny, J.   9-26, 16-43, 16-44, 16-45
Kenschaft, P.   13-04, 13-56, 14-02, 14-37, 16-72
Keyser, C.   1-10, 1-14
Kilpatrick, J.   14-28
Klamkin, M. S.   15-17
Klein, A.   13-58
Klein, F.   2-05, 3-11, 4-07, 12-02,
Kline, M.   1-24, 1-25, 1-45, 1-46, 2-14, 4-20, 10-18, 16-40
Knuth, D.   1-56, 8-36, 9-39, 10-36, 12-12, 12-13, 12-14, 12-25
Kolata, G. B.   14-13
Kolmogorov, A. N.   13-02
Kovalevsky, S.   8-20, 10-29
Krantz, S.   15-02, 15-03, 15-33
Kuratowski, K.   3-16
Kürschák, J.   5-05

Lang, S.   4-66, 5-11
Langer, R. E.   1-22
Lax, P.   3-29, 4-87, 9-40, 12-26
Lebesgue, H.   2-30, 16-21
LeCam, L.   3-30, 12-27
Ledermann, W.   14-03, 14-04
Lehmer, D. N.   3-04
Lehmer, D. H.   15-18
Lehr, M.   4-80, 8-33, 10-37
Lehrer, T.   15-41
Levine, A. T.   14-59
Levinson, N.   14-61
Lieber, L.   1-12, 2-04
Littlewood, J.   4-69, 6-22, 7-08, 7-15, 7-16, 15-46, 15-47
Love, A. E. H.   14-26

MSEB   16-81, 16-82
Mac Lane, S.   1-26, 1-53, 2-37, 4-70, 4-85
MacMahon, P. A.   9-36
Magnus, W.   14-41
Mal'tsev, A. A.   13-02
Mandelbrot, B.   3-25, 9-33
Manin, Y. I.   4-47
Massey, W. S.   2-40

May, D.   12-05
May, K.   12-18, 16-29
Merrill, H.   4-03, 16-05, 16-06
Milne, E. A.   13-55
Mirsky, L.   13-62
Moise, E. E.   12-21, 14-10, 16-46, 16-58, 16-67, 16-68
Montel, P.   13-64
Moore, E. H.   4-05, 16-09
Morawetz, C.   4-88, 4-89
Moritz, R. E.   10-09
Morse, M.   2-18, 10-22, 13-13
Mosteller, F.   8-39, 15-22
Murnaghan, F.   13-10

NCMR   16-10
NCTM Commission   16-77
NRC   16-78, 16-79, 16-80,
Nagel, E.   2-17
Neukomm, G.   5-04
Neville, E. H.   13-37
Newman, J.   1-09, 2-08, 2-17, 3-12, 10-12
Newman, M. F.   14-17, 14-18
Newman, M. H. A.   1-29
Newsom, C. V.   14-54
Niven, I.   14-01, 14-33, 15-20
Noether, E. P.   14-21
Noether, G. E.   14-21
Northrop, E. P.   1-13

Oleinik, O. A.   13-02
Øre, Ø.   14-25
Osgood, W. F.   5-18
Osofsky, B.   13-48

Papert, S.   2-34
Patashnik, O.   1-56, 8-36, 9-39
Peitgen, H.   10-33
Perfect, H.   14-03, 14-04
Péter, R.   2-22, 2-23, 8-11, 8-40, 9-41
Pierce, C. S.   1-02, 4-01
Pierpont, J.   2-02
Planck, M.   14-36
Poincaré, H.   2-03, 4-06, 6-03, 7-02, 7-03, 12-01
Polanyi, M.   4-40
Pollak, H.   1-32, 4-62, 9-22, 12-07

Pólya, G.   4-44, 4-45, 4-46, 4-63, 5-
    01, 5-03, 6-06, 6-08, 7-04, 10-35,
    13-15, 13-33, 13-34, 13-54, 14-55,
    15-10, 15-11, 15-12, 15-14, 15-15,
    15-19, 15-28, 16-15, 16-16, 16-30,
    16-31, 16-42
Priestley, W.   5-15, 10-31

Rademacher, H.   16-49
Ramanujan, S.   14-30
Read, A. H.   6-10
Rees, M.   1-51, 2-24, 2-25, 16-32
Reeve, W. D.   16-11
Reid, C.   1-30, 1-52, 8-41, 15-09, 16-69
Rényi, A.   8-13
Révész, P.   14-31
Richardson, M.   1-23, 16-18
Richmond, H.   14-14
Richter, P.   10-33
Robbins, H.   1-11, 2-09
Robinson, J.   4-71, 4-72, 14-48, 16-70
Rosenbaum, R.   4-35, 4-36, 9-23,
    10-23, 16-59
Rota, G.   4-81, 8-34, 10-38, 11-18,
    13-23, 13-35, 14-51
Royden, H.   13-12, 14-32
Rucker, R.   11-16, 13-40, 14-46
Rudin, M. E.   4-82, 4-83, 14-11, 14-34,
    14-35, 15-21
Russell, B.   3-05, 8-14, 8-15, 10-02

Sarton, G.   6-04
Savage, L. J.   8-23
Sawyer, W. W.   2-15, 2-16, 2-32, 4-26,
    4-27, 8-07, 10-20, 16-33
Schiffer, M.   14-29
Schoenfeld, A.   12-24, 16-71
Schwartz, J.   1-54, 9-37, 12-23
Scott, C. A.   13-21, 13-22
Serge, C.   4-02
Shapiro, H.   14-40
Shaw, J.   10-16
Simons, L.   14-42
Singh, J.   9-30
Slaught, H. E.   9-02
Slesnick, W.   16-37
Smith, D. E.   1-04, 3-03, 10-01, 10-04,
    10-06, 11-04, 11-07, 11-08, 16-07,
    16-08

Smith, M.   13-49, 14-43
Soare, R.   13-47
Steen, L.   2-33
Stone, M.   1-27, 1-33, 2-19, 2-20, 9-17,
    9-18
Straus, E.   13-29
Strichartz, R.   10-39, 15-37
Struik, D.   1-15
Suranyi, J.   5-04
Sutton, G.   14-68
Sylvester, J. J.   1-49
Synge, J. L.   1-28, 4-10, 4-11, 4-28,
    4-29, 8-08, 9-09, 11-11, 13-42
Szegö, G.   1-36, 4-44, 5-06, 8-12
Szekeres, G.   13-32

Talbot, W.   13-24
Tamarkin, J. D.   14-45
Tarski, A.   2-10
Taton, R.   8-24
Taussky-Todd, O.   4-67, 6-21, 8-30,
    10-32, 15-36
Taylor, A.   8-25, 8-26, 13-11
Taylor, S. J.   15-05
Thurston, W.   2-41, 12-28
Tietze, H.   5-08, 16-47, 16-48
Titchmarsh, E.   13-44
Toeplitz, O.   16-49
Trimble, H.   16-52
Trudeau, R.   1-42, 9-29
Tucker, A.   3-26, 4-58
Tukey, J.   3-14, 9-15
Turán, P.   8-17
Turing, A.   6-18

UICSM   16-22
Ulam, S.   4-31, 4-33, 5-12, 6-15, 6-16,
    7-06, 8-19, 9-32, 14-56, 15-27

Van Der Waerden, B.   14-22
Vandiver, H. S.   13-14
Veblen, O.   3-08, 13-36
Von Neumann, J.   1-37, 4-37, 9-13,
    9-25, 10-14, 10-15

Wall, G. E.   14-17, 14-18
Weidman, D.   4-41
Weil, A.   4-14, 4-15, 4-16, 4-21, 8-04,
    13-27, 13-41, 14-06, 16-20

Weil, S.   11-14
Weinstein, M.   4-48
Weizenbaum, J.   12-22
Weyl, H.   1-20, 2-12, 2-13, 4-12, 4-13,
    4-18, 8-03, 10-17, 13-52
Weyl, M.   14-58
Whitehead, A. N.   1-16, 4-04, 9-03
Whitehead, J. H. C.   3-08
Whitman, B.   14-19
Whyburn, L.   14-12, 16-55
Widder, D. V.   15-32
Wiegand, S.   14-65
Wiener, N.   4-23, 4-24, 6-09, 7-05,
    9-08, 9-16, 10-19, 13-43

Wigner, E.   1-31, 9-19, 9-20, 14-57
Wilczynski, E.   13-39
Wilder, R. L.   3-09, 5-17, 9-28
Wilson, R.   10-40, 15-35
Wren, F. L.   16-14

Yaglom, I. M.   13-67, 14-07
Young, G. C.   14-66
Young, W. H.   14-69
Young, M.   2-27

Zelinsky, D.   13-01

TOPIC INDEX

The numbers in this index do not indicate a page. The digit(s) before the hyphen refer to the chapter. The two digits after the hyphen refer to the number of the quotation within the chapter. For example, 4-34 indicates that the quotation is the 34th quotation in Chapter 4.

Abel, N.   4-34, 9-10, 14-36
absolutism vs. relativity   2-39
abstract mathematics becoming useful
   2-19, 3-22, 9-06, 9-25, 9-28, 9-40,
   9-41
abstract vs. concrete   2-26
abstractness of mathematics   1-02,
   1-08, 1-16, 1-18, 1-19, 1-20, 1-26,
   1-33, 4-19
   enjoyment of   8-20
   hindrance to learning   4-03
   related to concreteness   9-03, 9-18,
   9-23
Adams, C. R.   15-04
adventure
   fear of   6-04
   love of   6-04
advice
   to students   5-18
   to teachers   16-21, 16-30, 16-42, 16-
   44, 16-59, 16-62, 16-75
aesthetic criteria for mathematics   10-
   30, 10-32, 10-33
aesthetic pleasure in mathematics   4-
   10, 4-43, 9-31
agelessness of mathematics   1-06, 1-
   29, 3-12, 8-34, 10-05, 10- 06
Agnesi, Maria   13-73
Albert, A. A.   13-01
Aleksandrov, P. S.   13-02
Alexander, J.   14-15
algebra   3-26, 8-01
   and analysis   3-15
   as an axiomatic system   16-03
   definition of   3-10
   linear   9-06, 14-04
   love of   8-20
   unifier of mathematics   3-27
   word problems   15-47
algebra, abstract
   and algorithms   12-12

importance of problems in   4-11
   study of   4-48
algorithmic drill, dangers in   16-68
algorithms   12-14
   mathematics, a collection of   1-17
analysis   3-15, 8-27, 12-03, 12-04
analytic mathematics, characteristics of
   4-49
Anatolius of Alexandria   1-40
anti-semitism   8-12, 13-32
applications of mathematics in curriculum   16-34
applications of mathematics, teaching
   16-09
applications, test for validity of mathematics   1-05
applied mathematics
   balanced with pure mathematics   9-
   08
   compared to physics   9-34
   definition of   9-07, 9-21, 9-22, 9-27,
   9-34
   importance of   9-07
   importance to education   9-39
   of mathematical applications   3-14
   motivation for   9-31
   rewards of   9-38
   universality of   9-22
   use in teaching   16-19
archaeology and mathematics, comparison of   4-63
Archimedes   1-42, 8-13
architecture and mathematics, comparison of   10-02
Aristotle   4-78
arithmetic
   and abstraction   1-16
   beauty of   8-08
   cardinal   8-32
   confused with mathematics   1-21,
   10-29

definition of   3-24
development of   2-08
handmaiden of science   3-12
queen of science   3-12
teaching of   16-07, 16-22
Arrington-Idowu, E.   13-04
Artin, E.   13-05, 13-06
arts and mathematics, comparison of
    10-01, 10-08, 10-12, 10-14, 10-16,
    10-19, 10-20, 10-22
axiom of reducibility   2-29
axiomatization   2-13

Babbage. C.   12-14
Banach, S.   5-12, 6-15
Barbarossa   15-13
Bateman, H.   13-10
beauty
    of mathematics   1-04, 4-10, 8-02, 8-
        08, 8-10, 8-11, 8-13, 8-18, 8-27, 8-
        29, 8-31, 8-32, 8-37, 10-10, 10-21,
        10-33, 14-29
    criteria for   10-14
    in proof   10-07
    of pure reason   10-12
    guide in research   9-12
    guide of unconscious   10-13, 10-22
    test for significance   9-04, 9-12,
        10-10
Bell, E. T.   13-11
Bellman, R.   13-12
Bergman, S.   15-02, 15-03
Besicovitch, A.   15-05
Bevan, A.   15-35
binomial theorem   8-01
Birkhoff, G. D.   13-13, 13-14
Birkhoff, Garrett   8-26, 12-14
Bloch, F.   14-32
Boas, R.P.   13-18
Bochner, S.   15-06
Bohr, H.   13-15, 15-12
Bolyai, F.   6-20
Bolyai, J.   6-20
Borel, E.   13-16
Borsuk, B.   14-51
Bourbaki, N.   9-40, 13-17, 13-18, 13-
    19
Brauer, R.   13-20
bright idea   6-06, 7-04

Brouwer, L.   2-12
Burali-Forti, C.   2-02
Burgess, E.   15-21

calculators in mathematics education
    16-67, 16-76
calculus   3-17, 8-29, 10-31, 13-07, 15-
    41
Cantor, G.   11-16, 2-27, 2-31, 3-09,
    4-01
Cardano, F.   7-13
Cartwright, M.   7-16, 13-68
category theory
    applications of   3-22
    development of   3-22
Cauchy, A.   4-01, 6-01
Cayley, W.   9-06, 13-21, 13-22
certainty in mathematics   8-05, 11-11
certainty vs. conjecture   2-39
challenge of mathematics   4-66, 9-31
challenge, necessity of   16-58
characteristics of mathematics   1-04,
    1-28, 1-34, 1-35, 1-44
Chasles, M.   3-01
Church, A.   13-23
Claytor, W.   13-24
coincidence in mathematics   4-53
collaboration, description of   4-85
completeness   1-30
    vs. incompleteness   2-39
complexity reduced to simplicity   8-09
computer arithmetic   12-12
computer development compared to
    mathematical development   12-
    09
computer proofs   12-17
computer science
    and applied mathematics, compari-
        son of   12-15
    and mathematics, comparison of   12-
        09, 12-13, 12-23
    and numerical analysis   12-11
computers
    and applied mathematics   12-10
    extend intellectual horizons   12-07
    extend mathematics   12-14, 12-25
    dangers to mathematics   12-03,
        12-04, 12-27
    detriment to mathematics   12-08

a human creation   12-02, 12-06
  limits of use in mathematics   12-01,
    12-02, 12-05, 12-06, 12-20, 12-23
  in teaching, college   12-12, 12-24
  in teaching, elementary   12-22
  value to mathematics   12-06, 12-
    08, 12-16, 12-25, 12-26
computers' need for mathematics   12-
    03, 12-05, 12-21, 12-27
computing and computers   12-18
computing, definition of   12-18
connections to mathematics, finding   5-
    14
connections within mathematics   4-54,
    4-56, 4-85
  test for value   2-35
consistency   2-12
constructivism   15-44
contradiction   2-02
  in mathematical development   2-
    28
contrasts in mathematics   2-26
Copernicus   4-78
counterexample, value of   4-48
Courant, R.   13-25, 16-69
Cox, E.   13-56
creativity   12-06
  and humor   6-17
  joy of   4-43, 10-25, 11-12, 16-55
  in mathematics   6-03, 6-20,
    6-21, 9-11, 10-19, 16-39
  power of   2-17, 2-25
  in students, encouraging   16-44
criteria for good mathematics   4-07,
    4-17, 4-18, 4-35, 4-44, 4-70, 13-13
  false   9-17, 9-28
criteria for good teaching   16-57
curiosity in mathematics learning   16-
    07, 16-14, 16-15, 16-37
curiosity in mathematical research   6-
    04
curriculum
  content, static state of   2-04
  criteria for   16-32, 16-34, 16-48
  secondary   16-31
  criticism of   16-61, 16-63, 16-68,
    16-76, 16-81
    elementary   16-67
    secondary   16-33, 16-43

importance of change in   16-80, 16-
    82
  points for planning   16-25

D'Alembert, J.   5-15
Dantzig, T.   13-26
Darboux, J.   13-67
decimal system   2-30
Dedekind cuts   8-29
Dedekind, R.   2-27
deduction, origins of   2-11, 2-20
deductive reasoning   16-16, 16-19
  teaching   16-01, 16-03
definition of great mathematics   4-34
definition of mathematics   1-11, 1-14,
    1-24, 1-31, 1-40, 1-41, 1-52, 1-53,
    2-37
Dehn, M.   13-27
delight in mathematics   8-03, 8-14,
    8-25
delta-epsilon proofs   15-41
Denjoy's conjecture   13-03
Descartes, R.   3-01
desire to explore   4-27, 6-23
desire to solve problems   16-15
desire to study mathematics   8-15, 8-
    30
despair   6-20
development
  human soul and mathematics   1-48
  industrial, and mathematics   1-01
  intellectual, activity required for
    16-56
  intellectual, and mathematics   1-
    03, 1-24, 1-37, 1-46, 1-48, 16-10,
    16-20
  moral, and mathematics   1-03, 11-
    10, 16-18, 16-20
  spiritual, and mathematics   11-07,
    11-08, 11-10, 11-14, 11-16
devotion to mathematics   8-06, 8-12,
    8-13, 8-16, 8-19, 8-26, 8-35, 14-31
Dickson, L. E.   14-08
Dieudonné, J.   13-19
differential equations   14-52
difficulty of mathematics   1-38, 4-03,
    4-41, 4-43, 4-60, 4-66, 4-73, 4-89,
    16-06
Dirichlet, L.   1-19

discoveries, chain of   1-04, 4-40
discovery
    characteristics of   4-02
    of generalizations, teaching   16-23
    joy of   4-64, 4-74, 4-84, 7-18, 8-02,
        8-40, 14-29, 16-44
    mystery of   6-10, 7-07
    necessity of preparation for   5-02,
        6-02
    need for practice   16-38
    precedes proof   4-06
    rules of   6-06
    vs. invention   4-62, 4-75
discovery method   16-44, 16-63
    criticism of   16-24
discrete mathematics
    and computers   3-29
    vs. calculus-based mathematics   3-
        29
discrete vs. continuous   2-26
dislike of mathematics   1-21, 1-35,
        16-06, 16-17, 16-37, 16-49
diversity of mathematics   2-37
Dr. Matrix   15-45
dynamics of mathematics growth   1-
        06, 2-15, 2-16, 2-19, 2-23, 2-33, 2-
        38, 2-41, 3-01, 4-54, 10-15, 10-22
Dyson, F.   10-30

Edmundson, D.   14-02
education of the will   16-15
Ehrenfest, P.   7-14
Eilenberg, S.   4-85
Einstein, A.   4-60, 4-78, 11-13, 13-29,
        14-15, 15-08, 16-42, 16-43
elegance, guidance of   4-37
elements of mathematics   1-11
elliptical functions   8-10
encouragement, importance of   16-72
enjoyment of mathematics   4-27,
        4-59, 6-23
enormity of modern mathematics   4-
        56, 4-64, 13-28, 14-56
Erdős, P.   8-17, 13-30, 13-31, 13-32
Errara, A.   15-19
errors in mathematics   4-01
essentials of mathematics   11-08
Euclid   2-02, 2-31, 3-25, 9-29
Euclid's Elements   16-03

Euler, L.   14-56, 16-40
Everett, C.   6-16
examples, value of   4-48, 5-19

failure   4-61, 4-78
    description of   4-72
    in learning mathematics   16-80
    acceptance of   16-06
    usefulness of   4-77, 4-80
fascination with mathematics   8-01,
        8-05, 8-15, 8-20, 8-21, 8-23, 8-27,
        8-29, 8-32, 8-39, 14-49
Fejér, L.   13-33, 13-34
Feller, W.   13-35
Fermat's Last Theorem   4-55, 15-18
Fermat, P.   2-28
fifth postulate   6-20
Fine, H.   13-36
Flavius Josephus   15-40
flexibility in thinking   1-37
flexibility of mathematics   2-19
formal vs. material   2-26
formalism   1-19, 15-44
Forsyth, A. R.   13-37
Forsythe, G.   12-14
foundations of mathematics   2-02,
        2-12, 2-14, 16-40
four-color map problem   12-17
fourth dimension   11-04
fractals   3-25
Franklin, B.   16-12
Franklin, P.   15-32
freedom of mathematics from physical
        world   2-20
freedom of mathematicians   4-10, 4-
        15, 4-28, 4-39, 4-87, 6-13, 8-34,
        10-23
    limits to   2-09
freedom of thought, necessity of   4-
        78, 5-13
Frege, G.   13-38
Friedan, B.   13-45
frustration   4-41, 13-38
Fuchs, L.   13-39

Galois, E.   8-24
Gauss, C. F.   2-28, 5-19, 6-01, 16-40
general vs. particular   2-26
generalization   4-18, 4-46

danger of   13-11
  in geometry   3-02
  in mathematical curriculum   16-34
generating functions   8-39
genius, description of   14-50
geometry   2-05
  abstractness of   3-05, 3-07
  algebraic   3-23
  and analysis   3-04
  characterization of a   3-11
  compared to a mountain   3-03,
    3-19
  created by God   13-59
  defined by invariance   3-11
  definition of   3-08
  development of   2-08, 3-01, 3-03
  dynamic shapes in   11-03
  essentials of   11-08
  Euclidean   4-01, 8-05, 8-14, 8-37,
    16-40
  a game   10-01
  love of   8-21
  modern   3-02
  and nature   3-05, 3-25, 11-01
  non-Euclidean   4-01, 8-21
  pleasures of studying   3-21, 10-01
  subdivisions of   3-19
  teaching, goals of   16-01
  unity of   3-19
  value of   16-12
Gibbs, J.   15-34
girls' conditioning against mathematics
    16-02
goal of mathematics   1-53, 1-54, 1-56,
    11-19
God as mathematician   2-11, 11-01,
    11-06, 13-59
Gödel, K.   2-12, 2-17, 13-40, 14-15,
    15-08, 15-36
good students, definition of   16-83
good teaching, consequences of   16-
    60
Gosset, W. S.   15-09
Granville, W. A.   14-24
Grassman, H.   3-01, 4-36
group theory
  development of   3-20
  importance of   3-18, 3-20
groups, applications of   3-20

growth of mathematics   2-01, 2-04,
    2-10
  two forces of   2-24
guage theory   10-30

Hadamard, J.   13-41, 15-10
hallmarks of mathematics   1-41
Hamilton, H.   15-04
Hamilton, W.   3-01, 13-42
hard work, necessity of   4-41, 4-43,
    4-81, 5-01, 5-06, 5-08, 5-18, 6-02,
    7-13, 7-16, 14-26, 15-11, 16-47,
Hardy, G. H.   4-69, 13-43, 13-44,
    13-70, 14-30, 14-68, 15-11, 15-12
Harrison, K.   9-35
Hay, L.   13-46, 13-47
Hecke, E.   16-69
Herstein, I. N.   13-48, 13-49
Hilbert's tenth problem   4-72
Hilbert, D.   2-12, 4-52, 8-03, 13-50,
    13-51, 13-52, 15-13, 15-14, 16-69
Hille, E.   13-11
Hipparchus   13-42
Homer   1-40
honest inquiry, value of   11-08
honesty of mathematicians   11-09
honesty, intellectual   11-10
  in mathematics   1-23, 16-18
Hurewicz, W.   13-53
Hurwitz, A.   13-54, 15-15
hypercube   7-10
hyperspace   11-04

imagination   10-29, 12-22
  in mathematics   1-04, 4-82, 11-18
  necessity of   10-35
importance of mathematics   16-45, 16-
    59, 16-82
  education   16-79
impossible in mathematics   2-07
incompleteness   2-17
infinity   1-04, 8-11, 11-04, 14-46
  contact with   10-01, 10-06, 11-07,
    11-16
  finite from   1-54
  importance to growth of mathemat-
    ics   2-06
  in nature   11-15
  vs. finiteness   2-26

insight
    characteristics of   7-04, 7-07, 7-18
    necessity of   4-42
integral, Lebesgue   9-16
intellectual delight in mathematics learn-
    ing   16-32, 16-34
intuition   16-36
    characteristics of   4-19, 4-49, 6-10,
      6-11, 6-12, 6-18
    developing   16-40
    in development of mathematics   2-
      24, 4-04, 4-08, 6-05
    foundation of mathematics   2-14,
      9-14
    in mathematics and physics   9-32
    precedes deduction   4-76, 6-07, 6-
      08, 6-11, 6-12, 6-14
intuitive breakthrough   6-10, 7-12
    description of   7-02, 7-03, 7-05, 7-
      08, 7-09, 7-10,   7-11, 7-13, 7-14,
      7-15, 7-16
invention in mathematics
    sources of   6-04

Jacobi, C.   2-27, 8-04
jargon of mathematics   1-09, 16-51
Jeans, J.   3-18, 13-55
Jefferson, T.   16-12
Jones, E.   13-56
joy
    of achievement in mathematics learn-
      ing   16-29
    of contemplation in mathematics   9-
      31
    of creativity   4-43, 10-25, 11-12, 16-
      55
    of discovery   4-64, 4-74, 4-84, 7-18,
      8-02, 8-41, 14-31, 16-44

Kac, M.   13-35, 15-17
Kaplansky, I.   13-49
Keats, J.   10-30
Kepler, J.   11-12
Ketchum, P.   7-11
Kierkegaard, S.   1-20
Kirchhoff, G.   4-78
Klein, F.   2-37, 8-02, 13-36, 13-54, 13-
    57, 13-58, 13-67, 14-65, 14-66, 16-
    69

Kline, J.   14-62
Kronecker, L.   3-09, 8-12, 13-59

Landau, E.   13-60, 13-61, 13-62, 15-
    18, 15-19
Landau, H.   4-62
Lane, E.   13-63
language and mathematics, comparison
    of   1-29, 7-06
Laplace, P.   4-01
learning mathematics
    compared to learning sport   5-03
    by doing mathematics   5-04, 16-39,
      16-46, 16-50, 16-77, 16-78
    and girls   16-02
    natural approach to   16-07
    personal engagement in   5-18,
      16-78
    and women   16-82
learning to learn   16-52
Lebesgue, H.   2-18, 13-64
Lefschetz, S.   3-26, 4-60, 13-65, 13-66
Leibniz, G.   3-01, 10-31
Lévy, P.   15-19
Lie, S.   13-67
limitlessness of mathematics   1-30,
    1-40, 1-43, 1-47, 1-49, 2-01, 2-03,
    2-07, 2-15, 2-17, 2-31, 3-01, 8-04,
limits of mathematics   2-22
Littlewood, J.   13-68, 13-69, 13-70
logarithmic spiral   10-09, 11-02
logarithms, value of   16-12
logic
    compared to architectural structure
      10-02
    function of   3-13, 4-08, 4-19, 9-09
    hygiene of mathematics   2-14, 4-16
    importance to mathematics   3-13
    infinitary   6-13
    limits of, for understanding mathe-
      matics   4-12
    as poetry   10-07
loneliness of mathematicians   4-25,
    4-41, 4-43, 4-88, 13-38, 14-19
Lorch, L.   8-18, 13-71, 13-72
love of students   13-05, 16-08
Lovelace, A.   13-73

MacLane, S.   14-01

magic squares   16-12
Magie, W.   13-36
Marceli, D.   8-29
mathematical activity
    adequate time for   4-57, 4-65, 4-67,
        15-20
    beginning of   1-28, 6-22
    compared to civil service   4-67
    components of   1-32, 4-76
    description of   1-50, 2-34, 2-40,
        4-22, 4-52, 4-69, 4- 79, 4-81, 4-83
    diversity of   1-36
    inexpensiveness of   4-15, 4-24, 16-
        13
    motivations for   4-31
    two approaches to   4-38
    value of   4-59
mathematical method
    analogy   6-01, 6-24
    concentration   6-15, 6-16
    description of   6-14, 6-15, 6-16
        6-19
    detachment   4-37
    discernment   6-03
    experimentation   6-01, 6-08
    intuition   6-01
    optimism   6-01
    place of goals in   6-19
mathematical talent   4-14, 4-66, 4-81
mathematical understanding, levels of
    16-47, 16-49
mathematician
    description of   1-09, 1-47, 1-52
    making of a   16-29
    as consultant   9-15
    as painter   10-11
    as poet   10-06, 10-11, 10-28, 10-29,
        14-58
mathematicians   15-49
    characteristics of   4-71, 8-41, 15-35
    and computers   12-16, 12-17, 12-
        19, 12-20, 12-24, 12-28
    criterion for judging   4-51
    during World War II   9-02
    in industry   4-22
    and physicists, rift between   9-14
    social reaction to   15-01
    wives of   15-20

women   13-45, 13-46, 13-73, 14-02,
    14-13, 14-21, 14-35, 14-43, 14-59,
    14-69, 15-04, 15-21, 16-72
mathematics
    an adventure in ideas   1-15
    art of counting   3-12
    as an aspect of culture   1-01, 1-17
    characteristics of   1-04, 1-28, 1-34,
        1-35, 1-44
    in colonial times   16-12
    compared to a cathedral   1-04, 4-
        74, 11-19
    and cultural heritage   1-46, 16-27
    describer of universe   16-19
    and other disciplines, teaching   16-
        11
    escape from reality   4-03,
        4-20, 4-89, 8-04, 8-34
    as a filter   16-80
    as free creation   1-05, 2-27, 10-08
    as fun   1-42, 5-10, 8-36, 8-38, 8-41
    as a game   1-42, 8-11
    handmaiden of all disciplines   16-
        19
    a hypothetical system   1-02
    as an intellectual enterprise   1-14
    a language   9-26, 16-73
        of relationships   1-18
        of size   9-05
    a living subject   1-22, 16-13, 16-26,
        16-48, 16-66
        teaching   16-17, 16-27, 16-29, 16-
            35
    a logical system   1-05, 1-13, 1-14,
        1-18, 1-26, 1-55, 2-09
    mirror of the divine   1-03, 11-01,
        11-02, 11-06, 11-12, 11-15
    mirror of reality   10-28
    mirror of truth   13-27
    in nature, example of   4-04, 9-16
    not symbol manipulation   16-17, 16-
        37, 16-39
    as poetry   1-04, 10-26, 10-38
    queen of science   2-25
    a relational system   1-07, 1-33,
        1-53
    servant of science   2-25
    a way of thinking   1-13, 1-14, 1-37

mathematics department administration 15-27

Mayes, V.   14-02

Mazur, S.   6-16

meaning in mathematics   4-36
  pursuit of   4-29

memorization in mathematics   6-09, 16-71

memorization of tables   16-17

metamathematics   2-17

minorities in mathematics   14-33, 16-82

Mirsky, L.   14-03, 14-04

mistakes in mathematics   4-42

Mittag-Leffler, G.   14-05, 14-06

Möbius, A.   14-07

modeling   10-23, 16-28

models, criteria for   4-32

modern mathematics
  characteristics of   1-33, 2-08, 2-13, 2-21, 2-39
  development of   2-31, 2-32
  service given by   1-08
  understanding   16-17

Montaigne, M.   16-42

Montgomery, D.   14-15

Moore method   14-10, 14-34, 16-50, 16-54, 16-55

Moore, E. H.   14-08, 14-09

Moore, R. L.   14-10, 14-11, 14-12, 14-34, 14-62, 15-21, 16-54, 16-55

Morgenstern, O.   15-08

Morley, F.   14-14

Morse, M.   14-15, 14-16

music and mathematics, comparison of 10-03, 10-27, 10-36, 10-40

mysteriousness
  of mathematics   1-04, 9-19

nature and mathematics   2-31, 2-36, 3-25, 4-04, 10-07, 11-06
  conflict between   11-13

Neumann, H.   13-45, 14-17, 14-18

Nevanlinna, R.   13-03

Newson, M. F. W.   14-19, 14-66

Newton, I.   1-04, 2-31, 4-24, 5-02, 8-01

Neyman, J.   15-07

Noether, E.   4-46, 14-20, 14-21, 14-22

number and numeral, distinction between   16-22

number, abstract notion of   3-24

number characterizing periodicity   4-04

numbers
  created by God   13-59
  understanding of   16-22

number theory   2-05, 3-24
  and computers   12-12

numerals   15-45

numerical analysts   12-11

obstacles to mathematical progress   6-04

Olds, E.   8-39

Oppenheimer, J. R.   14-15

optimism, value of   5-12, 15-07

order, unexpected, and computers   12-01

origin of word 'mathematics'   1-39

painting and mathematics, comparison of   10-10, 10-24, 10-39

palaeontology and mathematics, comparison of   4-63

paradox   2-02

parallels, theory of   8-21

partial results, value of   5-12

passion for mathematics   4-29, 6-20, 8-04, 8-07, 8-24, 13-01, 14-42, 15-03, 15-32

passion for order   4-23, 13-61

passionate desire for results   4-72, 5-01, 15-13

patterns in mathematics   4-10, 8-27, 8-36, 10-10, 10-20
  fascination with   8-07

Peano, G.   2-31

Pearson, K.   15-09

permanence of mathematics   10-05

perseverence   5-15, 5-19, 6-15, 13-29, 16-15

persistance   7-13, 7-16, 15-46

pervasiveness of mathematics   1-10, 1-13, 1-24, 1-25, 1-44, 2-10, 5-14, 9-01, 9-05,   9-20, 9-24

philosophy and mathematics, comparison of   1-31

physical reality and mathematics   2-
    25
physical world and mathematics   1-
    45, 4-04
physics and mathematics   9-20
    comparison of   9-32
Piaggio, H.   8-22
Pierce, B.   14-23
Pierce, C. S.   16-34
Pierpont, J.   14-24, 14-25
Plato   2-11, 2-27
Platonism   4-75
plausible reasoning   6-08, 6-12
    description of   4-63
    importance for life   16-16
    teaching   16-16
playfulness   6-08, 6-11, 6-17, 6-24,
    8-11, 8-36, 14-44, 14-51
pleasure from useful results   9-18
pleasures
    of achievement   16-05
    of insight   16-05
    of intellectual pursuits   8-09, 10-01
    of mathematics   1-42, 1-43, 4-20, 4-
        25, 4-89, 8-17, 8-22, 8-28, 8-36, 8-
        40, 8-41, 9-23, 10-21, 10-25, 14-44
poetry
    and mathematics   10-35
    comparison of   10-04, 10-05, 10-
        10
        10-28, 10-31, 10-34, 10-37
    as mathematics   1-04
    proof as   10-18
Poincaré, H   2-18, 3-09, 9-10, 14-26,
    14-56,
Pólya, G.   13-03, 14-27, 14-28, 14-29,
    14-32,
Pope, A.   4-53
power of mathematics   1-01,
    1-07, 1-08, 1-12, 1-25, 1-35, 1-55,
    8-18, 9-26
precision of mathematics   1-50
prestige of mathematics   1-35, 1-51,
    16-13
principle of the excluded middle   2-12
probability   3-30
    an experimental science   3-06
    development of   3-28
    expectation   15-25

problem posing   5-10, 16-41, 16-64
problem solving   14-36
    attitude   5-06, 16-01, 16-61
    in teachers   16-30
    alternatives in   6-24
    delayed gratification in   5-15
    importance for college faculty   4-
        45
    importance of   15-40, 16-61
    importance of questions for   7-17
    joys of   8-28
    methods of   4-39
    necessity of practice   5-03
    proof of mathematical ability   16-
        51
    suggestions for   5-16, 5-19, 7-17
    teaching   16-15
    training youth for   5-06
problems
    compared to exercises   16-41, 16-
        71
    how to choose   5-19
    importance of   8-22, 16-41
    in teaching   16-66
    necessity of   16-48
    in teaching   14-48
    source of new   4-54
    value of   4-11, 4-16, 4-20, 4-33,
        4-55, 5-07
proof
    by intimidation   13-35
    makes everything trivial   15-06,
        15-48
    criterion for good   4-47
    qualities of a   4-50, 4-86
proofs
    beauty of   13-31
    honesty in presenting   16-36
Ptolemy   4-78, 13-42
puns   15-23, 15-48
pure mathematics
    balanced with applied mathematics
        9-17, 9-28, 9-29, 9-39, 9-40
    compared to applied mathematics
        9-09, 9-31
    definition   9-21, 9-29
    rooted in the physical   9-08, 9-13,
        9-14, 9-24, 9-33
    self-sufficiency of   9-29

uselessness of   9-10, 9-11, 9-25,
    9-29
pure mathematicians' disdain for appli-
    cations   9-10, 9-11, 9-18, 9-30,
    9-39, 9-40
purposes of mathematics education
    16-10, 16-19
    college   16-20
Pythagoras   4-04
Pythagoreans   2-11, 4-04

questions
    importance of   7-17
    value of   4-55

racism   13-04,   13-24,   13-56,
    13-72, 14-02
Rademacher, H.   15-20
Radó, T.   15-48
randomness   3-30
Rayleigh, J.   10-18
readers of mathematical papers   15-
    17
reading about mathematicians, impor-
    tance of   16-70
reading mathematics
    joy in   10-25
    suggestions for   5-04, 5-05, 5-09,
        5-10
reading the masters   4-34, 14-40
real world and mathematics   4-35, 16-
    26, 16-28
recursive functions   9-41
religion and mathematics, comparison
    of   1-20, 11-04, 11-11
religion and the mathematician   1-04
Rényi, A.   14-31
research
    compared to problem solving   4-45
    cooperation in   14-04, 14-45
    criticism of   15-39, 15-42, 16-53
    dangers of specialization in   4-13
    description of   4-65
    difficulty of   15-43
    need for flexibility in   2-40
    for publication, criticism of   4-45
    suggestions for   4-58, 5-14
    vs. practical training   16-20
    with students   13-03, 15-15

responsibility to science   2-09
rewards
    lack of, in mathematical activity   4-
        15, 5-06, 8-06, 8-17, 10-22
    of mathematics   1-25, 10-19
    of teaching   16-04
richness of mathematics   2-37
Riemann hypothesis   15-12
Riemann, G.   3-09, 9-10
Riesz, M.   14-32, 15-11
right answers, unimportance of   6-11
rigor   4-05, 9-32
    absence in discovery   4-02, 4-06
    compared to morality   4-21
    function of   4-21
    less important than intuition in teach-
        ing   16-40
    in mathematics growth   2-24
    preceded by intuition   6-01
Robinson, J.   14-33
roots of mathematics
    human experience   1-26
    nature   14-54
    real world   10-15
    scientific problems   1-53
Rudin, W.   14-35
Russell, B.   1-10, 1-33, 1-42, 2-02, 2-
    29, 9-35

Savage, L. J.   15-22
Schlick, M.   14-63
Schur, I.   14-36
science and mathematics   1-45
science is mathematics   1-27
science, source of mathematical ques-
    tions   4-54
scientific and spiritual attitude   11-05,
    11-09, 11-19, 14-16
Scott, C.A.   14-37
sculpture and mathematics, compari-
    son of   10-23
seduction by mathematics   8-10, 8-12,
    8-23, 8-33, 16-32
Selberg, A.   14-15
self-confidence
    building in students   16-55
    importance of   5-11, 8-09
serendipity   7-14
Serge, C.   14-38

series and sequences 15-37
series, infinite 15-31
Serre, J.P. 14-39
set theory 2-18, 14-46, 14-51
  a unifier of mathematics 3-16
  development of 3-16
Severi, F. 13-65
sexism 13-04, 13-07, 13-08, 13-72, 13-73, 14-37
Shakespeare, W. 10-31
Shields, A. 4-79, 14-40, 15-23
Siegel, C. L. 14-15, 14-41, 16-69
simplicity 1-54, 4-18
  of higher mathematics 4-26
simplification 4-50
  in problem solving 4-52
  of mathematical ideas 4-14
sleep 6-09, 7-01, 14-39
Slepian, D. 4-62
Smith, D. E. 14-42
social science and mathematics, comparison of 9-37
Socratic method 16-50
specialization 4-46
  dangers of 4-13, 9-36
  necessity of 13-28
  in problem solving 4-52
spiritual yearning for permanence and mathematics 1-10
statistics 3-30
Steenrod, N. 4-85
Steinhaus, H. 10-28, 14-44, 15-24, 15-25, 15-26
Strauss, R. 7-10
stubbornness in mathematicians 4-71
Student's t-statistic 15-09
students, gifted 16-32
subconscious work 6-07, 6-09, 6-21, 7-01, 7-08, 7-17, 10-13
  description of 7-02, 7-12
  initiating 5-01
subconscious, organization of 4-09
surprise 1-42, 1-43, 4-53
  enjoyment of 8-09
symmetry, value of 10-17
Szegö, G. 14-32, 14-45

Takeuti, G. 14-46,
Tarski, A. 14-47, 14-48

teach student, not subject 16-75
teacher preparation, college, criticism of 16-53
teaching
  compared to music 16-42
  compared to poetry 16-42
  compared to theater 16-42
  dignity of, college 16-53
  for future 16-25, 16-26, 16-45
  geometry, criticism of 16-35
  importance of enthusiasm for 16-30
  importance of subject knowledge 16-30
  necessity of unambiguous language 16-23
  nobility of 16-08
  as process 16-74
teaching mathematics
  compared to teaching a sport 16-47
  compared to teaching art 16-27
  compared to teaching language 16-31, 16-73
  compared to teaching music 16-49
  experimentation in 16-36
  goals of 16-08, 16-60, 16-61, 16-65
  laboratory approach 16-09
  primary 16-73
teaching style
  college 16-21
  criticism of 16-58, 16-61, 16-66, 16-68, 16-71
  description of 13-23, 13-35, 13-39, 13-60, 14-09, 14-23, 14-34, 14-60, 14-68, 16-24, 16-50, 16-54, 16-57, 16-63, 16-64, 16-69, 16-71, 16-74
technology, source of mathematical questions 4-54
theological techniques and mathematics 2-29
theology and mathematics, comparison of 11-17, 11-18
Thompson, J. 13-48
topology 3-26
  and analysis 3-15
  algebraic 14-51
  origins of 3-09
  point set 14-60

a unifier of mathematics   3-09
trigonometry   16-12
    curriculum, criticism of   16-43
truth
    absolute   10-01
Turán, P.   14-49
Turing, A.   9-35, 14-50

Uhlenbeck, G.   7-14
Ulam, S.   10-38, 14-51
ultimate reality and mathematics   2-11
uncertainty in mathematics   11-17
unconscious   6-05
unconscious work   10-22
understanding mathematics   4-12, 16-59
    lack of   15-38
unity of mathematics   1-44, 2-05, 2-13, 2-15, 2-35, 3-02, 3-04, 3-15, 4-24, 4-56, 4-59, 9-36
    for problem solving   5-17
    teaching   16-09, 16-11
usefulness of mathematics   1-04, 8-39, 9-02, 9-19, 15-38
    overestimation and underestimation   9-26
uselessness of mathematics   8-13, 9-35

value of effort   11-14, 11-16
value of mathematics   1-03, 1-04, 1-22, 1-45, 1-46, 1-48
    in education   1-13
Van der Pol's equation   7-16
Van Kampen, E. R.   15-16
Van Vleck, E.   14-52
Veblen, O.   3-18, 11-13, 14-15, 15-32
Voltaire   10-04

Von Kármán, T.   9-34, 15-28
Von Neumann, J.   12-16, 14-15, 14-53, 14-54, 14-55, 14-56, 14-57, 15-29, 15-30, 15-31

Walker, A. G.   14-04
Washington, G.   16-12
Weierstrass, H.   2-02, 14-05
Weyl, H.   10-30, 14-15, 14-56, 14-58
Wheeler, A.   14-59
Whitehead, A. N.   8-14
Whyburn, G.   14-60
Widder, D. V.   15-06, 15-48
Wielandt, H.   13-48
Wiener, N.   14-61, 15-32, 15-33, 15-48
Wilder, R. L.   8-23, 14-62
Williams, J.   15-22
Wilson, E. B.   15-34
Wintner, A.   15-48
Wittgenstein, L.   14-63, 15-47
Wolfskel, P.   15-18
writing a diary   14-03, 14-07
writing style   4-36
    choices in   4-30
    criticism of   4-13
    description of   13-33, 13-52, 13-53, 13-54, 13-55, 15-02
writing
    criteria for   4-36, 4-42, 4-68
    suggestions for   4-13, 13-20

Young, G. C.   13-58, 14-64, 14-65, 14-67, 14-69
Young, L. C.   14-64
Young, R. C.   14-64
Young, T.   13-09
Young, W. H.   14-67, 14-68

Zariski, O.   3-26, 4-80
Zermelo, E.   15-36
Zygmund, A.   10-39, 15-37